Faculty Identities and the Challenge of Diversity

Faculty Identities and the Challenge of Diversity

Reflections on Teaching in Higher Education

Edited by
Mark A. Chesler
and
Alford A. Young Jr.

with
Ruby Beale, Corissa Carlson, Jessica Charbeneau, Kristie A. Ford,
Megan Furhman, Laura Hirshfield, Tiffany Joseph,
Kelly Maxwell, Penny A. Pasque, *and* Elizabeth Ramus

Paradigm Publishers
Boulder • London

Copyright © 2014 Paradigm Publishers

Published in the United States by Paradigm Publishers, 5589 Arapahoe Avenue, Boulder, CO 80303 USA.

Paradigm Publishers is the trade name of Birkenkamp & Company, LLC,
Dean Birkenkamp, President and Publisher.

Library of Congress Cataloging-in-Publication Data

Chesler, Mark A.
  Faculty identities and the challenge of diversity / Mark A. Chesler, Alford A. Young Jr.
    p. cm.
  Includes bibliographical references and index.
  ISBN 978-1-61205-114-7 (hc : alk. paper) — ISBN 978-1-61205-115-4 (pbk : alk. paper) — ISBN 978-1-61205-224-3 (q)
1. College teaching—Social aspects—United States. 2. College teachers—United States—Social conditions. 3. Education, Higher—Social aspects—United States. 4. Multicultural education—United States. 5. Critical pedagogy—United States. 6. Educational change—United States.
I. Young, Alford A. II. Title.
  LB2331.C516 2012
  378.1'250973—dc23

                                                                    2012024525

Printed and bound in the United States of America on acid-free paper that meets the standards of the American National Standard for Permanence of Paper for Printed Library Materials.

Designed and Typeset in 10.5 pt. Minion by Straight Creek Bookmakers.

18 17 16 15 14   1 2 3 4 5

Contents

have examined the life of faculty members have looked broadly at the faculty in general or the faculty of particular races and genders. This book focuses on understanding the experiences of faculty members of various races/ethnicities and genders and, in particular, their classroom encounters with students and departmental encounters with colleagues. Because issues of equity in education occur in and are relevant to all classrooms regardless of discipline (albeit differently in different disciplines), the diversity of the data base for this book is reflected in interviews with faculty members of different races/ethnicities, genders, and academic disciplines. And the unique nature of this data base lies in its focus on faculty members whom peers have honored or nominated as "knowing how to deal with diversity in the classroom." Thus, the material in this book comes from a leading-edge cadre, and their wisdom and struggles illuminate both the limits of our current knowledge and skill as well as some of the best pedagogical options for the future.

Why Now?

At this time in history the United States continues to wrestle with the meaning and practice of race/ethnicity. The election of an African American president has ignited both hope and fear. It has led some to take courageous action to counter injustice and help realize the promise of a diverse democracy. It has led some to feel that our racial problems are solved, that race itself is a thing of the past and better ignored or left alone. It has stimulated others to express some of the worst aspects of our cultural ignorance and their opposition to difference, racial peace, and justice. Indeed, in the public sphere and within the academy we are witnessing all three types of response and now even increasing the challenge to the principles and practices of affirmative action, racial/ethnic diversity, and social justice.

It also is a time when public concern about public services, such as education generally and higher education in particular, has surfaced in critical ways. Concerns about the cost and efficiency of our academic system have led to higher levels of public judicial and legislative inquiry and challenge.

As these twin concerns meet, there is special focus on the amount and value of teaching that faculty provide as well as the possibilities of racial peace and justice in the academy. The inquiry in this volume sheds light on some of the dilemmas faculty experience in diverse classroom settings, some of their innovative strategies for dealing with these issues, and their own efforts to help realize the educational promise of race and gender diversity. It also provides some guides for efforts to increase the skills and pedagogical options available to other faculty in such circumstances.

Why Us?

If the issues are important and if now is an appropriate time to work on these issues, why are we—Mark Chesler and Alford Young Jr.—appropriate research leaders and authors? We are both veteran faculty members. Young is a departmental chair, and Chesler has been an instructor in faculty development programs. Both have received awards for our teaching and institutional leadership on issues of racial equity. Both are experienced researchers and have published previously on issues of race in community, organizational, and academic settings.

Young is an African American, and Chesler is white; thus, we represent an interracial collaboration. And the team of postdoctoral scholars, graduate students, and undergraduate students we bring together on this project represent a race- and gender-diverse team. Thus, multiple perspectives have been brought to bear on this project.

Mark Chesler

My interest in the issues central to this book stretch back over forty years, beginning with research and consultant efforts to help secondary school systems dealing with desegregation and integration. It was clear to many of us that physical desegregation, or structural diversity, was only the tip of the iceberg of racially/ethnically mixed education. What went on in the classroom when students of different races/ethnicities learned (or tried to learn) together (interactional diversity) was the crux of the issue. And it soon became clear that many schoolteachers didn't know what to do in racially diverse classrooms: What, if anything, should they do differently?

Forty-plus years of teaching in a major university has taught me that these issues are just as present now in our predominantly white colleges and universities. I see them being replayed in both student and faculty communities in the current context of efforts to increase the representation and quality of education for students of color. I also see the importance of understanding and challenging especially the orientations of young white men and women as they seek to create meaningful relationships with students of color and grapple with life in a more racially diverse society. Thus, I have changed my own classroom approaches and have been involved in creating innovations in interactive and experiential pedagogies and programs, including Community Service Learning and Intergroup Dialogues. In all this work I have often found myself at the edge of my own identity, knowledge, and skill, seeking collegial assistance and support.

With colleagues, I have researched and consulted on efforts to alter the embedded racism and sexism of our colleges and universities, on the ways in which white students and students of color experience racially diverse classrooms, and on how faculty members might alter or improve their own pedagogies—including their identity management tactics—in the interest of creating more effective classrooms, classrooms that are not only diverse but also equitable and multicultural. I know we cannot accomplish this without challenging the racialized and gendered organizational culture and structure of higher education institutions.

Given this background along with conversations with colleagues who care deeply about these issues as we struggle with them, it seemed natural to begin a serious inquiry into faculty members' actual experiences and options in increasingly diverse collegiate environments. When the opportunity arose to work with a challenging and knowledgeable partner like Alford Young Jr., the die was cast.

We come from different social and intellectual backgrounds but from similar political and educational orientations to the academy. Hence, our intellectual orientations and sociopolitical worldviews have come together in the production of the material that is now before you.

Alford Young Jr.

For those familiar with my scholarship, contributing to the project that results in this book may seem like a far stretch from my long-standing interest in the life chances of low-income African American men. Yet there is a strong link between these two pursuits. Much of my commitment to research has involved bringing the experiences and findings concerning the men who I study into the higher education classroom; that is, as an instructor I have dedicated my effort to teaching students about the experiences of marginalized populations, especially low-income African Americans. In teaching on the matter I have been, at various times, intrigued, confused, thrilled, and disappointed by students' reactions to the material about these and other disadvantaged people. Positive feelings surface when my students realize that the lives of such people are as complex as their own. At these points my students endeavor to more thoroughly explore and dissect commonalities and distinctions in the views, opinions, and outlooks of the people being studied and draw comparisons to their own lives.

My disappointments have to do with, among some other occurrences, moments when students expect that my courses be simpler or easier than others because mine are largely based on the study of socially disadvantaged people. The feeling on the part of some of these students is, "How hard can it be to understand these people?" or "Don't they really just really need to stop misbehaving, get jobs, and take better care of their children?"

It is during these moments that I must maintain a careful balance of encouraging critical inquiry while tempering the desire to advocate. As an African American faculty member who largely (though not exclusively) researches and teaches about a social category in which I hold membership, my classroom experiences involve moments of conflict and mild turbulence that I sometimes encourage, sometimes receive as unplanned for, and often explicitly involve my own identity.

My reflections about my teaching, a part of my service as a professor that I take as seriously as my research, led me to take much time over the years to think and talk with my colleague, Mark Chesler, about what goes on in the classroom for faculty in higher education. Talking together led to an effort to plan a research project on teaching in regard to diversity, and that project has resulted in this volume.

Mark Chesler and Alford Young Jr.

Abbreviations Used in This Book

(Used following quoted material from interviewees)

AfAm   African American
ArAm   Arab American/Middle Eastern
AsAm   Asian American
L   Latino/a
NA   Native American
Wh   white
M   man
W   woman
H   humanities
NS   natural science
SS   social science
NS   natural science

Chapter 1

The State of Research with Faculty Identities in Higher Educational Classrooms and Institutional Contexts

Mark A. Chesler

Faculty members are not simply lone scholars and researchers, isolated teachers, or freewheeling entrepreneurs in the university. Much of what they do—or can imagine doing—is affected by the disciplinary, departmental, and organizational context within which they work, teach, and learn and by their relationships with their peers and students. The different missions, operating structures, cultures, and resources of varied higher educational organizations affect support for and resistance to departmental/peer climates and classroom experiences that might improve the quality of life for all faculty, especially for white women faculty and men and women faculty of color. They also impact faculty members' pedagogical options and encounters with students. These organizational contexts often are not conducive to good teaching and learning, let alone to creating effective and

1

diverse environments in which faculty can realize the goals of a critical multicultural community and the creation of generations of students prepared to live in a diverse democracy. Any serious analysis of the professional lives and practices of faculty members as well as of race, gender, and class equity or discrimination in higher education must take account of the organizational cultures and structures within which faculty operate.

This chapter establishes a context and background for the chapters to follow by (1) discussing the raced and gendered nature of these institutions that provides the setting within which faculty members enact their pedagogical and organizational practices, (2) reviewing some of the scholarly and anecdotal literature about the experiences and pedagogical approaches of faculty members of different racial/ethnic and gender identities, and (3) introducing the empirically based chapters that follow and their links to this established literature. As such, it relieves the following chapters of creating lengthy independent reviews of the scholarly literature except insofar as there are sources that pertain most directly and uniquely to their foci. A common understanding of the cultural and structural characteristics of higher educational institutions and related research is background for the following chapters' descriptions and interpretations of the experiences of faculty members of different social identities.

Higher Education as Raced and Gendered Culture

Our research-oriented higher educational institutions (R-1s) and their curricula, pedagogies, and scholarly traditions have been developed principally by—and for—members of privileged social groups and have been maintained more or less in this fashion until very recently (and how much "more or less" is a matter of considerable debate). These systems have privileged white and male faculty members and students and have provided the basis for exclusion and discrimination against members of various racial/ethnic groups and white women. As Jayakumar and associates (2009, 555) note, such privilege may or may not be known or sought: "White faculty benefit from institutional racism irrespective of whether they are consciously aware of or actively support racist attitudes, practices, policies." The benefits to white faculty—and disadvantages to others—include the treatment of some kinds of cultural stances and priorities as legitimate and others not, some faculty scholarly pursuits as normative and others not, and some ways of teaching and relating with students appropriate and rewarded and some not.

Many of the core cultural priorities and practices of higher educational institutions have played significant and positive roles in the history of education and science in our nation. But in their extended application in Historically White Colleges and Universities (HWCUs, also known as Primarily White Institutions,

PWIs) they also sustain and reproduce race and gender inequality and discrimination. Some of these traditions clearly work to the detriment of all scholars and students, but they fall especially hard on people who come from backgrounds supporting alternative values, who are less socialized into or comfortable negotiating the academic culture (a culture dominated by white and male and relatively affluent lifestyles and norms), or who have experienced a history of educational and societal disadvantage, exclusion, and oppression.

These traditions include a focus on the individualistic value orientation of white culture and on individual achievement as the standard for faculty members' scholarly and teaching performance and for student performance. They are reflected in the academic emphasis on and greater reward for single-authored papers or for being the "lead author" on multi-authored works. Individualistic norms also diminish the importance of teamwork and skills in interactions among the faculty, often sapping the vitality of groupwork, communal styles of working and relating, thereby leading to a lack of community or "hollowed collegiality" (Massey, Wilger, and Colbeck 1994). And as Creamer (2006, 74) argues, "The individualistic values that are at the center of the traditional academic reward structure offer one explanation why early career faculty often voice a concern about a sense of isolation and lack of community." They also affect the career trajectories of women colleagues and colleagues of color who may adopt a more collective or communal orientation to departmental life or classroom instruction.

The emphasis on individual achievement also leads to pedagogical approaches that treat students as individual learners, minimizing consideration of their cultural and socioeconomic identities, backgrounds, and peer group relationships. Moreover, because groupwork or teamwork is seldom employed as part of instructional designs, the potential power of collaborative learning is lost. One result of these pedagogies is that generations of students have not learned how to work effectively as team members and especially not as members of diverse teams nor with people of different racial/ethnic backgrounds.

A second tradition emphasizes universalistic norms/definitions of merit and the utilization of standardized—universally applicable, assumed to fit to everyone regardless of cultural background or style—tests or criteria as indicators of such merit. This orientation (along with concerns about bureaucratic efficiency) led to the use of SATs and GREs as admissions criteria, which we know now are culturally biased and systematically disadvantage certain racial/ethnic groups of students and those of lower-class origins, especially those who have been tracked or segregated into inadequate forms of elementary and secondary education. They also privilege students whose prior cultural, socioeconomic, and educational experiences and resources enable them to fit neatly into these narrow definitions of talent and merit. The failure to recognize and act on the limits of universalistic assumptions and policies minimizes race/ethnic, gender,

and class differences and justifies the mythology of a meritocratic system that is open to all.

At the faculty level narrow definitions of merit promote a set of orthodoxies that limit the possibilities for diversity in faculty ranks and work and lifestyle. To be sure, different disciplines have different criteria for excellence, but by and large the range is narrow and privileges research topics and methods that can gain publication in prestigious academic journals that are read primarily by elites and are typically unavailable to the general public. They constrain the hiring, retention, and promotion of faculty members who have opted for lifestyles that may have delayed their entry into the academic job market (i.e., nonaffluent men serving in the armed forces in order to generate the resources to pay for continued education, women bearing and raising children, people of color struggling to overcome societal barriers to educational opportunity). Thus, scholars coming from or committed to serving the interests of women, racial minorities, and working-class or poor communities may face exclusion, punishment, or sanctions in hiring searches or at tenure reviews. Tate (1994) argues that universalism, with its emphasis on transcendency, acontextuality, and single truths, is a worldview that "tends to minimize anything that is historical, contextual or specific with the unscholarly labels of *literary* or *personal*" (249). The universalistic tradition obviously erects barriers to retrieving or using such different perspectives and the potentially unique contributions or stances undertaken by many scholars of color and feminist scholars (and students), thus negatively affecting their advancement within traditional notions of scholarship. As a result, the academy loses the expertise of faculty from different racial/ethnic, gender, class, or cultural backgrounds who are likely to bring unique and valuable insights to the table—to the curriculum, to views of students and pedagogy, to decisions about hiring and promotion, and so forth.

Culturally narrow notions of merit also mean that "On and off college campuses [the products of] white status and privilege are often mistaken for meritorious privilege" (Feagin, Vera, and Imani 1996, 152). Thus, by being seen as "normal," whiteness dominates the culture of the academy and the knowledge it produces and disseminates. In like fashion, Auster and MacRone (1994) discuss how the "masculine" nature of the educational system, reflected in public displays of superior knowledge, argument, and challenge, is seen as a common form of intellectual exchange.

A third major tradition is the generally low priority for undergraduate education in our large, prestigious research universities. Despite rhetoric about commitments to undergraduate education, the recent report on undergraduate teaching at Harvard notes that "The problem lies, for the most part, not in individual values but in what the institution seems to prioritize and reward in its official, publicly visible routines. In principle, FAS (Faculty of Arts and Sciences) expects all faculty members to do what many in fact do: devote comparable time during

the academic year to teaching and research, and teach undergraduates as well as graduate students. But in institutional practice cutting-edge academic research is what FAS celebrates and most consistently rewards" (Harvard 2007, 6–7).

To the extent that white women faculty and faculty of color are likely to spend more time than do white men on teaching and service roles (see, among others, Antonio, Astin, and Cress 2000; Bellas and Toutkoushian 1999), they are disadvantaged by the priority on research as the primary—if not sole—criterion for academic advance. Further, the research priorities of these institutions encourage a form of academic specialization that, as James J. Duderstadt, former president of the University of Michigan and author of the visionary *Michigan Mandate,* (2007) recently pointed out, often prevented or delayed the hiring of minority scholars/teachers who could enhance departmental strength even if they did not fit a narrow (sub)disciplinary need.

Large and prestigious research-oriented universities along with their stellar departments gain their reputations and enhance their own sense of excellence via the activities of research scholars and the production of research. These scholars, especially the senior research-oriented faculty, enhance and enrich the intellectual environment of the university and often are beacons of light and stimulus for interested and committed colleagues and students. At the same time, as academic administrators Cross and Goldenberg (2009, 1) point out, "Today, outstanding teacher-scholars spend much more of their time and energy on their individual scholarly work and their national and international networks than they spend on their local institution." Clearly, not all these senior scholars are interested in or committed to undergraduate education or are effective undergraduate classroom teachers.

The research priority of many R-1 institutions also is reflected in the overrepresentation of the newer generation of junior scholars in nontenure-track roles (often women faculty and faculty of color), in the instruction of large introductory lecture classes, and in some institutions doing the bulk of undergraduate teaching. Cross and Goldenberg (2009, 71) further argue that R-1 institutions' growing rise of non-tenure-track faculty (NTTs—lecturers, instructors, part-timers) is due partly to deans who are "more powerfully driven by academic research and scholarly needs than by teaching needs." These NTT colleagues' lower status conveys important messages about the relatively low priority of such instruction and of the appropriate roles for white women and men and women of color in the larger frame of organizational responsibilities, assignments, and rewards.

An additional result of the low priority on undergraduate teaching in general is a press for efficiency, an emphasis on mass production of students, and an assumption that one type of instruction works best for all faculty and students, regardless of their cultural background or style. The dominance of large lecture-style and "transmission belt" forms of pedagogy (see Freire 1970) fit best, if at all, with white- and male-oriented styles of being, relating, teaching, and learning. Indeed, Johnsrud (1993, 13) argues that "Traditional academic values of autonomy, competition and individualism are called into question as women and, to some extent, minority faculty counter with values of community, connectedness and collaboration." Some of this "countering" is reflected in research by Lindholm and colleagues (Lindholm and Astin 2008; Lindholm and Szelenyi 2006; Lindholm et al. 2005), suggesting that women faculty and faculty of color are more likely than white men faculty to use a wider range of nonbanking and nonnormative approaches in class—student-centered and participative techniques such as open discussion, peer evaluation, dialog, and so forth.

Such alternative approaches are critical because racial/ethnic diversity (called "structural diversity" by Gurin 1999) is a necessary but not sufficient condition for an effective multicultural learning environment. The level and quality of interaction among students (and among students and faculty) of different backgrounds is the crucial added element (see the distinction between "structural" and both "classroom" and "interactional" diversity in Gurin 1999; Gurin et al. 2004; Gurin et al. 2002). Marin (2000, 64), among others, continues this emphasis on pedagogy as she argues, "interaction—in the form of discussion and other active learning techniques—is essential if the potential of multi-racial/multi-ethnic classrooms is to be maximized." Such active and learner-centered pedagogies are quite different from the more typical teacher-centered and lecture-based approaches to teaching (Maruyama and Moreno 2000; Nagda, Gurin, and Lopez 2003).

Finally, contemporary standards of scholarly work in our elite and trendsetting institutions emphasize the production of research that advances academic theory and disciplinary goals over the expansion of public knowledge. The very nature of scholarly activities that focus on limited methodological and epistemological designs and that privilege disciplinary agendas results in work that is read by and generally serves narrow professional audiences and ruling public elites—white and affluent constituencies, for the most part. And even work that might serve the interests of poor people or of communities of color seldom finds its way out of academic texts and journals into the hands of members of these communities.

Many white women and men and women of color—and a good number of younger white men—enter the academy with strong commitments to reduce race and gender oppression and to do scholarly work that links to the needs and interests of disadvantaged or oppressed constituencies in student or civic communities. When their commitments lead them to spend considerable time advising white women students or students of color or otherwise work in ways and on issues not valued or rewarded by traditional academic norms (Tierney and Bensimon 1996; Turner 2003), they may be seen as deviants or transgressors. Then the power of the dominant normative system works to threaten, constrain, or sanction them for their alternative choices, both in formal tenure and promotion reviews and in informal everyday forms of interaction.

Tierney and Bensimon (1996, 10) suggest that as a result of some of these conventions, core norms, or sacred cows, "The social fabric of the academic community has been torn asunder." A focus on diversity efforts in R-1 institutions and the evidence in this volume regarding the different classroom, pedagogical, and collegial experiences of their white faculty and faculty of color as well as their women faculty and men faculty lay bare the narrow and elitist cultural assumptions and organizational practices that govern higher education and help explain much of the underlying lack of community and civility of discourse within academe.

The Campus and Classroom Climate

The demographic realities and cultural traditions identified above set the stage for how faculty members approach and respond to what goes on in the classroom, the central arena for student learning and faculty teaching. And the faculty's approach to the classroom, the pedagogical and curricular choices they make, determines much of students' experiences. Of course most faculty members care about the instructional process and try hard to be effective teachers. At the same time, however, many have not been trained to, do not know how to, are not rewarded for, and are not provided with the support to be effective in diverse and multicultural classrooms. Faculty members' own race/ethnicity, gender, and age, separately and together, also affect their expectations and approaches to the classroom and how students anticipate and respond to them. The application of universalist norms about academic performance that do not attend to these potentially different realities fails to assess adequately or accurately diverse forms of academic merit and style.

We know that white students often enter into higher education from race—and class—segregated communities and schools, experientially ignorant about race and unaccustomed to interacting with students and faculty of color. Students of color, especially African Americans, also often arrive from segregated backgrounds and may only know others as they have been depicted in the media (Massey and Denton 1993; Orfield and Gordon 2001). Once in college, many students continue to mirror what they learned previously and what they see and hear about race in the media and in public policy disputes.

Despite the existence of different perceptions and experiences as well as the pockets of separation and conflict that occur, some data also show that many campus settings are not highly segregated by race (Antonio 2001; Gurin 1999). Many students and faculty enjoy substantial interaction across race/ethnic lines, and those who take the opportunity to explore such issues can contribute to the development of a diverse democratic society. Indeed, classes and programs that provide students with more sustained intergroup exposure lead to greater growth in active thinking processes, intellectual engagement, academic skills, and more intergroup friendships (Gurin et al. 2002; Gurin, Nagda, and Lopez 2004). Such experiences can only occur when faculty members understand and deal with the likely effects of prior patterns of separation, ignorance, and awkwardness.

Although many students of color can identify faculty members who have had a positive influence on them and faculty teaching strategies that were successful, many others (often the same people) report feeling excluded from the curriculum and the classroom. Research extending back more than two decades indicates that some faculty members, especially white faculty, do not expect students of color to do well in class, treat them as all alike (i.e., stereotype them and fail to see individual or subgroup differences among them), single them out as racial "experts" or spokespersons, and express discomfort in relating with them (Allen 1988; Duster 1991; Trujillo 1986). Students of color are not alone in reporting these problems in relating with university faculty; LGBT students (Rhoads 1997), white students from working-class backgrounds (Black 1995; Peckham 1995), and students with physical disabilities (McCune 2001) often report similar experiences.

Helping students of any social background learn about the contributions of different social groups, their own privilege or lack thereof, the nation's history of social discrimination and oppression, and how to get the most out of their interactions with others is not merely a matter of curricular content. Classroom pedagogies that do not engage students in positive and mutually productive classroom interactions with diverse peers, that reproduce or fail to interrupt discrimination or unequal treatment from other students, or that fail to provide access to affirming relationships with faculty members diminish all students' collegiate experience.

This brief discussion of the student and classroom climate further sets the stage for understanding the literature discussing the approaches and experiences of faculty members of different racial/ethnic and gender identities, both in and out of the classroom.

Research on Faculty Members' Social Identities and the Academy

The raced and gendered context of the academy, including colleagues' and students' assumptions and reactions, affects how faculty members operate in the classroom and in their relations with their colleagues. The literature about the role of faculty members' social identities in their classroom, departmental, and collegiate experiences comes mostly from a series of first-person anthologies and essays (women of color: Berry and Mizelle 2006; Latino/as: Castellanos and Jones 2003; African Americans: Cleveland 2004; faculty from working-class backgrounds: Jacobs, Cintron, and Canton 2002; Dews and Law 1995; African American men: Jones 2002; Asian women: Li and Beckett 2006; African American women: Mabokela and Green 2001; women: MacDonald and Sánchez-Casal 2002; lesbian faculty: Mintz and Rothblum 1997; faculty of color: Stanley 2006a; TuSmith and Reddy 2002; women faculty of color: Vargas 2002). However, there exist relatively few monographs or anthologies that are explicitly comparative in design and presentation. A significant exception, albeit with a small sample, is the work of Turner and Myers (2000).

In dramatic contrast to this list and to the many articles cited throughout the literature there is relatively little published work that explicitly examines the relationship between white male faculty members' identities and their classroom approaches or departmental experiences—historically, their racial/ethnic identities are treated as irrelevant, as the unspecified "given" or "norm" from which "others'" experiences can be examined (for exceptions see Giroux 1997; Lea and Helfand 2006); Weinstein and O'Bear (1992); also see Gillespie, Ashbaugh, and DeFiore 2002; Maxwell 2004; O'Brien 2006; Wagner 2005—are rare among white faculty as they write about their personal awareness of their race/ethnic identities (among others) and the way these identities impact their pedagogical choices and relations with students of varied backgrounds. Fortunately, in the past decade a series of articles exploring these issues have been appearing in journals such as the *Journal of Diversity in Higher Education* and *Race Ethnicity and Education*. Jessica Charbeneau and Mark A. Chesler's chapter (7) extends this literature with a detailed analysis of the ways white faculty in this sample deal with race and their own and students' racial relationships in their classrooms—either reproducing or transforming normative notions of race.

Many white faculty and faculty of color along with many men and women faculty detail some of the joys as well as dilemmas they experience in a diverse environment. They report the richness of teaching and learning experiences, their pleasure at working with diverse groups of students and colleagues, and their feelings of effectiveness in a diverse community. With such excitement and opportunity for growth, however, often comes a series of struggles or dilemmas. Quite clearly white men faculty, compared with white women faculty and men and women faculty of color, experience the academy—classrooms, colleagues, students, departments, and institutional environs—differently (see Johnson-Bailey and Cervero 2008 for a joint report by an African American woman and a white man on their divergent faculty experiences in the classroom). Many white men faculty can automatically expect to be treated with respect and deference—and are surprised when they are not. Many faculty members of color cannot make that assumption; they often experience substantial hostility, or at least distance and caution, from white students—and sometimes from students of color as well. Faculty of color often highlight the tensions of being negatively stereotyped with regard to their cultural styles or characteristics, having to prove their competence and counter assumptions of incompetence, being the target of direct or indirect insults, and dealing with requests/expectations from students and peers that they conform or assimilate to white cultures and norms (Harlow 2003; Messner 2000; Sánchez-Casal 2002; Stanley et al. 2003; Turner and Myers 2000; TuSmith and Reddy 2002). In somewhat similar fashion, women faculty, of whatever racial/ ethnic origin, more often report being challenged by students and diminished or not supported by their colleagues. Further documentation and analysis of students' challenges to both the subject-matter expertise and the classroom authority of faculty members of different races/ethnicities and genders is provided in Alford A. Young Jr., Megan Furhman, and Mark A. Chesler's chapter (4).

Some faculty reports and comments on these dynamics also reflect the "double jeopardy" that often accompanies the intersectionality of race and gender experienced by faculty women of color (Bavishi, Madera, and Hebl 2010; Myers 2002). Not only is this double jeopardy especially problematic in its own right; it also often has the additional confusing result of causing faculty women of color to wonder whether it is their race or gender (or both) that is in play. In chapter 8 Kristie A. Ford analyzes the ways in which these pressures and challenges affect how faculty women of color (especially) focus on "managing their bodies and selves" in the classroom.

Faculty of color, regardless of their teaching competencies, often receive lower teaching evaluations from white students than do their white colleagues (McPherson and Jewell 2007). And the same dynamic may occur for white women faculty (Reid 2010). Students often have differential expectations of how men and women instructors ought to behave and, therefore, may respond to and evaluate their teaching differently vis-a-vis men. For instance, Fiske and colleagues (2002) report that women faculty, more than men, are judged partially on the basis of student perceptions of their warmth and accessibility. Men are more likely to be judged independently of students' contact with or accessibility to them, and their level of preparation and organization is more likely to be assumed and not questioned. But even when men and women or white faculty and faculty of color receive roughly equivalent quantitative evaluations, this apparent parity often masks some of the qualitatively different aspects of their experiences and students' reactions to them (Kardia and Wright 2003; Russ, Simonds, and Hunt 2002).

Overt disrespect, questioning of competencies, differential expectations and evaluations, and occasional name calling or epithets are all forms of harassment (Myers 2002). In more covert form they represent micro-aggressions, "those brief and commonplace verbal, behavioral and environmental indignities that often unintentionally convey hostile, derogatory or negative racial insults" and that wear on the spirit of the recipients (Sue et al. 2009, 1092; see also Solorzano, Ceja, and Yosso 2000). One result of these expectations and challenges is that faculty of color may experience greater amounts of race-based disappointment, anger, and stress and may suffer from "battle fatigue" (Smith 2004; Smith and Witt 1993). Many faculty of color and white women faculty also feel they have to work harder than do white men faculty to establish their credentials and maintain their roles as instructors and scholars (Laden and Hagedorn 2000; Turner and Myers 2000). The added burden of dealing with such racial and gender dynamics or of preparing oneself to face them makes life harder for white women faculty and men and women faculty of color, lowers their satisfaction with professional and institutional life, and deprives students and the institution of some of their talent (Stanley 2006a; Turner and Myers 2000).

Faculty members' social identities also seem to play important roles in the choices they make about curricular content and pedagogical tactics, albeit often unconsciously. Using data from a national survey of faculty, Lindholm and colleagues (2005) report that more women faculty than men faculty feel it is "very important" to help students develop knowledge and appreciation for other ethnic groups. And faculty members from underrepresented groups agree more often than do white faculty that "racial and ethnic diversity should be more strongly reflected in the curriculum" (15). Of course, to the extent that academic instruction and classroom management of race and gender dynamics are seen as only discipline-specific matters (e.g., relevant only in the social sciences and some humanities), it is easy to understand why they are not often accommodated or accounted for in other disciplines and courses. But the reality is that race and gender as well as the dynamics of historic advantage and disadvantage are alive in every classroom, regardless of the subject matter.

With regard to pedagogical choices, on the basis of a survey of over sixty-five thousand college and university faculty, Lindholm and Astin (2008, 187) also report that "women, faculty of color, and younger faculty are more inclined than men, white/Caucasian, and older faculty to employ student-centered approaches to teaching" (see also, Lindholm and Szelenyi 2006; Maruyama and Moreno 2000). Such student-centered or active learning approaches include an emphasis on discussion rather than lecturing and the use of experiential exercises, community-service learning opportunities, and student-initiated activities. Kumashiro (2003, 58) argues that such pedagogical approaches respond more effectively to different groups of students' diverse learning styles and needs and that "Educators who presume that their teaching consists solely of the formal curriculum cannot help but teach in ways that repeat the often oppressive curricula." In a similar vein Scheurich and Young (2002, 225) note that "If a university's standard pedagogical method is culturally congruent with the culture of white students but not with the culture of students of color, this is institutional racism." Lindholm and Astin

(2008, 187) suggest, then, that "in an era characterized by increasing diversity among college students with respect to past educational experiences and learning styles, the merits of incorporating learner-centered approaches to teaching may be especially compelling."

It is important to recognize that such pedagogical approaches may challenge some core assumptions about teaching and learning along with the place of students' subjective experiences and emotional responses, that are rooted in a predominantly white male academic culture (O'Brien 2006). Indeed, as Bernal (1998, 557) argues with particular concern about the field of education, "Theories of cognitive development still espoused in many teacher education and educational psychology programs are normed on the behaviors of white, middle-class, male students, and are ignorant of or misapplied to students of any other identities." And in institutions with a generally low priority on attending to the needs and styles of undergraduates, there is likely to be even less attention to the needs and styles of students from historically underrepresented communities.

The reality of both societal and academic dynamics of racism and sexism (and classism, homophobism, etc.) is that conflict around these social phenomena is a natural feature of all classrooms. Lack of knowledge, awkwardness, and suspicion between white students and students of color are almost always present in classrooms. Sometimes such conflicts are overt, public, visible, and admitted; sometimes they are covert, invisible and unacknowledged, operating under the radar. In chapter 3 Alford A. Young Jr. provides a conceptual scheme for understanding the constitutive elements of classroom conflict—students, the faculty member, the curricular material, faculty members' pedagogical approaches, and the physical space of the classroom (see also Marin 2000).

Boysen and colleagues (2009) report a variety of ways in which faculty members respond to incidents of racial bias in the classroom, ranging from challenging them via direct confrontation and providing information to overlooking or ignoring them. And in Sue and colleagues' (2009, 1096) intensive research with a small sample of white faculty, "Two major characteristics emerged that made facilitating racial dialogues difficult: (a) fear of losing classroom control and (b) the dialogues' emotionally charged nature."

Despite—or perhaps because of—these concerns, some faculty actively seek the positive value of conflict as a learning tool, utilizing the psychological principles of ideological incongruence, cognitive dissonance, or disequilibrium as part of their pedagogical approach (Bowman 2010; Gurin et al. 2002; McFalls and Cobb-Roberts 2001). By surfacing or creating tension and conflict and by challenging students to confront the differences between their own world views and those of others or between their own understanding of social phenomena and the empirical reality of the social environment, cognitive dissonance can actively contribute to new understandings of self and other. McFalls and Cobb-Roberts

(2001) and Wagner (2005) suggest that faculty can increase the chances of more positive responses by preparing students to expect, recognize, and deal with the challenging nature of dissonant material ahead of time. Other analyses and guides for faculty members' skillful use of such dissonance have been discussed especially in the context of multicultural pedagogies (Nagda, Gurin, and Lopez 2003; Rich and Cargile 2004). Two chapters in this volume explore student classroom conflict and faculty members' proactive or reactive responses to them. Penny A. Pasque, Jessica Charbeneau, Mark A. Chesler, and Corissa Carlson (chapter 6) examine whether and how faculty members perceive, acknowledge, and respond to student conflict as well as the extent to which their responses varied by race/ethnicity and discipline. Kristie A. Ford and Kelly Maxwell (chapter 5) report on the pedagogical principles, practices, and skills a subsample of faculty members employ in their efforts to deal with such classroom events. All these and other investigations into student-peer conflict emphasize the need for faculty to create a relatively safe space—for both faculty and students—in which all involved can more or less freely explore themselves and others and respectfully express their views and hear others' views. Safe space is relative, however, because absolute safety is neither an attainable nor advisable component of a learning enterprise.

It is not just students (or colleagues) who may stand in the way of such curricular or pedagogical innovation; faculty members may be their own serious restraints. Chesler, Lewis, and Crowfoot (2005, 238; and see table 12.1 in this volume) illustrate what curricular content, instructional strategies and activities, and assessments of student knowledge and classroom dynamics might look like in a more multicultural classroom environment. The inclusion of nondominant group perspectives in the curriculum, interactive learning designs that center on the personal experiences of students from different groups, assessments that focus on action-oriented projects, and equity in student participation all are noted therein. In turn, the active resistance or passive failure to adopt diverse curricular and pedagogical content and approaches is another example of how traditional teaching styles may be based on universal assumptions about learning and thus end up being culturally and politically biased.

Many faculty of color suggest that the expectation that they will be especially attentive to the needs of students of color often leads to a form of extra duty or "cultural taxation," which occurs especially when there are only one or a very few faculty of color or white women in a department or college (Balderrama, Texiera, and Valdez 2006; Jayakumar et al. 2009; Stanley et al. 2003; Turner and Myers 2000). Then they may be called upon to advise many or all the women students or students of color in their departments, teach primarily race- or gender-related courses, take on the mentoring of many junior faculty of color and junior women faculty because no one else may be doing it, serve on many committees in order to ensure token representation, be called upon to "handle" racial or gender conflicts, or feel compelled to respond to academic and service requests from many campus and community constituencies. In chapter 10 Tiffany Joseph and Laura Hirshfield examine the cultural taxation encountered by white women faculty and men and women faculty of color and enrich prior discussions of this issue with an analysis of the crisis of legitimacy and identity that some faculty experience as a result.

One result of these increased academic and community requests and pressures is that faculty members of racial/ethnic minority groups may find themselves moving back and forth between two communities, responding both to conventional departmental and university assignments and serving as special resources to students and communities of color (Conway-Jones 2006). Under these circumstances many faculty of color struggle to adopt a bicultural stance and often "code-switch" or negotiate between the cultures in which they were raised and live and the culture in which they now ply their trade (Sadao 2003; Segura 2003; Stanley 2006b).

In Departments and with Peers/Colleagues

The dominance of the white male culture of the academy is also reflected in the collegial and departmental relationships reported by white women faculty and men and women faculty of color. The underrepresentation of women faculty and faculty of color sets up the possibilities of "solo status" or "token status" that often leads to more explicit and/or implicit stereotyping, scrutiny, and ignorant or negative judgments (Niemann and Dovidio 1998; Valian 1998). Many white female faculty and faculty of color also report a range of subtle but nevertheless problematic challenges with their peers, often including not feeling listened to, difficulty gaining and being treated with respect, being treated unfairly, and being pigeonholed on account of their racial/ethnic or gender status. Concerns also often arise in these faculty members' relationships with departmental structures, norms, and resource allocations.

It is obvious that the classroom and faculty members' classroom approaches and experiences are not separate from the nature of the academic environment and culture in which they teach and conduct research. Aside from the classroom itself, the importance of the local departmental climate and disciplinary culture and priorities for faculty members' curricular and pedagogical choices is highlighted by Mayhew and Grunwald (2006), who report that instructors' propensity to incorporate diversity-related content into their courses was related to their department's emphasis on this approach, to their chair's commitment to it, and to the accompanying rewards for such innovation. Boudreau and Eggleston (2002) document their own experience as white faculty members trying to alter traditional classroom approaches and to incorporate an antiracist stance. They encountered collegial resistance that was couched as appeals to traditional curricula content and pedagogical approaches. Colleagues may sanction white women faculty and faculty of color who identify "too closely" with teaching and with students, potentially undermining their departmental standing and careers. These reports again reflect the low priority given to undergraduate education in general and especially to faculty efforts to expend energy incorporating innovative material or pedagogies in their courses, particularly materials related to race/ethnicity, gender, and sexual orientation.

Women faculty often report a poorer departmental climate, less support, and less effective mentoring compared to men faculty (although relatively universal, these issues are especially potent in the natural sciences, math, and engineering; see ADVANCE 2002; Chesler and Chesler 2002; Monroe et al. 2008). Moreover, the lack of culturally relevant and effective mentoring of white women faculty often is one factor in their reports of lower levels of job satisfaction (Bilimoria et al. 2006; Callister 2006). Tillman (2001, 310) notes that African American faculty often are satisfied with the career mentoring they receive from white faculty but that "same-race mentor-protégé relationships provide significantly more psychosocial support than cross-race relationships." Obviously both types of mentoring and support—professional/technical and psychosocial—from whatever sources, are necessary. A closely related result of such marginalization is less access to social/professional networks and the "tacit knowledge" that helps young scholars progress effectively through the institution (Jordan and Bilimoria 2007; Rankin, Nielsen, and Stanley 2007).

Reports of sexual harassment and discrimination in the academy in general often center on issues of gender stereotyping, marginalization, harassment, policies regarding salary equity and promotions, and the lack of accommodations for faculty attempting to fulfill both academic and family/home obligations (Gunter and Stambach 2003; Monroe et al. 2008; Settles et al. 2007; Valian 1998). For some observers, the norms of competition and individual achievement that guide the promotion system themselves reflect traditional definitions of masculinity and male dominance (Gunter and Stambach 2003).

Similarly, faculty of color, in addition to being underrepresented, more often than white faculty report a "chilly" departmental/university climate; lower satisfaction with resource allocations; higher levels of racial stereotyping from colleagues; more tokenism; racist and disparaging remarks, such as questioning whether they were "affirmative action hires"; and a greater sense of exclusion or marginalization (Hobson-Horton 2004; Smith 2004; Thomas and Hollinshead 2001; Turner 2003; Verdugo 2003). Harlow (2003) also emphasizes the implications of intersectionality in discussions of such marginality, noting the double jeopardy that many women faculty of color face along with Asian American faculty's reports of feelings of greater institutional isolation than their white peers.

Departmental chairs also play a significant role in faculty members' sense of satisfaction. For instance, in a study conducted with women faculty in the natural sciences, Settles and colleagues (2007) report significant relationships between these faculty members' views of their chairs' leadership and their perceptions of a negative and sexist departmental climate along with a minimal sense of their own "voice" or ability to influence departmental procedures and decisions. These negative climate factors, in turn, are significantly related with lower job satisfaction and feelings that their professional success was not important to their colleagues and chair (ADVANCE 2008).

In sum, on the basis of a sample of over thirty-three thousand faculty, Astin and colleagues (1997, 25) report that "Compared to White faculty, faculty of color are less satisfied with nearly every aspect of their jobs." Seifert and Umbach's (2008) later research with a NCES sample of over eighteen thousand faculty respondents indicates that the lower satisfaction reported by women faculty and faculty of color typically is not due to the intrinsic nature of academic job and roles, per se, but rather to their extrinsic characteristics—relations with coworkers, rewards and resources, promotion possibilities, respect, and collegiality. The lower level of satisfaction appears most dramatic among those white women faculty and men and women faculty of color who have solo status—who are the only member of their social group in the department or area (Niemann and Dovidio 1998). Ultimately, faculty who report less satisfaction are more likely to state a desire to leave for another institution—and perhaps to actually leave (ADVANCE 2008; Jayakumar et al. 2009).

Because many faculty of color enter the academy with an explicit desire to provide service to their racial/ethnic communities, they are especially likely to respond to service requests and demands from these local communities, off campus as well as in the classroom and university. However, Akbar (2002) notes that responding to these community requests, though burdensome, can also be a source of agency and positive energy and another, perhaps alternative, source of scholarly credibility, personal esteem, and job satisfaction. Faculty members' experiences in this arena expose structural forms of racism and challenge the meritocratic and individualistic views of race and racism that prevail in the society and the academy—sometimes to the detriment of the particular scholar—and of course to the detriment of an open and multicultural academy (Bonilla-Silva 2001). Indeed, Maher and Tetrault (1997, 72) note that "A necessary part of perceiving how the assumption of Whiteness shapes the construction of classroom knowledge is understanding its centrality to the academy's practice of intellectual domination, namely, the imposition of certain ways of constructing the world through the lenses of traditional disciplines. Such domination is often couched in the language of detachment and universality, wherein the class, race and gender position of the 'knower' is ignored or presumed irrelevant."

In a similar vein Padilla (2003) and Ibarra (2003) discuss how research issues and problems related to the Latino/a population may be seen as irrelevant to mainstream scholars and established (often disciplinocentric as well as traditional) scholarly paradigms; as a result, their academic credibility may be challenged by colleagues as "marginal," "lacking objectivity," "watered down," or "oppositional" (Balderrama et al. 2006; Valle 2002). Stanley (2006a) also comments on the reports of similar pressures experienced by Asian American and Native American faculty (see also DeLoria 1998; Nakanishi 1993).

These reports and analyses indicate that, despite some noteworthy individual efforts, organizational norms and established patterns of intergroup relations continue to typify collegial interactions in ways that often create a negative climate for white women faculty and faculty men and women of color. They also typify some of the experiences of faculty members from working-class backgrounds (Centra and Gaubatz 2000; Dews and Law 2005) and those with LGBTQ sexual identities (Mintz and Rothblum 1997; Russ, Simonds, and Hunt 2002).

Many of these pressures and consequent difficulties for scholars of color emanate from the dominance of western European and white American cultural values present in the academy as well as their potential difference or distance from the core values of African American or Latino cultures. They are the daily and common enactments that flow from academic commitments to universal standards for performance and to a priority on scholarly detachment and objectivity. These strains and the additional time and energy it takes to deal with them often are invisible to and not understood by members of the majority community and, thus, often are overlooked when assessing the workload and accomplishments of white women faculty and faculty men and women of color (Harlow 2003). Kolodny (2000) calls this a "hidden overload." In addition, the very nature of these added burdens reflects elements of the monocultural style of most colleges and universities, wherein a lack of systematic and proactive attention to the particular needs of minority students, colleagues, and communities is part of a passive racist and sexist organizational posture. The questions for many faculty of color and white women faculty, especially those without tenure and especially for faculty women with families, is whether and how to adapt to the traditional white male academic culture and its racial/ethnic- and gender-based norms as well as how much time and energy to invest in challenging this culture or evading it. To be sure, many young white male scholars also suffer from the pressure on them arising from the older white male academic culture, and some of them, along with white women faculty, either leave or elect not to seek employment in the R-1 university system. Mason, Goulden, and Frasch (2009) comment on the concerns that both men and women graduate students—potential future faculty members—have about these pressures and the lack of attention to work-life balance and the importance of family-friendly environments in the academy: 35 percent of the male graduate students and 53 percent of the female graduate students they queried indicated that they were "very concerned" about such issues.

The range of issues raised above draws our attention beyond faculty representation and demographics and beyond individual student/classroom and peer/ departmental interactions to organizational patterns of cultural ignorance or disregard, outright insensitivity, messages of exclusion, and various subtle and not-so-subtle expressions of cultural dominance and privilege. They reflect some of the same issues reported about intergroup interactions and organizational discriminations in relationships and institutions in the society at large. And they draw our attention to the need to challenge some of the core norms and traditions of the higher education enterprise. Such change must be undertaken at both the individual and the systemic level in order to alter effectively both institutional structures/cultures and individual patterns of expression and interaction. Ruby Beale, Mark A. Chesler, and Elizabeth Ramus (chapter 11) detail how some faculty engage in various forms of "engaged scholarship" in their teaching, research, and service efforts and elect to be conscious advocates of diversity and diversity-related concerns in classrooms, departments, and local communities.

Agency in the Face of Such Pressures

No set of racial or gender interactions in our society is "all good" or "all bad" nor are the problems and dilemmas reported above etched in stone. Although it is important to acknowledge the organizational forces that so clearly affect the quality of life of all faculty members—particularly so for white women faculty and men and women faculty of color—no one should imagine that these colleagues and their white and men allies are rendered powerless, disabled, or solely as victims in their daily classroom, peer, departmental, and career struggles. Many faculty members develop ways of establishing and asserting agency, of finding ways to cope with these situations, to learn from them, to survive and even thrive in their midst, and hopefully to improve the quality of life, learning, and social justice in their institutions. All faculty bear the responsibility for personal and organizational changes in the academy, but because white faculty dominate the academy, Messner (2000, 464) argues that they especially should use their authority to adopt practices that challenge and disrupt "the commonplace, liberal, white male habitus that is, perhaps unwillingly, complicit with the devaluation of women, and women and men of color."

Park and Denson (2009) created a measure of faculty "diversity advocacy," basing it on faculty members' professed value of diversity and their notions of the goals their institutions should adopt to promote understanding. Their concept of institutional goals is limited to the inclusion of racial/ethnic issues in the curriculum, but even so, it is clear that white women faculty and black faculty were most likely to adopt a diversity advocacy perspective—indeed, all faculty of color supported this stance more than did white faculty. In addition, faculty in education, social science, and humanities were most likely to endorse this commitment, whereas colleagues in engineering, physical sciences, and mathematics were least likely to do so. A more elaborate set of conceptualizations of diversity advocacy and a wider set of examples of faculty approaches to such agency are explored further in Beale, Chesler, and Ramus's chapter (11) on diversity advocacy.

White women faculty and faculty women and men of color seldom are passive victims of these cultural and structural forces and their reflection in the daily enactments of racial and gender discrimination by white students and faculty peers. Women faculty of color, especially, are not victims, even when victimized; they are unlikely to internalize these messages about being inadequate, less than, or a token. Several authors commenting on the marginalization and discrimination felt by many white women faculty and faculty men and women of color argue that there can be benefits as well as drawbacks to disparagement and exclusion (Monroe et al. 2008; Settles et al. 2007; Thomas and Hollinshead 2001; Turner 2003). Echoing hooks's (1990) notion of using the margin as a "space of resistance" they discuss the importance of building communities of marginalized faculty and of linking to their communities and interest groups in civic arenas outside the academy. For some faculty of color, strong connections with and service to local racial/ethnic communities are positive responses to feelings of marginalization and alternative sources of validation and usefulness. They may set the stage for the critical agency that counters feelings of isolation and injustice and that redefines academic structures and culture. In these spaces faculty can seek to transform elements of the dominant white male academy and perhaps even the structural/cultural contexts described earlier. Such efforts stand as alternatives to accepting or internalizing disparaging messages from students or colleagues or deciding to "opt out" (or be pushed out) as a way of escaping from a distressing and dangerous environment.

Several of the chapters in this volume examine the kinds of agency undertaken by faculty members in their own classrooms. In chapters 11 (Beale, Chesler, and Ramus) and 12 (Young and Chesler) authors discuss faculty agency in a wider range of perspectives, arenas, and actions.

Chapter 2

Issues of Research Design and Reflexivity

Penny A. Pasque, Mark A. Chesler,
and Alford A. Young Jr.

The purpose of this study is to explore the ways in which faculty members' social identities impact their experience in the university, especially but not solely in the classroom. We focus on their personal sense of their racial/ethnic and gender identities, their approach to pedagogical and curricular issues, their experiences in diverse classrooms and with diverse student bodies, their relationships with their peers, and their general outlook on university life.

This project was initiated and led by two senior male faculty members in the social sciences, one African American and one white. Over several years two postdoctoral colleagues, thirteen graduate students, and fourteen undergraduates were involved in the varied processes of designing and carrying out the research. Among this total team of thirty-one persons were seven men and twenty-four women: fifteen whites, eleven African American or Afro-Carribbeans, two

Latinas, two Asian Americans, and one person of Middle Eastern origin. The core members, over time, included the two senior faculty, one postdoc scholar, nine graduate students, and six undergraduates.

During the years of data collection and analysis some undergraduate and graduate students finished their degrees and left the university and others entered the project in their stead. Faculty members, postdocs, and graduate students conducted all the interviews; undergraduates were involved in all other aspects of the process, including reviewing literature, coding and analyzing data, and engaging in the interpretation, theory development, and writing.

The entire research team consisted of volunteers, of researchers for whom matters of race and gender—identity group membership, social location, organizational structures and cultures, teaching and pedagogy—were primary in their studies and work. Many were practicing or committed to learning how to practice pedagogical approaches that respected and responded to the role of such issues in the classroom. Given the expertise and personal intellectual involvement of team members in the issues guiding the project and in the interest of mobilizing their voluntary energy, team members were encouraged to determine their own particular points of interest in the data. More importantly, there was minimal epistemological or theoretical orthodoxy for approaching the data. Hence, different peoples' work (as represented in the following chapters) defines and prioritizes the issues in different ways, and the comparative approaches taken toward the data are multifold and overlapping.

Several graduate students discussed how they were drawn to the project because of their interest in advancing their own understanding of teaching and conducting research in multicultural environments. They focused on learning more about themselves and people who shared their racial/ethnic identities who were successful teachers, researchers, and scholars. For instance:

> I became interested in the experiences of the women of color faculty. In particular, the poignant stories of the black female faculty struck me, in part because the issues of legitimacy/authority raised by these participants were concerns that I have encountered—and would continue to encounter—as I moved through the various realms of academic life. (African American, woman)
>
> I was really interested in learning from some folks who'd had success. As a graduate student I think I was also motivated by wanting to one day be one of those faculty who was known for being good at this. (white, woman)

These reflections from graduate student researchers focus on the academic as well as life and career-relevant lessons gained as well as the potential for applying such information to their own academic futures. In this sense, all the researchers learned from the narratives and experiences the informants shared as this process facilitated connections between theory, practice, and reflection.

Participation in the project provided graduate and undergraduate students access to evocative and useful stories not generally shared in typical classroom and advising contexts. This connection between research and teaching and between experience and reflection epitomizes the learning objectives of the larger research project and one of the goals of this book—that readers will also learn from the information and views both informants and researchers express here.

Indeed, several former team members now teaching in the academy reflected back on how work with the project reverberated currently in their academic careers.

> As a new faculty member, and more specifically as a new faculty member who is *also* a young black woman, it is surreal that I am now experiencing much of what I abstractly researched during my graduate days at the university. (African American, woman)
>
> Aside from my academic focus on race/ethnicity and teaching, there are three primary ways my involvement with the project has shaped my graduate education: access to mentorship and a community of scholars; development of theoretical, analytical, and practical research skills through applied practice; and exposure to the benefits and challenges of collaborative research. (white, woman)

The first colleague reports how her current experience mirrors that of the faculty she interviewed as a graduate student. What once may have been abstract notions and theories are now part of her daily experience as a new faculty member. And she is now aware that her experience as "a young black woman" in the academy is not unique to her as an individual. The second colleague expands on these reflections to identify the ways in which this volunteer research involvement shaped her graduate experience. Access to mentoring and a community of scholars in real-time and collaborative research was instrumental in shaping this junior scholar's graduate research experience.

Design Decisions

The Interview/Informant Sample

In gathering the data we constructed a sample pool of faculty members who had received university awards for their teaching and diversity-related service along with additional "snowball sample" nominations by these awardees. We relied on face-to-face interviews with this sample of sixty-six faculty members at a major midwestern Extensive Research (R-1) university. The final sample was diverse on several dimensions (the following abbreviations will be used from this point forward in this volume following excerpts from interviewees and interviewers):

thirty-two women faculty (W) and thirty-four men faculty (M); eighteen white faculty (Wh), twenty African American faculty (AfAm), fourteen Asian American faculty (AsAm), eight Latino/a faculty (L), four Native American faculty (NA), and two Arab American/Middle Eastern faculty (ArAm); twenty-five social science faculty (SS), twenty-two natural science faculty (NS), and nineteen humanities faculty (H).

Faculty selected for inclusion in the sample all had reputations as outstanding instructors and as especially thoughtful practitioners of teaching in diverse classrooms. No attempt was made to gather a representative sample (for survey data with a more representative character see Astin et al. 1977; Lindholm et al. 2002; Lindholm et al. 2005) but instead to solicit the most advanced thinking and experience on these issues from what is, in many ways, a particularly sophisticated cadre. That sophistication is reflected by the numerous awards and citations for campus diversity leadership or teaching excellence that members of this sample have garnered as well as their nomination by their peers as leaders in teaching innovations and diversity efforts. Moreover, many of these faculty had publicly asserted their commitment to teaching, to teaching effectively in a diverse environment, and to employing unique, progressive, or innovative approaches to that endeavor in a university that is intensely committed to research.

Selection of a sample on these bases may have implications for the issues we explore herein: these colleagues may be more aware of, sensitive to, and adept at dealing with these issues than their less-experienced or less publicly noted or rewarded colleagues. Their wisdom and the problems they nevertheless face should be most valuable. What they have to offer about teaching philosophies and practices can be taken to represent faculty who are most committed to undergraduate education and to attending to issues of race/ethnicity and gender equality in education. If their wisdom does not always represent "best practices," they do reflect some of the strongest and longest-standing efforts to struggle with and commit oneself to the tenets of multiculturalism and diversity. However, the price of such a leading-edge sample is that it will be dangerous to generalize facilely from their experiences to the larger faculty population that has not demonstrated either such interest/commitment or reputational expertise.

Although faculty members of color constitute a large proportion of the sample, this is not characteristic of the population of the faculty at large at this university. Consistent with national patterns, a significant racial and gender gap persists at this institution in tenured and tenure-track ranks, despite its national reputation as a leader in efforts to create faculty and student diversity. According to the *Chronicle of Higher Education* (2011, B53), 19 percent of all full-time tenure-track faculty at this university are members of racial/ethnic minority groups (of this total, 12 percent are Asian Pacific Islanders, 4 percent are black, 3 percent are Hispanic, and less than 1 percent are Native American). Twenty-six percent of all tenure-track faculty are women. The lack of an organizational critical mass of some racial/ethnic minorities or of white women, especially in some fields, can be expected to affect the nature of informants' classroom experiences and their relationships with departmental colleagues.

Once potential participants were identified, the two project directors sent each of them a formal letter describing the purpose of the project, why and how they were invited to be part of the sample, an indication that the project had received clearance from the relevant IRB, an estimation that the interview would take an hour to an hour and a half, and contact information for reaching them. Within ten days a team member followed up with an e-mail or a telephone call seeking to arrange an agreeable time and place for a taped interview.

A total of seventy-three faculty members were contacted, and only seven colleagues either refused to be interviewed or failed to respond to repeated efforts to schedule an interview, resulting in a positive response rate of 90 percent (sixty-six out of seventy-three). Three of the sixty-six informants requested that their interviews not be taped (all three were junior faculty members not yet tenured and undoubtedly feeling particularly vulnerable). Interviewers took copious notes in these circumstances.

In the assignment of interviewers to informants, attention was paid to the creation of cross-racial/ethnic encounters insofar as possible, given scheduling difficulties (i.e., white interviewers were assigned to interview faculty of color, and interviewers of color were assigned to interview white faculty in thirty-three of the sixty-six interviews). Our reasoning was that in such encounters faculty members being interviewed might enact their own sense of and ability to cross racial/ethnic borders and display their skills (or lack thereof) in such intergroup settings. As indicated below, the protocol contained an opportunity for reflective checking on just such issues.

The Interview Protocol

The original members of the project team together constructed a protocol of open-ended and broad questions. As the interview process unfolded and as the team debriefed their early-stage experiences, we revised the protocol to better explore emerging agendas and clarify core questions. Although the dynamics of each interview situation and each interviewer and informant required each interview to differ slightly from the official protocol format, team training and constant debriefing ensured that no interview diverged far from the overriding goals of the project. Efforts were made to conduct interviews in an open-ended and conversational manner, and interviewers were encouraged to deviate from the official progression of questions if appropriate and to follow informants' lead if they brought up new or tangential issues of interest.

The protocol sought information around eight topical areas: (1) personal racial/ethnic biography and self-expressed social identity; (2) teaching biography or academic career path; (3) pedagogical approach to teaching and learning; (4) views of the impact that their own social identities had on their approaches to and experiences with students and classroom teaching; (5) experiences of and approaches to conflict and tension in the classroom; (6) raced and gendered experiences with their peers, departments, and the structure/culture of the university; (7) views of general issues of diversity in higher education; and (8) roles as agents in supporting or creating change related to diversity and multiculturalism. A final question asked whether and how the interview might have been different had the interviewer been of a different racial/ethnic or gender identity; this was included as a way of checking on the potential impact of matched (or unmatched) interviewer and informant identities. The entire protocol is presented in Box 2.1.

The Interview Process

Interviews were generally conducted in an open-ended and conversational manner. Some of the graduate student researchers worried about doing the interviews "right" and sticking to the agreed upon protocol. Others recounted their concerns or discomfort with issues that arose in the interviewing process, explicitly in the racial, gender, or status (e.g., graduate student interviewer and faculty informant) dynamics between interviewer and informant. For example, a consequence of our commitment to interview with deliberate regard to racial cross-matching was made evident by one researcher, an African American, whose first interview for this project was with a white woman. Upon first encountering this faculty member in order to convene the interview, the researcher was greeted quite politely and a bit cautiously. He was then asked to say something about himself and how he got involved in this project. It was immediately clear that he was being asked to explain himself in ways that were strikingly different from the kinds of initial inquiries that were made to him by African American informants in his other research activities. He explained to other members of the research team that when African Americans asked him to explain himself, he was accustomed to their wanting to know how someone who was much like them decided to conduct research about them. In this case, however, the racial background of the informant created an unfamiliar scenario for the researcher, one in which the power of race and gender difference was such that he first had to confront the social distance that existed between himself and the white woman across the table. Similar situations engaged research-team conversations and deliberations about our procedures as well as findings.

Box 2.1 Interview Protocol

First, I have some general questions about your academic and teaching background.

Biographical Questions Regarding Academic Career
1. How central is teaching in your life as a faculty member?
2. What kind of classes do you teach? (graduate/undergraduate, required/ optional, large/small, etc.)

Teaching Philosophy and Practice
3. What kind of teacher are you trying to be? How would you describe your teaching styles?
    3a. What are your greatest strengths as a teacher? Areas for improvement?
4. What makes you feel successful in the classroom? What does it look like when you are doing a successful job in the classroom?
        Tell me a story about a good teaching moment.
        Tell me a story about a classroom experience you wish you'd handled differently?

Now I want to talk with you about your own personal understandings and experiences with race. Please answer in the way that is most comfortable for you.

Personal understandings about the importance of race
5. Do you feel like you are a member of a racial group?
    [if YES] Which? What does it mean to you?
6. What role do you think race has played in your daily life?
    6a. Do other people find your race to be important? How? In what ways?
7. Have you had much experience with racially diverse situations? [probe for details]

Now I want to ask you a few questions about the role of racial diversity in your teaching....

Teaching and Diversity
8. How do you deal with issues of racial diversity and multiculturalism in your classroom? Do they have an impact on your teaching practices? On your students? [probe for concrete examples]
9. How did you learn or first consider how to deal with racial diversity in the classroom?
    9a. What have you found useful in helping you to improve your ability to deal with diversity in the classroom successfully? [probe]
10. What kind of *knowledge, skills, and temperament* do you think a faculty member needs to possess in order to be able to do a good job teaching in a racially diverse classroom? What is most important? [probe for concrete details]

box continues

Box 2.1 continued

11. Can you remember a time in class when a racial "event" created strong emotional feelings for you? [ask for a fearful time and an angry time]
    11a. What happened? What did you do?
12. Are there things you can and/or can't get away with or do or can do easier because of who you are (in terms of race, gender, status)?
13. Can you teach effectively without paying attention to issues of diversity in the class?

Now I'm going to ask you some questions about white students and then about students of color:

14. Where are white students on these issues of racial diversity (how do they react)?
    14a. Have you ever proactively dealt with them on these issues?
15. What's going on with students of color? Where are they on these issues of racial diversity?
    15a. How do students of color react in class?
    15b. Do students of color and white students generally have the same skills, talents, and learning styles? If not, how do you deal with the differences?
16. How do you deal with conflict between racial groups (or racial conflict) in the classroom? Can you remember any specific examples?
17. Do you see yourself as a "diversity advocate"?
    [If YES] What does that mean for you? What things do you do as a result?
18. Have you ever been accused either by students or colleagues of being racist?
    [If YES] What happened? What did you do?
    18a. Have you ever been accused of being soft or of bending over backward for minorities? [What happened? What did you do?]
    18b. Have you ever been accused of being soft or bending over backward for white students? [What happened? What did you do?]

And now a few questions about your colleagues and department:

19. Is there anything more about how you are perceived by your colleagues on these issues? How do you know? Are they supportive?
    19a. What happens when racial issues come up with colleagues more generally? What brings them up? What do you feel or do *when these issues come up*?
20. What advice would you give a new faculty member of your race/ethnicity at this university about the kind of issues we've been talking about?
21. There's been a lot of debate about Affirmative Action, about who ought to be a part of the university community. What's your take on what's really going on in the debate? Where are you on what kind of students and faculty ought to be a part of the university?And finally,
22. Do you think this interview would have been different, would your answers have been different, if I had been more like you in terms of race, gender, discipline, and so forth? If yes, how?

Graduate students often recounted their concerns or discomfort with racial, gender, or status issues that arose between themselves and informants during interviews. For example:

> Sometimes I was respected; other times, I felt that my graduate student status, social identities, or both caused a few faculty members to approach me in a condescending manner. One informant in particular talked down to me at various points during the interview process. Although this may be her typical demeanor, I would presume that she would have trusted and respected me more if I was a well-known faculty member. (L, W)
>
> At the time I understood the dynamics in these two interviews to be racialized and gendered and also to be shaped by generational or status at minimum. They both seemed to engage and answer in gendered ways—for example, with their own authority and interactional styles. They also felt gendered in that both responded to my gender and generation—as younger, female, graduate student. Perhaps a little of "you'll know what I'm talking about some day." (AfAm, W)

These reflections about the interview process, shared in team meetings, provide a glimpse into the struggles and tensions researchers experienced. The examples of power dynamics within the interviews reflect some of the complexities of power dynamics within the academic structure, particularly around issues of race/ethnicity, gender, and status. Open discussion permitted all team members to analyze how these dynamics, intentionally or unintentionally, may have shaped the research process and findings.

In a similar vein, some researchers reflected on their own "self talk" during the interviews.

> At times I'm sure I was worried about whether there was some way to convey to the interviewee that I was, to put it crassly, "down," that I got it, that I was the kind of white person that would understand, that he could speak to openly. At one point we were talking about racial profiling and he used the acronym, "DWB" and then felt the need to explain it. I said something to make it clear that I knew what it was.... My race [white] clearly mattered in the interview process, and I think I was more meta-aware during our conversation of what my identity might be signaling to him and how I needed to monitor that. (Wh, W)
>
> When I interviewed a woman faculty of color who I did not know beforehand, she challenged me by saying, "I don't know why you're talking with me. You should be talking with white faculty—they're the issue." I responded that we were also talking with white faculty but that was barely the point. Under the surface I think this was an example of a faculty of color feeling overused by and perhaps distrustful of the system—a white system that I was part of whether I wanted to acknowledge that or not. (Wh, M)

Researchers encountered little overt or obvious resistance to the interview questions from those informants who agreed to be interviewed. Most faculty expressed the view, directly or implicitly, that the conversation had been interesting and/or useful to them. Sometimes that was a function of their commitment to and/or interest in the goals of the study; sometimes it was a response to their prior knowledge of the study, codirectors, or some of the interviewers; and sometimes it was because they wished to respond supportively to graduate student interviewers. Several informants indicated that they were grateful that these issues of classroom diversity and pedagogy were being pursued, and others indicated that the interview experience had provided them with some new ideas or new things to think about.

With particular respect to the issue of interviewer-informant interaction around racial/ethnic and gender issues, forty-nine of the sixty-six informants were asked and answered whether they thought their answers to our questions would have changed if the interviewer had been of a different race/ethnicity (only forty-nine were asked this question directly, mostly because this question was included only after the first series of interviews). Nineteen of the forty-nine indicated that their answers would have or probably would have changed. Seven of those answering "yes" were white, five were African American, one was Latino/a, four were Asian American, and two were Native American. The yeses were approximately evenly split between men and women faculty. Finally, the yeses were evenly split between those faculty interviewed by members of their own racial identity group and those interviewed by members of a different racial group.

Several informants said that they would have (or might have) answered differently had the interviewer been of a different race/ethnicity. In one case an African American man responded to his African American woman interviewer with

> Yes, absolutely. By having someone who you think is a member of your community, you assume that there's some experience in their life that's going to allow them to hear your answers. If somebody from another … does not share that experience, then they will misconstrue what you've said to them. There's also a presumed intimacy, right? That's very important in terms of me being more candid. I think I was more candid with you than I would be with someone, you know, an upper-middle-class white person. Not because of the class issues but because of the experience of the life experience issues. (AfAm, M, H).

In a similar vein a white man said to his white man interviewer,

> Sure, I think if you were an African American woman coming in, I don't know how, but I can't imagine it would be the same. Probably I would be more concerned about how to say things. There's all sorts of gender dynamics to think about. I think we have a comfort level as men. And if you were an African American man,

the conversation also would have gone differently—not so much consciously but unconsciously. (Wh, M, NS)

Most informants who indicated that their answers would not have changed were quite direct in saying, "No, it would not make a difference," or "No, not an iota." But others provided fuller responses, as an African American woman elaborated to her African American female interviewer:

> I don't think that my answers would have been different if you had been a person of a different race or gender. I think it is important to give my true events of my experiences because I think it probably provides a unique perspective. It'll be very difficult to get perspectives of African American female scientists in research I universities. There just aren't that many of us. So I think it's important to tell you exactly what happened without adding a sugarcoating or without making it seem more difficult than it was for me either. (AfAm, W, NS)

Data Coding and Analysis

All taped interviews were transcribed. Interviews that were not taped relied on extensive handwritten notes and postinterview reconstructions made by interviewers and then were transcribed. Interviewers then read through the transcriptions of all interviews they had conducted in order to clarify transcription unclarities, errors, or omissions. Prior to analysis all transcripts were read by two team members and cleaned of all personal and departmental identifiers (identifiable personal history references were eliminated, specifically named courses were disguised, and all references to specific disciplinary or departmental names were replaced by the generics of "natural science," "social science," or "humanities"). In a few cases, in which there were only a very few faculty of a particular race/ethnicity or gender in a discipline, even those disciplinary markers were omitted. The potential loss of personal information embodied in these disguises or eliminations are more than compensated for by the necessity of confidentiality and pseudo-anonymity in a single, local campus environment.

Data analysis typically proceeded via the general principles of grounded theory and relatively inductive analysis (Emerson, Fretz, and Shaw 1995; Glaser and Strauss 1976). Team members working on different analytic projects started with an orienting concern, an a priori hypothesis, or general question, read through each interview multiple times and identified core themes or subthemes through selective processes of open coding and, later, more focused coding. Different team members used somewhat different coding systems and also varied in the access to and use of software packages to aid in the coding and thematizing process. Some used "scissors and scotch tape" to code and cluster responses, and others used NVIVO to help organize the data around themes that they had identified and generated.

All coding was done in teams of at least two persons (usually also involving undergraduate team members), and in those cases of different reading/coding of the material a third person was brought in to resolve disputes and increase coder reliability. Exemplars of coded material were used as the basis for identifying and generating themes and writing memos that helped interpret the data. Eventually, as part of the process of sharing early ideas and memos with other team members, integrative memos and essays were developed to make theoretical sense of the data and help link these interpretive frames to other literature and other theories of pedagogy and intergroup relations.

Analytic designs varied, although almost all used some form of comparative analysis. Most of the following chapters used data from all sixty-six informants. However, in some cases team members focused on the experiences, outlooks, or approaches of a particular identity group, such as white faculty or faculty women of color, and so forth. For instance, Charbeneau and Chesler (chapter 7) used data from only the eighteen white faculty informants, Ford (chapter 8) used data from only the twenty-one faculty women of color, and Young (chapter 9) examined only the responses of faculty men of color. Ford and Maxwell (chapter 5) started their inquiry by examining the interviews from all sixty-six faculty members but elected to analyze in depth only those twenty-three faculty who discussed their approaches to classroom peer conflict in detail. Even these efforts contrasted and compared faculty across other identities or social locations (gender or discipline) within those broad groupings. In other cases team members directly explored the experiences or outlooks of faculty members of different racial/ethnic or gender groups with regard to particular issues, such as ways of responding to conflict, dealing with challenges by students to their expertise and authority, collegial relationships, and other daily experiences.

Some of the analyses in the following chapters started with broad code categories based on issues raised in prior literature or in team conversations. For instance, Young, Furhman, and Chesler (chapter 4) started with a desire to explore and eventually document the literature's suggestion that the faculty's race and gender influences student challenges to faculty classroom authority and expertise. Charbeneau and Chesler (chapter 7) used a mix of focused and open coding procedures, moving in an iterative fashion between themes derived from the literature on whiteness and white faculty members' reports of their pedagogical approaches, "testing" these themes against the data. However, most analyses relied initially on one or another form of open or inductive coding, often followed by focused efforts: Ford and Maxwell (chapter 5), Pasque, Charbeneau, Chesler, and Carlson (chapter 6), Ford (chapter 8), Young (chapter 9), Joseph and Hirshfield (chapter 10), and Beale, Chesler, and Ramus (chapter 11). In many of these cases the open coding process generated themes and subthemes that took these investigators beyond their original broad categories and beyond themes previously generated in the scholarly literature. Other details of the different coding and analytic processes that are uniquely germane to different team members' work are explicated where relevant in the following individual chapters.

Team Operations/Interactions and the Processes of Positionality and Reflexivity

What is represented herein is a collective effort. The entire team (or whoever was in town or available by telephone at a particular meeting time) met about once a month, and individual team members consistently met to work in smaller combinations between meetings. As individual team members shared their work, we were able to develop and introduce some of these core narratives into individuals' analytic and writing efforts. Typically, two or more team members of different racial/ethnic or gender identities worked together on an analytic piece and on what ultimately became an article or a chapter to follow. Even team members who worked alone engaged in and benefited from extensive and intensive conversations and exchanges with other team members. In all cases the writings of individuals or team members working together were reviewed, discussed, and critiqued individually and in team meetings.

Research on matters of social identity and equal/unequal treatment often engage scholars' own values and experiences. We all see, experience, and interpret the world through lenses and tools shaped by life in a racialized, gendered, and classed society. In this respect a number of scholars argue that overt inquiry into and discussions of researcher positionality can strengthen research, especially qualitative and interpretive research (Jones, Torres, and Arminio 2006; Lather 1991; Richardson and St. Pierre 2005). In addition, Milner (2007, 388) argues that, especially in the case of research involving issues of identity, "when researchers are not mindful of the enormous role of their own and others' racialized positionality and cultural ways of knowing, the results can be dangerous to communities and individuals of color"—and, we may add, to everyone involved, including researchers.

During one of our discussions of methods a team member emphasized these suggestions for quality improvement and developed an open-ended questionnaire that invited others to respond to a series of retrospective questions about our own experiences with ourselves, other team members, informants, and the operation of the research project (see box 2.2). Nine of the most heavily involved colleagues (out of twelve solicited) provided written responses to this e-mail inquiry. Through the subsequent process of participating in a series of reflexivity exercises and conversations, we shared and discussed the role of our own social identities, individually and collectively, in relationship to the research effort—an exercise in increasing trustworthiness.

Explorations of researcher positionality include attention to assumptions researchers have about the topic, their relationships to the topic, and reflexivity about their own identities and/or feelings connected to the topic. Thus, we were concerned that explorations of academic life in diverse environments that failed to consider the racial and gender (and perhaps disciplinary) identities of researchers/ interviewers as well as informants might lead to unforeseen dangers in our own and readers' interpretations of the interviews and of the reported findings. As a result, team members' conversations and memos occasionally focused on how their own identities might have affected the racial, gender, and status dynamics in the interviews and in how team members' with different identities and social locations engaged and dealt with one another.

> There were issues of race and gender to discuss as well in interviews, in research meetings, and in collaborative projects. This impacted my sense of propriety or lack of propriety regarding issues, silenced me, inhibited or challenged communications in ways I was aware of on different levels and puzzled by to various degrees. At times it felt like I was speaking past other members of the group and wondered if it was about identity. Other times I stayed quiet either out of uncertainty, respect for the power dynamics around the identity of the member speaking, who I thought might want the space to speak, or out of fear. (L, W)

This woman graduate student of color discusses her feelings of insecurity or anxiety, illustrated in part by her decision to remain quiet in research team

---

Box 2.2 Reflexivity Questions for Team Reflection/Writing

1. What do you remember most about the interviews?
   Did your social identities (particularly race and gender identities) make a difference in the interviews? If yes, how?
2. What interactions with informants created particular feelings for you? Did you have any "friendly interactions" with the interviewees? Or were there any tense situations that stand out for you?
   In what ways did your own intellectual and research interests play a role in your participation in this research project?
3. In what ways did your own social identities and experience with multicultural teaching pedagogies play a role in your participation in this research project?
4. Describe your participation in the FacDivProj. research team. How did the group work (or not work) together? What was your role in this process?

If you are doing an analytic piece from the project, how have your identities and values influenced what you are writing (or considering writing)?

meetings. As she connects her feelings and participation to other examples of uncertainty and power dynamics in the group, she identifies them as important power dynamics across race and/or gender interactions in general.

Despite these expressions of concern—or perhaps because of the group's ability to surface and work on such issues—many team members (including the colleague quoted above) talked about the team's positive intellectual and emotional atmosphere and the rewards of participating in a relatively open and challenging group process.

> I thought the group worked together quite well—it was very collegial and democratic. We all brought ideas, concerns, insight, special knowledge and shared it openly. I remember it being fun—the early planning, the coming together to discuss the interviews as we were collecting the data, the early analysis. Clearly, we were a group of people who were focused on teaching in a not-so-teaching-friendly kind of place. The group was probably therapeutic in some ways in asserting a kind of alternate value system. (Wh, W)

This comment addresses how well the team worked and how freely sharing occurred, apparently in contrast to this person's prior experience with the more formal and hierarchal values and styles of the academy.

An important part of the dynamic of this research team effort, over time, was the nature of the leadership exerted by the two senior investigators/project initiators. One graduate student and one of the senior investigators reflected on these dynamics as follows:

> I think it's fascinating that despite cultural stereotypes that suggest women are more collaborative and cooperative than men are, this group headed by two men is the first collaborative research group I've had the chance to work with since I came here to this university. Stereotypes would suggest that the group would be likely to form a distinct hierarchy of power, yet the two men heading up the project seem very comfortable without a clearly defined structure of command and seem happy enough to allow the group to make democratic decisions, and so forth. (Wh, W)
>
> My role as a senior faculty member working with the graduate students often was to convene meetings, keep up the level of excitement, try to keep things moving. I am sure that my investment in our early thinking and approaches as well as my race, gender, and style stifled some conversations and perhaps even initiations by graduate students in the later stages of his project while encouraging others. I did try to stay alert to these dynamics. (Wh, M)

In the first excerpt the gendered social identity of the primary investigators is dissected in relation to a graduate student's surprise with the way the senior men led a group with an informal (relatively nonhierarchical) structure and a collaborative, group-initiated process; such group leadership is traditionally—and narrowly—associated with women leaders. In the second excerpt the senior researcher reflects on his own race, gender, and seniority as a faculty member as well as his interactional style as it may have played out in the dynamics of the group.

As team members undertook this effort in reflexivity and shared their written and verbal reflections about the project with one another, one graduate student colleague noted that

> The conversations we have had around this reflexivity process have been some of the most dynamic and insightful. It has brought our collaborative work to a deeper level by constructing the space for us each to step out into the group a bit further. We had been invited to offer our reflections along the way; however, my guess is that the reflections offered here are richer, denser, than our individual bits and pieces. (Wh, W)

The continuing process of sharing and reflection that characterized the team's approach, codified in the reflexivity exercise, provided an opportunity and a context for intentionally thinking about the importance of identity and power in the research and in the lives of the researchers. Reports of such deliberate explorations are often omitted from research project activities and from published academic work. These brief narratives portray how we, as researchers, positioned ourselves, the faculty being interviewed, and others on the research team.

Throughout this volume we provide a good deal of quoted material from informants, letting the voices of these faculty members come through, not only as a sign of our respect for informants' wisdom and struggles but also so that readers can "see for themselves" and on occasion reflect on our interpretations. These concrete and practical illustrations and examples of pedagogical and collegial behaviors may enlighten and guide other faculty throughout the higher education system. Even so, it should be clear that the work presented here reflects faculty members' own perceptions and interpretations—not those of their students and colleagues—as received, organized, and interpreted by various team members.

Chapter 3

A Schematic for Analyzing Conflict in the University Classroom

Alford A. Young Jr.

The consistent recognition of conflict between the various partners in the higher educational system was a central part of the research project that led to the creation of this book emerging from the data. According to the 2011 edition of Merriam-Webster's dictionary, conflict is a "competitive or opposing action of incompatibles," an "antagonistic state or action (as of divergent ideas, interests, or persons)" or the existence of "a mental struggle resulting from incompatible or opposing needs, drives, wishes, or external or internal demands." Conflict is a resulting property of social relations, especially when such relations occur in milieu where people promote and defend clear and deliberate objectives for engaging each other. Such conflict can result from engagements that concern disagreements about beliefs as well as about access to and utilization of material resources.

Conflict is a seemingly endemic property of educational environments; that is, as much as student-teacher and student-student interactions are pivotal for the learning experience of students, these interactive domains also serve as the sites for students to express and act on their reactions to their learning experience and for faculty members to react to the newer generation's cultural styles (especially as reflected currently in their preferences for social media and technology). Higher education is an institutional setting that involves consistent interaction among parties that promote and defend varied objectives. Students, who function as clients and consumers in that institutional sphere, are subordinate to the faculty, who provide the principal service but who are also charged with informing the client/consumer about what will be the constituent parts of that service. Accordingly, the subordination of the client/consumer in relations with the service provider is a unique pattern for the social dynamics occurring in a formal institutional setting (Freire 1970). This is the very case of social relations between students and faculty in educational institutions.

These developments take unique form in higher education, where students have often reached a level of social, intellectual, or physical maturity such that they feel a greater sense of efficacy in reacting to their instructor's pedagogical style, course objectives, and course material. Moreover, as noted in chapter 1, they often are learning in an academic environment where faculty may pay relatively little attention to their developmental status and where undergraduate students' needs are not a high-priority matter. Of course, students may also feel such efficacy in responding to the behavior and reactions of their fellow students. Hence, taking all of these factors into account, conflict can be expected in any educational setting. Undoubtedly then, conflict is a critically important issue to unpack, explore, and interpret, not simply as a social phenomenon worthy of intellectual investigation but also for the purpose of developing preventative and remedial approaches.

Furthermore, when social characteristics such as gender and race are taken into account (as well as, presumably, a whole range of other characteristics—sexual orientation, religion, etc.—that may matter in any particular institutional setting), the pattern of subordinate to superior relationships becomes all the more potent. This is especially the case if the instructor, who is traditionally in the superior status, possesses characteristics that are more commonly associated with subordinated status. The arrival of African Americans, Latinos, Asian Americans, Native Americans, and women (of various racial and ethnic groups) into higher education as faculty has exacerbated this condition, especially for majority students. It is also the case when faculty who are from dominant or majority backgrounds encounter students who are from traditionally subordinated and excluded racial and ethnic backgrounds; faculty may not know how best to teach or relate with them. These interactions all occur within what has been described in chapter 1 as the raced, gendered, and classed structure and culture of higher education.

Any effort to explore conflict systematically as a social phenomenon must begin with the premise that it has been sorely underinterrogated in terms of its constitutive elements and the diverse ways in which those elements can lead to the emergence of distinct and diverse forms of that phenomenon, especially in demographically diverse settings. This chapter defines the constitutive elements of conflict and deciphers how varied forms of conflict emerge given the different ways in which these elements converge. The purpose of highlighting these differences is to offer greater understanding of the nature of different kinds of conflict in higher education (and, by extension, in education more generally) not only so that a broader array of responses to conflict can be identified but also so that greater appreciation for the pedagogical role that conflict can play may also be elucidated and advanced in the theorizing and practice of higher educational instruction (and, by extension, education more generally). Admittedly, the end goal is vast and complex, and fully articulating how this can be achieved is beyond the scope of this chapter. However, this chapter does provide an incremental step toward understanding the mosaic of elements and patterns of classroom-based conflict and sets the stage for issues elaborated in empirical detail in later chapters.

Conflict as a Property of Social Relations and the Constitutive Elements of Conflict in Education Settings

In order to specify and delineate the types of conflicts that emerge in the higher education classroom, it is crucial to explain each of its constitutive elements—human and material. Although conflict in higher education most visibly surfaces in the interaction between people and, in this case, between faculty and students and faculty with other faculty, a sociologically grounded interpretation of such conflict must also take into account the role and significance of cultural or material resources (e.g., pedagogical approaches and curricular material, such as teaching philosophy/style and course text books/educational material) and the location and arrangement of the physical space where such conflict may surface (e.g., size of classrooms, public classrooms or hallways vs. private spaces such as faculty offices).

There are five major constitutive elements of conflict in the educational setting: the instructor, the student, the instructor's pedagogical approach, the classroom space, and the course material. Each can potentially contribute to the emergence of specific incidents of conflict as well as influence the pattern and duration of any emergent conflict. We now turn to discuss the dimensions and characteristics of each element. Thereafter, we explore some potential ways in which these elements can connect in the formation and maintenance of overt conflict.

The Instructor

As the central agent for the transmission of knowledge and/or the creation and direction of a learning environment, the instructor's agency in regard to conflict cannot be understated. The instructor's identity traits and related behaviors and how these features are read by students, the other central agents in the emergence of conflict, shapes whether and how conflicts emerge and the form they take.

In sociology, identity is construed as a social phenomenon; that is, people come to know who they are by interacting with others (or imagined others) and knowing (or imagining) how others see them (Cooley 1902; Mead 1934). Some of the identity traits that are crucial for situating the instructor in the emergence of conflict are racial and ethnic background, gender, age, indication of sexual orientation, manner or style of social interaction with students in the classroom, and professional status. As has been commonly documented in research and elaborated empirically in chapters 4, 8, and 9 in this volume, instructors who are members of underrepresented ethnic and racial groups often face more direct confrontation or are at least more critically evaluated than are those who represent majority racial and ethnic groups (see the many first-person anthologies cited in chapter 1 and, especially, Bavishi, Madera, and Hebl 2010; Grahame 2004; Turner 2002; Turner, Gonzalez, and Wood 2008). This is also a consistent pattern with younger faculty, women faculty, and (at least in some instances) faculty who appear to be or who overtly identify themselves as gay or lesbian. Accordingly, conflicts can emerge for these faculty because students may feel more agentic in expressing anger, frustration, or anxiety about any aspect of their course or classroom experience with such individuals.

Pedagogy

Another relevant factor for conflict is the pedagogical approach, the course aims and activities and the teaching style, adopted by the instructor. Pedagogical approaches can include or involve the instructor's sociopolitical orientation toward the topic matter for the course as well as his or her educational objectives for a particular course, style of instruction, and approach to student evaluation. It is often the case that an instructor's pedagogical style may be inspired by some aspect of his or her identity. For instance, white women instructors and those from underrepresented ethnic and racial groups may be especially attentive to including in their teaching emphases on people who traditionally have not been well represented in course literature. Of course, instructors may feel the impulse for such inclusion without holding membership in the social categories and groups that pertain to the silenced or less-represented parties. As one might imagine, however, the identity status of an instructor can have profound effect on how students react to the ways in which course material is presented, and such reaction can range from extreme satisfaction on the part of students through passive resistance to extreme hostility (the latter, of course, are overt exemplifications of the constitutive conflicts).

Of course, a part of the instructor's package of pedagogical style and objectives may be to foster conflict (albeit in a controlled way) in the classroom. In this case, the instructor may desire to create an atmosphere where students vividly recognize and must confront the tensions they experience with the course material or with the views and expressions of other students. Alternatively, instructors may not desire and thus avoid or try to deflate any such conflict from surfacing in the classroom. The exploration of such pedagogical options are documented and discussed in chapters 5, 6, and 7 in this volume.

The Student

As the consumer or target of instruction and knowledge transmission, the student contributes to the potential for conflict in how he or she responds to the social, physical, and pedagogical contexts of the learning environment. These potential reactions and responses are predicated on a series of factors. One set (as previously discussed) involves the students' own identity traits, which include racial and ethnic background, gender, age, sexual orientation, manner or style of social interaction with the instructor and with other students in the classroom. These issues are especially potent in the situation where students (and faculty) from largely racially segregated backgrounds, who may not have had much experience interacting across such borders, begin to encounter one another in a diverse collegiate environment. Another set involves the pedagogical and educational interests and expectations that a student has for the course that he or she is taking.

In taking the agentic capacities of students into account, they may also try to take advantage of incidents that arise or otherwise engineer or promote visible conflict as a means of acting on their own dissatisfaction with a course, its instructor, the course material, or fellow students. In this case, conflict emerges not in the more passive sense of students maintaining a negative response to one or more of the other constitutive elements but in aiming to assert themselves as challengers and instigators of conflict as a result of having been affected by one of these elements.

Course Material

As previously stated, material refers to the documents, devices, and instruments used to deliver instruction (e.g., books, articles, audio-visual materials, etc.).

Although these materials comprise the core resource base for the pedagogical practices and objectives of the instructor, they clearly are distinct from those practices and objectives. A primary example as to how this is the case is that a series of documents may be used to serve the instructional aims of a course on race relations in the United States. Irrespective of the pedagogical practices and objectives of an instructor, students may react differently to the inclusion of material produced by seemingly extreme racists than that produced by proponents of racial integration and harmony.

A more subtle but equally revealing example is the utilization of a book on American slavery that was written by advocates of that practice (seemingly ridiculous by contemporary perspectives but common in the early part of the twentieth century) in comparison to a book written by a critic of that practice. An even more subtle point of consideration is the kind of examples or cases drawn upon in a classroom to illustrate a point. Again, not very long ago it was not uncommon to use examples from slavery to discuss economic theory (with African Americans referred to as material commodities) rather than widgets. Moreover, many white students and students of color suddenly exposed to alternative historical or structural explanations of racial or economic inequality may be shocked and react vigorously to documentation and analyses that markedly contrast with their high school history lessons (see, for example, Zinn's 1980 alternative view of early US history).

In all of these cases, the very kind of material brought into the learning experience can serve as a source of conflict depending on how students react to it or how they respond to other students' or the instructor's reaction to the material. Clearly, the specification of such possible materials—and perhaps even their existence—will vary substantially depending on the academic discipline involved. Several later chapters present faculty informants' comments on conflicts generated in response to the use of such challenging curricular materials.

The Physical Space

The final constitutive element of conflict is the classroom, the very space in which the learning experience unfolds. Essentially, the size and dimension of the classroom space allow for specific degrees of proximity between students and between students and the instructor that can either facilitate or inhibit the emergence of conflict. A larger classroom can promote more anonymity in terms of student conduct and expression and, therefore, less willingness on the part of others in that space to engage or incite a moment of conflict. In contrast, a smaller classroom allows many—and in some cases all—students to learn one another's names and observe how each is reacting to the other elements of the learning environment (the instructor, pedagogy, other students, and course material).

Accordingly, the smaller classroom removes anonymity from and can intensify the intimacy of such conflict.

Of course, the larger classroom creates unique opportunities for conflict, as it can be a site for the collective expression of angst, confusion, or anger (and the mere appearance of such collective forms of expression may create or exacerbate conflicting feelings in other students). The distance that instructors have from students (and given the size of some university lecture halls, that distance can be quite substantial) can also allow them to avoid, ignore, or manage conflicts in ways that cannot occur in a smaller classroom space. For instance, an instructor can more easily avoid responding to a student who may be expressing a sense of conflict with some aspect of the course by intimidation or by the elicitation of contrasting comments from other students. In contrast, the instructor also can mobilize or encourage large numbers of students in ways that engage or advance the expression of conflict—and either approach can be undertaken consciously or unconsciously by instructors. All together, then, the physical space of the classroom serves as a crucial structuring element of the emergence, endurance, or minimization of conflict in the higher educational environment.

The Nature of Classroom Conflict

Any emergent conflict can take one or more of the following forms: instructor-student, student-student, student-instructor's pedagogical approach, or student-course material. It is possible for any form to be combined with another—or all of the others—in the formation of a particular pattern of conflict. It is also the case that each configuration may serve to mitigate, inhibit, or facilitate the emergence of conflict. Although a minimum of two elements must be present in order for conflict to surface in the classroom, up to all five may be implicated in its underlying dynamics. Taken together, then, a faculty member's identities and his or her pedagogical styles and objectives serve to create images in the minds of students about what to expect and, consequently, how they might respond to the classroom experience. Those interpretations and reactions are developed as a result of the students' own identities, interests in the course, considerations of course material, and conscious or subconscious recognition of what kinds of behaviors can be enacted in the physical space in which the class is being held. All these elements provide grounds for how students construct meanings about their courses and, thus, enact, pursue, or become engulfed in conflict in or in regard to the classroom.

Sociologists define the general process of meaning making referred to above as social constructionism. That concept posits that all knowledge is partial, constructed by individuals and groups based on their historical and cultural locations (which include the identities that they claim) (Berger and Luckmann 1967; Harding 1991). Scholars in the social constructionist tradition maintain that identity categories exist in and through their social meaning, and these meanings may change over time and have different degrees of salience to different groups of people.

A related construct, symbolic interactionism, adds some specificity to the theory of social construction by suggesting that social groups are constructed through human interaction using symbols, such as language and bodily gestures (Blumer 1969; Goffman 1963; Strauss 1959). When engaged in social interaction, individuals use certain symbols that the other person(s) in the interaction read and respond to. These symbols can include identities (in this case the identities of faculty and students) and objects (in this case course material). It is the amalgamation of readings of identities and objects in social interaction that give rise to conflict, either for people with other people (students with students, students with faculty) or people with the meanings apprehended from objects (students with course material). Both constructs—social constructivism and symbolic interactionism—are key to the analytic and interpretive processes used throughout the other chapters in this volume.

Part II Difference and Diversity in Classroom Interactions

Chapter 4

How Race and Gender Shape Perceived Challenges to Classroom Authority and Expertise

Alford A. Young Jr., Megan Furhman, and Mark A. Chesler

"But there's always, always, one male student, at least one white male student that I have, at least one in the class, who always wants to challenge me, you know." (AsAm, W, H)

The increased race and gender diversity of higher education faculty presents many students with the relatively rare situation of dealing with people in positions of authority who do not look like traditional white male authority figures. Students' preconceived notions of what faculty members are supposed to look like and what they might expect from them often are rooted in traditional race and gender stereotypes. These notions shape the ways that students react to their instructors and their classroom pedagogies, often resulting in a series of covert

45

and overt student challenges, especially to white women faculty and men and women faculty of color. Student orientations and behaviors also affect how faculty members anticipate and enact their roles and deal with students' reactions to them.

In this chapter we examine how the social group identities of faculty members are reflected in some of their pedagogical encounters and practices. More particularly, we consider how faculty members of different social group identities deal with two issues commonly faced by all faculty: (1) embodiment of the authority of the faculty role, and (2) assumptions about their subject matter expertise. Although related to one another, faculty authority in the classroom and faculty expertise concerning subject matter are two distinct phenomena. The first has to do with how students evaluate, interact, or otherwise respond to the faculty member's power and status to make and enforce decisions. The second has to do with students' perceptions of the instructor's repository of knowledge about the course matter or topic. In the case of men and women faculty of color and white women faculty, research has demonstrated that both groups are often covertly or overtly challenged by students on these bases (Gitli 2002; Harlow 2003; Hendrix 2007; Hubbard and Stage 2009; Perry et al. 2009; Thompson and Dey 1998). Our objectives here are to explore whether and how faculty members experience, think about, and navigate the challenges they perceive being received from students, and if so, how they see and react to these challenges differently based on their race and gender. In so doing we shed empirical light on several of the constitutive elements of classroom conflict identified in the prior chapter—instructors, students, and pedagogies.

We anticipate that faculty members of color and white women faculty experience more challenges and more intense challenges to their authority and expertise than do their white men colleagues. In addition, we suggest that faculty whose social identities are comprised of more privileged characteristics (i.e., whites, men) are able to demonstrate greater agency in handling classroom issues concerning their academic credentials and subject matter knowledge than do (or can) white women and men and women of color. This is also the case for how these scholars express themselves in regard to their institutional role as faculty and the authority presumably associated with traditional student behavior (e.g., respect and deference, acceptance of the status hierarchy, grading practices, etc.); that is, those faculty who possess more privileged social identity characteristics are less likely to be challenged and less likely to feel challenged about these matters (or to feel distressed by such challenges) or to seriously consider that students or others in the university community might issue such challenges.

Analytic Strategy

We approached this inquiry with an intent to examine these two types of challenges. Thus, we read through all the interviews and coded the challenges faculty members reported into these two major categories. We then discovered and focused on some different subthemes within each major category.

One example of a challenge to authority is reported by an African American faculty who shares a story about an experience in the classroom that she wishes she had handled differently.

> I haven't figured out how to effectively deal with my white males who are resistant to me for I guess a number of reasons ... snide looks, rolling their eyes, I mean it's a lot of even nonverbal aggression—and I haven't figured out how to deal with that because it's not overt. (AfAm, W, SS).

Her response does not speak to a specific classroom situation but instead to a continuing problem she faced with white men students.

This same young African American woman faculty member who discusses students' challenges to her authority also reports several challenges to her expertise. In one example she describes a white male student e-mailing her regarding his desire to do a final paper on a topic not covered in the syllabus because he felt it should have been covered and that it was more important than the topics the professor had chosen. She goes on to say,

> I think that kind of challenge as to why I would organize a class and not include his particular topic comes out of how he's situating me and would he have been so vocal if I assumed a different identity? I don't think so, I could be wrong, but I doubt it. (AfAm, W, SS)

Analysis of these data yielded four types of reported challenges to authority and two types of reported challenges to expertise. The challenges to authority include mistaking or addressing faculty as nonfaculty, expecting faculty to be parental figures or servants, in-group boundary breaking, and disrespectful or harassing behavior. The two types of challenges to expertise include not being perceived as an expert and thus having to prove credibility and accusations of biased curriculum or behavior. The data also reveal that some faculty discuss receiving no challenges, feeling that their authority and expertise are safe from students' challenges in the classroom and/or that they dismiss these challenges easily.

Findings

Table 4.1 presents the aggregate number of faculty reports of challenges (combined challenges to authority and expertise) by the race and gender of the faculty member. This table makes abundantly clear that faculty members of color report substantially more challenges than do white faculty members, and that this trend is true for all racial/ethnic categories of faculty of color. The eighteen white faculty report a total of 15 challenges, or less than 1 per person, whereas the forty-eight faculty of color report 125 challenges, an average of 2.6 per person. Among faculty of color African Americans report the most challenges (per person) and Asian Americans the least. Moreover, it is clear that in each racial/ethnic category women faculty report experiencing more challenges than do men faculty. Overall, the thirty-two women faculty report 95 challenges (an average of 3), whereas the thirty-four men report 45 (an average of 1.3). Moreover, when we disaggregate the data, the above trends hold true for both types of challenges—to authority and to expertise.

Table 4.1 Total Challenges to Authority and Expertise, by Race and Gender

Race/ethnicity	Women (n = 32)	Men (n = 34)	Total challenges mentioned and means
Faculty of Color (n = 48)	82	43	125 (2.6)
African American (10W, 10M)	38	23	61 (3)
Asian American (7W, 7M)	22	8	30 (2.2)
Latino (4W, 4M)	14	8	22 (2.75)
Native American (2W, 2M)	8	2	10 (2.5)
Other (2M)	0	2	2 (1.0)
White (n = 18) (9W, 9M)	13	2	15 (.8)
Total challenges mentioned and means (n = 66)	95 (3.0)	45 (1.3)	140 (2.1)

Challenges to Authority

Mistaking or Addressing Faculty as Nonfaculty

Both in and out of the classroom faculty members of color disproportionately perceive challenges to their authority that come in the form of not being recognized or addressed as a person holding their professional status. However, no white faculty members spoke of not being recognized or addressed as a faculty member. For instance, an Asian American woman faculty member explains that

> People would always stop at my office and ask questions. I was not [in the] office at the end; I was fourth in. But people would look in and figure woman, woman of color—secretary. (AsAm, W, H)

This colleague attributes the mistake about her professional status to the stereotype of a woman of color that allows people not to consider her as a person of authority and professional status. She goes on to say that such interactions initially left her feeling very angry, but they were not unfamiliar: "I frequently get the feeling that people have absolutely no expectation that I can be a faculty member" (AsAm, W, H).

In the classroom arena as well several women faculty of color report being mistaken for a graduate student, an undergraduate, or even a staff member. As an African American woman reports, this occurred "even by my own students in the classroom. It was very odd, because all I was seen as was a black American" (AfAm, W, H). She attributes this lack of recognition of her status and authority as due to her race and argues further that a black American does not fit the phenotype that students generally associate with faculty members and, thus, do not acknowledge her as an authority figure.

Both women of color indicate that these initial student perceptions and reactions to them make it more difficult and take longer for them to establish their appropriate classroom role and authority.

Even when they are recognized as faculty members, some faculty of color report that students sometimes choose not to address them as doctor or professor; instead, students may address them by their first name or simply avoid calling them anything. Although these faculty members are not being mistaken for non-faculty, similarly stressful and intense feelings are involved in these approaches:

> I think students are very, very careful not to reveal their source of domination, or they may not be aware that they're feeling more comfortable attacking me because I'm an Asian or an immigrant or a woman. I think women as a whole and women of color faculty [in particular] are an easier target [for students]. And I think a lot of times it's very unconscious on the part of the students. In a situation where there are male faculty and female faculty, a student may call male faculty Dr. So-and-So [and call the female faculty by her first name]. (AsAm, W, SS)

This Asian-American woman faculty member grapples with the issue of intent or consciousness behind a student's choice of forms of address. She believes that either students do not realize their biases about faculty of color and women faculty or that they intentionally keep their challenges covert so they cannot be proven to be race or gender motivated.

Reports such as these are confirmed by other informants and have been consistently confirmed in the literature (Harris 2007; Takiff, Sánchez, and Stewart 2001). Whether such challenges are made consciously or not, these incidents are examples of a more general and problematic trend. Harris explains why behavior like not calling a professor by her title, which she calls a "very casual approach to faculty-student interaction," is problematic. She argues that such interaction is a way that students "try to define, determine or shape a professor's identity through the messages communicated" (2007, 57). It also places an extra burden on the faculty member to assert or defend their professional role and status and its accompanying legitimate authority.

One Latino professor reflected on the duality of his role as a faculty member and a member of an underrepresented group and how the constant feeling of having to prove himself is transferred into his interactions with students. He says,

> While I recognize myself as a Latino who is capable of performing as an academician, sometimes … it almost feels like I always have to prove myself, to prove I belong here. When I come into the classroom I say, "If some of you think I'm here to fix some of the equipment or something like that" or "If maybe I lost my way to the garden" or "What's the janitor doing in here?" (L, M, SS)

His anticipation that students are likely to see him as a blue-collar worker rather than a professional has a powerful impact. Whether or not any students have actually responded to him in this way is unclear in the interview, but the emotional impact of the possible challenge is strong enough for him to identify and discuss it with students ahead of time.

This example perhaps is the best indicator of a unique form of stereotype threat that many faculty have encountered. Stereotype threat has traditionally been studied in terms of how students from racial, ethnic, and gender groups that often have underperformed on standardized achievement tests or other academic evaluative measures continue to do so precisely because of the angst they feel given their knowledge of that history of that performance (Aronson and Steele 2005; Steele 1997, 2007, 2010). The stereotype threat has also been extended to explore how it relates to faculty members' feelings of tokenism (Niemann 1999). The instructor above reveals that rather than simply withdraw into some sense of inner angst or turmoil, he publicly foregrounds a negative identity that can be attributed to him on the basis of his ethnicity in order to challenge others to dismiss that negative image and, instead, regard him as worthy of being regarded with authority.

Expecting Faculty to Be Parental Figures or Servants

Some faculty members report that students treat them like parental figures, not as people operating in a professional instructional role. Faculty members who express this feeling do so with intensity and, unlike some other challenges to authority, say conclusively that they receive this type of challenge because of their racial and/or gender identity. Although there is a relatively low frequency of such reports, they occur particularly in the interviews with Latina and African American women faculty, and the intensity and specificity with which it is described warrant it being a separate category. One African American woman tells the story of a time when a student expected motherly treatment from her (she also reports that this happens often to African American women).

[A student left me a message saying,] "I'm joining your class tomorrow, and I realize that I'm joining late and that I have heard about the books, and … now I would like for you to call me back and I would like to have the syllabus and I want to know exactly what readings we're going to be doing for tomorrow, and I expect to hear from you, and here is my number." … I thought, please never mistake kindness for weakness. So don't call me up [saying,] "Oh, yeah, well you're just going to be around to do blah-blah-blah." No, I'm not. Never. Ever. (AfAm, W, SS)

This scholar continued to say that she was going to have a face-to-face encounter with this student to address the assumptions that went into the student's lack of deference.

One of the key dilemmas reported here and in several earlier comments is the tension between authority and warmth or kindness and the ways in which accessibility, warmth, or pedagogical innovation on the part of white women scholars and women scholars of color may be interpreted and reacted to by students as signs of weakness or loss of traditional forms of authority (Fiske et al. 2002). Men who are not expected to be particularly warm and friendly have greater freedom in their approach to an available and relaxed classroom demeanor/role.

The prior excerpt is wrought with emotion about how African American women are stereotyped and mistreated as a result of these stereotypes. An African American man explains why he thinks students treat African American women in stereotypic and disrespectful ways:

If they've always had maids, then they can respond to you the way they've responded to their maid. Yes, there's genuine affection. You're a member of the family.… There's patronizing behavior that's as offensive as someone calling you a nigger. (AfAm, M, H)

He argues further that this challenge can be so detrimental that it can seriously hinder an African American faculty member's career, either through alienating him or her from the academy or forcing him or her to accept a position of little authority and control in the classroom. As in the case of mistaking or addressing faculty as nonfaculty, these challenges are perceived to be the result of students' stereotyping their professors and expecting things from them based on those stereotypes rather than on their true positions of instructional authority.

In-Group Boundary Breaking

Some scholars of color indicate that challenges to their status and authority were not made exclusively by white students but also by troubling interactions between themselves and students who share their race/ethnicity. These interactions come in the form of expecting special treatment, grading, and attention from their instructor and/or expecting him/her to act in certain ways based on assumptions or requests for racial/ethnic loyalty (Guiffrida 2005). It is only faculty members of color who experience this with their students; white faculty members do not talk about any of their white students having similar expectations for special treatment or grade leniency on the basis of common racial group membership.

Because faculty of color are often expected to be role models for students of color, these students may feel a special bond with their professors and look to them for guidance and support. However, some students appear to take this bond too far and push the boundaries of the student-professor relationship. An African American woman shares a story about a situation that she feels a white male professor would never have to deal with:

> I run into black students who do the "You're my sister, and I don't have to do any work." ... One woman wrote a paragraph in pencil ... big, old letters for her final project ... So, I wrote in pen, big bold letter, F. And, she was like, "You know, but my family ... and I'm taking care of me." And she did this whole thing about, you know, "You're the first black professor I've ever had." ... Then I said, "You should know better.... You would never turn that in to a white professor. Never, ever in your life." So I get those every once in a while. (AfAm, W, SS)

This faculty member perceives that the student blatantly uses their common racial group membership race in an attempt to bargain, hoping their in-group bond will trump the more typical student-faculty relationship. She clearly objects to the way the student sees their shared identity as more salient than her position of authority.

In a similar example a Latina faculty member explains how two of her Latino students reacted when they felt they should have received better grades:

> In terms of authority, an experience with this one student was a good example [of my authority being undermined]. He actually accused me of giving grades preferentially. He said that I was grading the Anglo students much easier than I was grading the Hispanic students. I also had an experience with another Latino male student who did not like the grade I gave him at the end of the semester, and then I found out later that he had been talking to other students. Those have been experiences where students have defied my authority. (L, W, H)

This example is slightly different from the prior one because here the professor believes that the student feels she is biased, but she similarly suggests that these students who share her racial/ethnic identity were challenging her authority.

Grading is often a bone of contention between students and any faculty member, but here it is turned into a loyalty test.

Minority in-group identity sharing also becomes problematic for professors who are verbally attacked for not representing their race or ethnicity in the way students feel they should. A Native American man explains that more than one student has challenged his ethnocentricity and racial group representation:

> There was this woman who called me out in class for not being Native enough. They say, "You're not Native enough." There is always this thing between Natives, "You're not brown enough," She really unleashed her anger at me. (NA, M)

By using the language "they call me out in class" and repeating it several times (some of which do not appear in the portion of text above) this colleague notes the intensity of this challenge by its repetition and the length of time he talks about it. Although minority in-group identity sharing allows many students and faculty to bond, in the classroom it sometimes can lead to students crossing an authority boundary that faculty believe should be steadfast in any student-faculty relationship.

Disrespectful and Harassing Behavior

Another type of challenge to professorial authority arises in faculty members' reports of students engaging in disruptive and disrespectful behavior toward them in the classroom. Women faculty of color more often report disrespectful behaviors or perceive them at a higher level of intensity than do men faculty of color or white men and women faculty. For example, in one interview a white woman faculty member briefly mentions students sleeping or reading the newspaper in class but is very quick to move past it and does not bring it up again. Although she affirms that students have slept or read during her class, she is not distressed enough to dwell on it and does not attribute the behavior as racially (or gender) based. She is, of course, pleased when students do pay attention and are engaged in the work. African American men's quotes about disrespect generally follow a pattern whereby they report what the disruptive behavior is, how they responded to it, and that their response put a stop to the behavior. Most faculty of color suggest that this behavior is racially based and cannot be attributed solely to students' lack of respect for "people in general." Women of color report such challenges in a variety of ways but generally do not say they are able to stop the behavior easily. This loss of agency reflects the ways in which such challenges can lead faculty members—especially women of color—to wonder whether they really have the power and authority to be in charge of the classroom.

It is not possible for us to say that white faculty members do not experience students disrupting or disrespecting them in class as often as do faculty of color. But whether or not it is happening to white professors with the same frequency that faculty members of color experience it, white faculty do not feel it is important enough to mention in interviews. This suggests that they seldom perceive it as a significant (even of low intensity) challenge to their authority. It is possible, of course, that faculty of color expect their authority to be undermined and interpret it in the context of a history of racial/ethnic slights, whereas white faculty members do not expect it and thus do not interpret or react to students' disrespectful or disruptive behavior in the same way (a potential outcome of "stereotype threat").

A white woman colleague emphasizes the importance of gender in discussing her classroom experiences and struggles in comparison to other professors:

> I think men have it way too easy in the classroom. They don't have a clue how much harder it is to have authority and to get respect and to just not have to deal with a lot of bullshit from some students. I mean, I take a real risk, because I do break down authority relations and so then I have to deal with the people who want to exploit that and abuse that and are more likely to do that because I'm a woman. (Wh, W, SS)

As a tenured professor, this scholar benefits from having a privileged identity characteristic—seniority—that allows her to navigate the challenges that she faces because of her gender identity (of course, her privileged identity of whiteness may also be a factor in her agency). Accordingly, she speaks as if she has achieved a secure level of comfort and security in dealing with such challenges.

This commentary also is verified in the contrast a senior African American man draws between the relative ease with which he functions and what he believes women faculty of color in particular have to deal with in the classroom:

> So I let the students start off. And so long as I can get them where I want them to go without telling them, you get the same result each time, but never the same route. And that's easy, see, that's fun. I don't know why we don't do that more often. I think it's because, you know, many teachers are insecure. They'd enjoy teaching more if they weren't. And when I mention to younger colleagues that this is the way I do it, especially black women can't fathom going into a classroom that way. Because, you know, they're concerned that their authority will be undermined. They say, "You're male and you're older." (AfAm, M, SS)

With disrespectful behavior, like many challenges to authority, it often is particularly difficult for faculty members to identify the basis of the challenge. Often they are not sure if they are experiencing it because of their race and/or gender or if it a common occurrence in all professors' classrooms. This uncertainty makes teaching even more confusing for faculty members who frequently perceive such challenges.

At the extreme of disrespectful behavior, some faculty members tell stories of feeling harassed by students, reporting serious disrespect, often experienced with great intensity, distress, and emotion. These unacceptable behaviors are most often reported by women of color, and are perceived by both women of color and white women as usually coming from men students of various races/ethnicities. One woman faculty member says that she has a number of issues with male students challenging her authority, and in one particular case she says that a white man went so far as to "sexually harass me in front of the other students in the class" (Wh, W, SS). When she later shares an experience of feeling humiliated by a black male student while teaching a class on race and ethnicity, she says,

> White guilt intervened in how I handled that situation in ways that I think inhibited me from probably handling it the best way possible. (Wh, W, SS)

Although she felt this challenge to her authority was related to her race and gender, the racial dynamic she felt between her and the African American man student may have prevented her from effectively dealing with both the student's behavior and her own feelings of humiliation. This dilemma in dealing with unacceptable and humiliating behavior provides a good example of how difficult it can be for faculty members to address the challenges they perceive occurring in a racialized situation.

The preceding comments demonstrate that mastery of course content is far from all that is necessary to ensure that faculty of color and female faculty secure the kind of respect and deference accorded to higher education faculty who occupy more privileged identity categories. They reflect what it means for some professors to appear in front of a classroom in possession of bodies that do not correspond with the image that many students, of whatever race or gender, associate with the professoriate.

Challenges to Expertise

University faculty, especially those in prestigious institutions, may be expected to have technical expertise in their fields, and students can be expected to receive them as such when they enter the classroom. As the dominant face of the faculty, white men faculty members can make and can assume that students will make just such assumptions about their high level of course content mastery and general subject matter expertise. White women faculty and men and women faculty of color cannot always make these assumptions.

Not Being Perceived as an Expert and Having to Prove Credibility

Faculty members almost always attribute perceived challenges to their expertise as related to one or more of their social identities—race, gender, age, nationality—and sometimes their personal/political views. Several informants of color feel that if they were white men, the students would not question their expertise. These findings reproduce Harlow's (2003) research with a sample of fifty-eight white and black faculty members at a Midwestern state university. She reports that black professors believe that students question their intellectual competence but that very few white faculty say the same thing. Several similar reports exist of the ways many faculty of color and white women faculty, especially young women of color, feel that students test their expertise, almost regardless of the class's manifest content, and especially so when the subject matter is not directly linked to their race or gender (see chapter 1 of this volume and Harlow 2003; Messner 2000; Turner and Myers 2000; TuSmith and Reddy 2002).

One woman faculty member reports that the combination of being young, a woman, and a woman of color made it particularly difficult for her to feel accepted as an expert by students. She says,

> [It was hard to get] students to take me seriously when I started out when I was younger. Now I'm feeling older, but looking young and being a woman, and being a woman of color, there are always these issues of [students asking,] "How are you qualified to teach me?" (NA, W)

Whether students actually ask her how she is qualified to teach or she just perceives that they wonder about this, she still feels that her expertise is challenged and that she has to work harder than some other professors to convince students to trust her qualifications.

An African American natural scientist also discusses his experience as follows:

> When I walk into the classroom, my anticipation is that I will be challenged, that's why I've got to be prepared, and I think that with that philosophy, it's easier for me to be well prepared, because I expect and anticipate, you know, the worst. (AfAm, M, NS)

He clearly expresses an anticipatory vigilance and even sense of dread accompanying his entry into a challenging and potentially disconfirming environment.

An African American woman faculty member says that she gets a similar feeling from students, and this affects what she can do in the classroom:

> I don't walk into a classroom expecting that, especially, my white students, and particularly my white male students, will automatically accept that I'm a scholar in my area. My white colleagues can do that. And I think a lot of students come in expecting that "Oh, a black professor. I'm not going to learn that much and not going to learn that much about anything that's real." I think my white colleagues can teach about lettuce heads for like a whole semester, and that's got nothing to do with what they're supposed to be teaching and it's automatically assumed that, really the knowledge is there, but this may just be sort of an eccentric person. I could not get away with that. Not at all. No. (AfAm, W, SS)

The high intensity of her comment is made clear by the dramatic example—white colleagues being able to "teach about lettuce heads for an entire semester"—of the expertise students automatically attribute to white professors.

Many faculty women of color suggest that especially white men students' challenges are rooted in their disbelief that a woman of color could have the knowledge to teach the course. In the following excerpt an African American woman discusses her experience with white male students directly challenging her expertise in the classroom:

> Now I can't prove that these are racial events, but I have some supposition that they may be racially motivated. One of them is the occurrence of white males coming into my class and questioning my expertise. I can't prove this, but I don't believe that they go into their [science] class and challenge their chemistry white male, perhaps, or even Asian [professor]. I would think now that it may be gender as well as race. Because I just don't think that they'd go to some of their other classes and question or challenge their professors in ways that I've been questioned or challenged. (AfAm, W, SS)

In this situation perceptions of racism and sexism are so fused that the respondent cannot tell which she is experiencing, as is often the experience of double discrimination. The interconnectedness of these "isms" compels her to experience this challenge in a way that a professor who does not have two marginalized identities would not experience.

This is not a burden of self-presentation for most white faculty members, especially white men faculty. As the expected and normative inhabitants of the faculty role, very few of the white faculty interviewed expressed concerns about how their own academic background or technical credentials would be received by students. Nor did many of them anticipate or encounter a challenge to their expertise. Indeed, when faced by the occasional student challenge to this expertise, they responded with relative ease. In fact, one white man faculty member indicates that he can afford to be challenged and even to make mistakes.

> *Are there things that you can do in the classroom because of who you are, that you can get away with, that other people can't?*
> Fabulous things, absolutely. Oh, my God! [laughs] I can make errors, I can make mistakes, I can have a bad day, I can be disorganized … I can use terms incorrectly, which most people of color can't use … or they'll be nailed—not only by the majority but by the minority students. (Wh, M, SS)

This colleague clearly recognizes that his privileged status as a white man leads students automatically to assume he is expert even when he performs less than perfectly. He also confirms the notion that his colleagues of color do not have this privilege. His perception of how students react to him positively based on his race supports the contention of faculty members of color who believe that students are less apt to trust their expertise than that of white men.

Accusations of Biased Curriculum

Some faculty members report that students sometimes make accusations that the curriculum material or professor is biased and/or racist. For example, some professors perceive that students challenge their expertise by suggesting that the material covered in a class is too focused on women or on people of a certain race or ethnicity. Others feel that no matter what or how they teach, students perceive their actions—and thus their expertise—through their stereotypes of the professors' identities.

An Asian American female faculty member talks about how difficult it is for her to teach Asian-related material because of students' challenges to her expertise:

> I used to teach a course including work from Chicano writers, African American writers, Asian American writers, and some Native Americans. But I found that when I taught the Asian American section, they responded to me in a totally different way; they perceived me as representing this group. That made me very nervous. I felt like that was inhibiting their experience; it made me uncomfortable. It felt like after that moment they always saw me as somebody who was speaking for minority issues. (AsAm, W, H)

Although this informant teaches a large variety of writers from different racial and ethnic backgrounds, she feels that some students frame or stereotype her in a way that makes her uncomfortable. The high level of intensity she feels is demonstrated throughout her interview as she talks about it several times.

In one of the few instances in which a white woman reports a challenge to her expertise, this colleague indicates that some students have complained about the gendered focus of her course materials:

> I've had the comment in a class that I taught that it was much too much about women, that one lecture about women [scholars] was fine, but thirty was way too much. I saved the comment. And I think that even if they don't say so, they sometimes feel that way. White maleness is invisible, it's just normal. And when we put other things in like disabilities, broader ethnic concerns, different mixes of scholars, or some not known to them, they think that is all we covered in the course, that it is way too much. And I understand that it doesn't have to be very many to seem way too much to these students. (Wh, W, H)

She feels that if she covers even a limited amount of material that is not about white men and their works, her students sometimes feel that it was all she covered, especially when it is about women.

Within this category of accusations of biased curriculum one challenge stands out because it comes from a white man, one of only two white men who talk about perceiving any type of challenge to either their authority or expertise:

> I had this one black woman who was a basketball player, female basketball player, and she was quite militant, and she did speak out in class, and a number of white students were angry and didn't like that. And so they would, you know, jump on her. And they always felt I was taking her side. And they wrote letters saying that I was a racist. They wrote these letters saying that I was antiwhite [and saying that] … it was impossible for white students to take my classes because I was so prejudiced.… You know, there's no way you can respond to student evaluations. So I think I carried those evaluations around with me a few times, showing them to people and saying, "Isn't this unfair—you know I wouldn't say that." That was a bad moment. (Wh, M, H)

This perceived challenge is by far the most intense of any mentioned by a white man informant. He clearly is distressed at the white students calling him "antiwhite" and accusing him of teaching the material in a racist way. His intense reaction—even showing the evaluations to colleagues—is an indication that it is not easy for faculty members, white faculty or faculty of color, to dismiss such challenges.

Once professors begin teaching materials related to their own race or gender, students often start to see the class material and the professor as focused on that one group or particular point of view to the exclusion or minimization of any others, even when many other points of view are taught. Furthermore, several faculty suggest that any diversion from white-centeredness (and, to some extent, men-centeredness) may be very disconcerting to students who are accustomed to learning primarily about and from white men. And when the normative forms of racial power are disrupted, as when the white colleague above acts to slow down attacks on a black woman, white students may become distressed and react accordingly.

Faculty Members Who Mention Not Feeling Challenged

Not all faculty informants perceived challenges to their authority or expertise. Many men, both men of color and white men, talk about the authority students naturally attribute to them in the classroom. They often use terms like "confidence," "personality," and "privilege" to describe why they believe they easily receive students' respect. In reciprocal fashion, they often say that they feel their self-confidence, personality, expertise, or presence shape how students receive them. In particular, one white man informant specifically says that he feels he has never said anything that would cause him to be challenged by a student in the classroom (of course, most of the women and minority faculty quoted earlier also feel they said nothing offensive but were challenged anyway).

> I've never had the experience, thank goodness, where I said something that was offensive to a student and they challenged me in class. I don't think I have. And if I did, like I said, I sort of have this sense from my reputation or something that people don't take offense as quickly as they might if I said the same thing and was somebody else. So I don't think there's ever been a situation where I said something terribly offensive. (Wh, M, SS)

He is aware that students do challenge professors in the classroom, but he does not experience this himself, and he attributes this to his or others' reputation or personality (not to his or their gender, race/ethnicity, or seniority). This tendency to minimize the categorical or structural impact of race and gender and to reduce matters to individual factors such as personality and personal characteristics is, itself, a mark of privilege—and close to color-blindness or gender-blindness (Bonilla-Silva 2001, 2006).

For some, intellectual respect comes automatically, and thus, potentially difficult situations or feelings do not arise. However, as we have shown, many professors do not perceive that their title automatically earns them authority and credibility with their students; in fact, some perceive that they are not even always perceived as a person with the title of a faculty member. Thus, whether these men escape challenges because of their gender and/or race—or for other reasons like personality—they do not face the same emotional taxation as do professors who perceive intense challenges.

Conclusion

The material presented here indicates that some professors perceive that students challenge their authority, their expertise, and sometimes both. Although analytically distinct, these two types of challenges often are interwoven in everyday experience. The challenges that faculty members perceive differ in type and intensity, but some general trends are clear. First, challenges to faculty members' institutional role and authority status as well as their standing as subject matter experts can occur to anyone, regardless of race, gender, or seniority. However, the racial and gender (and, in some cases, seniority) status of professors directly affects the degree to which they feel challenged about their classroom roles and pedagogical approaches, how much or what they know about their topic, and the manner by which they interpret and respond to such challenges (including whether they feel inclined or obliged to respond at all).

Second, challenges of any type do not have to take the form of aggressive or pernicious interactions. Alternatively, they can occur as students try to reposition faculty members as fulfilling supportive, nurturing, or intimate roles rather than professional ones. This is done—or at least expected—precisely because such faculty members stand in social identity categories that have not been traditionally associated with faculty status in the academy. Although faculty in such "nontraditional" identity categories sometimes may be seen as particularly expert in course content that addresses issues of race, ethnicity, multiculturalism, or social inequality, their very location in these categories can lead to them being challenged with regard to their expertise in other areas.

Third, the extent to which professors occupy dominant identity categories (e.g., male, white, tenured) reflects the extent to which they are able to discuss and respond to these challenges without an extensive degree of threat or anxiety. However, faculty with less privileged identities meet more such challenges and are more likely to anticipate and be concerned about such threats or anxieties such that they become consistent and durable points of concern in their everyday lives in the academy.

Finally, the relevance of faculty members' social identities is apparent in many ways. Although women of color talk about receiving challenges from students of varied social identity groups, they especially and repeatedly talk about experiencing problematic behavior from white men students. This specific mention of white maleness illuminates the particular way that race and gender power dynamics can affect professors. Women of color and occasionally white women and men of color not only perceive more frequent challenges to both their authority and expertise than do white men, but they also interpret the same behaviors from students very differently. Harris (2007, 61) suggests that although whites can dismiss challenges from students as "infrequent, impersonal infractions, marginalized individuals perceive them as a lifetime of repeated exposure to racial offenses, with an emotional tax that affects their psyche in various ways."

Given our nation's complex racial history, faculty of color standing in the front of a classroom immediately and starkly become visible examples of difference for their students. At the least, for many students they appear as unusual or unfamiliar images, given most students' limited contact and negative stereotypes regarding members of underrepresented groups in positions of authority or as models of scholarly expertise. Indeed, Purwar (2004, 53) argues that "Because they are not the 'natural' bodies for academia, black academics [sic—and other academics of color] have to endure a burden of doubt from those around them. And it comes with a level of hypervigilance, giving a feeling that colleagues and students are more likely to pick up on any mistakes and see them as signs of misplaced authority." This perspective on the ways in which faculty expertise may be perceived as a function of race/ethnicity is commonplace in the experience of faculty of color interviewed here.

Some faculty members of color also suggest that repeated past incidents of racial offense cause them to anticipate receiving challenges from students, such as worrying about being perceived as someone other than a professor, being thought to be less credible than white men faculty members, or even being harassed by students. A few white women also anticipate receiving challenges from students. These are good examples of how one's recognition or memory of past discrimination may create future expectations and perhaps hypervigilance. However, neither the experience of hypervigilance nor stereotype threat suggest that such memories of anticipations are divorced from the social reality of what happens in intergroup relationships.

It is not unusual for historically—and currently—marginalized group members to see the world differently and to anticipate challenges and interpret experiences differently than do members of more privileged groups. However, the great differences in numbers of challenges mentioned and the rarity of any mention of challenging student behavior in white faculty men's interviews strongly suggests that the actual frequency of students behaving in challenging and disrespectful ways does vary depending on the race and gender of the faculty member. These reports and prior literature (see chapter 1) suggest that we are not simply dealing with differential sensitivities or misinterpretations of challenging behaviors; white women, women of color, and men of color do receive more frequent and more intense challenges from students than do white men. Ultimately, whatever the causes of perceived challenges to authority and expertise, the key pedagogical dilemma for faculty is to work at ensuring and preserving the authority that has a place in relationships with students while also maintaining an inquiring, empowering, and vibrant educational climate.

Chapter 5

Identity, Power, and Conflict

Pedagogical Strategies for Successful Classroom Peer Dynamics*

Kristie A. Ford and Kelly Maxwell

Although there is a small but growing body of work that focuses on how to resolve student-student classroom conflict around social justice issues, such as racism, sexism, and heterosexism (e.g., Fox 2009; Goodman 1995; Meyers 2003), the research on faculty skill development around these issues is minimal. Instead, much of the existing research on teacher competence and training focuses on grades K–12 and/or exists within non-US university contexts (e.g., Brouwer and Korthagen 2005;

*Travel for this research collaboration was supported by the National Science Foundation and ADVANCE Grant 082008. Any opinions, findings, and conclusions or recommendations expressed in this material are those of the authors and do not necessarily reflect the views of the National Science Foundation.

McAllister and Irvine 2000). Accordingly, in this chapter we explore the following questions: How do faculty of differing social and professional identities navigate issues of race, gender, and sexuality in the classroom? What teaching moments enable faculty to recognize their strengths and weaknesses with respect to these issues? What pedagogical strategies do they employ to deal successfully with specific moments of student-to-student conflict? The exploration of these issues illuminates the interaction of the student element of conflict noted in chapter 3 and poses some options regarding the instructor and pedagogical elements.

For the purposes of this chapter we present data from a subsample of the twenty-three interviews in the study's data set that describe, in detail, challenging student-to-student interactions and/or describe pedagogical strategies for discussing difficult issues in the classroom. These participants, who provide insight into the role of identity, power, and conflict in the classroom, represent a diverse range of social identities: eleven women and twelve men; sixteen people of color (which includes faculty who identify as Hispanic/Latino/a, African American/black, Asian/Asian American, and Native American), and seven White faculty; and disciplines, ten social scientists, six natural scientists, and seven faculty in the humanities.

Theoretical Framework

Most college instructors in the United States have not been formally prepared for their roles as teachers (Kane, Sandretto, and Heath 2002), and fewer have had specific training related to managing bias or conflict in the classroom (Weinstein and O'Bear 1992; Meyers 2003). According to Paige (1986, in Weinstein and O'Bear 1992, 49), successful classroom management of conflict requires a number of skill sets and traits, including:

- tolerance of ambiguity
- cognitive and behavioral flexibility
- personal self-awareness, strong personal identity
- cultural self-awareness
- patience
- enthusiasm and commitment
- interpersonal sensitivity, relations
- tolerance of differences
- openness to new experience, peoples
- empathy
- sense of humility
- sense of humor

Meyers (2003, 94) also recognizes the propensity for conflict in the classroom and believes that faculty are underprepared to address it effectively: "Although faculty members report that they perceive classroom conflict to be distressing and disruptive, they are often reluctant to take active measures to resolve the disputes. One likely reason why inexperienced and even seasoned instructors ignore conflict is that faculty are not effectively prepared to handle these situations." Consequently, Meyers offers strategies to prevent conflict (if possible) or reduce conflict (if necessary).

Although Meyers (2003) emphasizes a prevention-based model of conflict, opposing research views conflict as pedagogically useful—philosophically and practically—if employed responsibly. Using a cultural diversity course as an exemplar, Roberts and Smith (2002, 293) focus on the importance of emotion management strategies in the classroom and their impact on student learning, arguing that "teaching is a service-oriented occupation that requires emotional labor: instructors must monitor and manage students' emotions as a routine part of their job." They highlight several different pedagogical tactics for effectively engaging with contentious diversity-related topics (e.g., establish rapport, create a sense of safety and trust, model appropriate conflict responses for students). Finally, McAllister and Irvine (2000) note that instructor cross-cultural competence, which is crucial to dealing with identity-driven classroom conflict successfully, involves understanding the worldviews of students, confronting internalized biases, learning about students' cultures, and viewing society through a variety of cultural lenses. Some of these same themes emerged from our study described below.

Findings

The subsequent results sections of this chapter are informed by three primary themes that emerged inductively from the data: (1) how student-to-student conflict around issues of race, gender, and sexuality manifests itself in the classroom; (2) how peer conflict may become amplified if faculty are unsure about appropriate ways of dealing with this conflict and the resulting emotions; and (3) how faculty use specific pedagogical approaches to engage with these emotionally laden issues successfully.

Student-to-Student Conflict

Given raced and classed residential segregation patterns in the United States (Krysan and Farley 2002), it is likely that students have had minimal contact with people of differing racial backgrounds prior to college. Once in college, intergroup friendships and interactions are often limited; moreover, honest conversations about diversity-related issues are hindered by fears of conflict, a climate of political correctness, and inexperience with effective models of dialogue across social identity groups. In interactions among students, faculty, primarily in the social sciences, highlight how identity politics, tokenization, racial stereotyping of classmates' intellectual abilities, discrepancies in student awareness or naïveté about structures of power and privilege, feelings of empowerment (e.g., having a voice) or disempowerment (e.g., being silenced), and perceptions of vulnerability or safety within the classroom can significantly affect group dynamics. In particular, discussions about controversial race- or gender-related issues with students from diverse backgrounds and identities tend to elicit a range of emotions, including anger, frustration, and fear. Underlying these emotions are unrecognized assumptions and stereotypes, often due to students' lack of contact and resulting ignorance with groups of people different from their own. A white faculty member in the natural sciences, for instance, notes that students in his courses often stereotype peers, particularly African Americans, when paired in team projects:

> It generally involves issues of teamwork problems, where students often have low expectations of African American team members. I've heard this from both minority and nonminority students, so I think they want so desperately to have students who are really strong, especially when most of their grade comes from a team effort. (Wh, M, NS)

Although it is unclear whether the African American students involved were aware of their team members' perceptions, raced or gendered stereotypes often do emerge in small-group interactions. They can reinforce notions of stereotype threat in which students representing nonprivileged or targeted social identities fear confirming pervasive stereotypes about their group's intellectual abilities (Steele 2007). Consequently, stereotypic race-related expectations of certain group members' academic competencies can negatively affect class dynamics, particularly when grades are in question. Contrary to this instructor's observations, however, literature also suggests that small group interaction with diverse peers can be a helpful way to break down stereotypes among groups.

Like the colleague above, another faculty member discusses how difficult group dynamics can affect a class if left unresolved throughout the course of the semester:

> Toward the end of the course, we were kind of summing up—in fact, it was on the last day—we were summing up and talking about what we had learned and such. We drifted into this conversation where the black students were expressing dissatisfaction that they felt like the white students weren't contributing enough when the conversations were about race. So they kind of felt like we were all talking about

discrimination and prejudice and stuff, and the black students were voicing a lot about it, talking about experiences they had or talking about their views on it. And the white students aren't saying anything. But like (the black students ask) "What are you guys thinking? And does it exist and do you see it? Is that what you talk about in other groups of other white friends?" And then it became this really kind of strange and kind of a tense situation for I think the white students who felt kind of on the spot ... it was one of those teachable moments for me, I guess. You know, there is this imbalance, and it was interesting to understand why, try to understand why students might be hesitant to speak about this. But we didn't get a lot of closure on it on that day. (NA, W)

In this instance, lingering racial tensions eventually emerged about how much black and white students were contributing to conversations about race; although a contentious issue, this "teachable moment" might have provided an opportunity for the group to better understand the role that voice, identity, and power play within the classroom space.

In contrast to the underlying tensions present in the above class, an African American male faculty shares an incident in which a student directly challenges other socioeconomically privileged students' perceptions of people from low-income, urban environments:

We were talking about a book on urban issues, and one of the more outspoken students, who didn't have a lot of the formal academic skills but was probably one of the most critical thinkers I've met as an undergraduate, had said a lot about himself in this class. I don't think the other students always got how personal he was in what he was saying. But at one point in the discussion of this book he said, "You all are talking about these people like they are foreign beings you never come in contact with. That's me, and I used to be on the corner. If I could have been on the corner at one point and be here with you now, it's a different way to think and talk about these people, and a different kind of understanding that you need to have." And everyone just sort of froze at that moment. We got a real live person from this book. (AfAm, M, SS)

As this passage indicates, it may be disconcerting for some students, naive to others' lived experiences, to encounter people who previously only existed in their social world as abstract characters in novels, ethnographies, or media reports. When confronted with a disconnect between their previously held beliefs about a particular social identity group and their interactions with a student who is representative of that group, students may be forced to reexamine and renegotiate their relationship to the "other." This is consistent with psychological theory on disequilibrium, in which people may experience a crisis of self by being presented with information that is unfamiliar or new (Bowman 2010; Gurin et al. 2002;

McFalls and Cobb-Roberts 2001). Students who are members of privileged groups may seek to reduce dissonance by altering their views of students from less privileged groups or by questioning these students' experiences as real. Although we do not know the resolution in the situation described above, the emotional real-life testimony provided a unique challenge and learning opportunity for the class.

Finally, a white man social science instructor discusses his need to intervene when a straight student, seemingly unaware of the heteronormative socialization process of sexuality in the United States, made a comment that reflected her ignorance:

> I was teaching a course, and during the discussion one of the students who identified herself previously as being heterosexual and very naive said, "I wasn't raised to be heterosexual." And the majority of the class responded pretty negatively to this comment, saying, "Everybody's raised to be heterosexual. We all were. That's why we have internalized homophobia." Out of their anxiety and their angst they wanted to battle and crush her and just run her over. I intervened, I calmed it down, but I didn't stop it. (Wh, M, SS)

Although the issues are different across these four passages (i.e., race, social class, and sexuality), at the core these incidents reflect students' inability to engage effectively with people who are racially or culturally unfamiliar to them. More concretely, privileged students' lack of exposure to other (usually marginalized) social identities and inability to examine their relationship to structures of power and privilege often clashes with students from targeted identity backgrounds who cannot understand why they have never heard or experienced perspectives similar to their own. Taken together, these episodes often result in emotional exchanges and conflict between students.

Faculty Dilemmas and Responses to Student Conflict

Student uncertainties can become heightened when faculty are unsure about how to appropriately engage with peer conflict and the resulting emotions that emerge. For instance, an Asian American man instructor provides an example of how student-to-student conflict around a film that documents eight men's experiences with and pain around race and racism in the United States may have been amplified by his inability to redirect the conversation in a constructive manner.

> We were watching this movie called *The Color of Fear*. It was a real heavy movie. A number of the white students in my class were in tears, having come to this realization suddenly that they are contributors to the cycle or dynamics of oppression. Students who never thought that they were. So we were having this very emotional discussion, and one of our female students of color raised her hand and said, "You know,

all of you folks here crying think that you know what it's all about now, well, you don't. This movie was the G-rated version of reality, and this was nothing." She was giving voice to her own frustration while very much minimizing the experiences of everyone else in the classroom. And there was a lot of anger that I just didn't handle. I got into this one-on-one discussion with her and I said, "Well, tell us the R-rated version. Don't pull any punches here—tell us the R-rated version. We want to hear it." And I don't think that this person was ready to articulate that and instead came back at me with "Well, in this course we're really not getting into the real issues." And then I started to take it a little bit personally and I said, "Well you know, everybody is at different levels. Some people are here and some people are here and we got to learn to teach other folks." It didn't even sound right to me when I was saying it. It almost sounded like I was being defensive. I didn't do a good job, I didn't handle it well.... The students of color are already so disempowered in our classes as it is, especially because there are only a few of them in our classes. I really should have done a better job, validating what she had said and just leaving it at that as opposed to try to take it personally. (AsAm, M, SS)

This faculty member realizes that he did not handle the incident particularly well and offers alternate ways of approaching difficult classroom situations better in the future. Often, decisions about how and when to intervene are recognized after the incident and resulting emotions have subsided. To that end, a white woman faculty in the social sciences explains one scenario in which a difficult and potentially personal topic for some students, rape, becomes heated along gender lines.

We were discussing rape. There were one or two guys in the class, and a guy in the class asserted very angrily that rape was not just a women's issue; it was a men's issue too. And he meant being raped. A woman in the class was impatient with this and said, "You know, that's ridiculous. It's disproportionate. You're trying to make something equal that's not equal." He had a point, she had a point, and I didn't intervene much. I just let it play out. I think the discussion didn't get anywhere helpful, and he was disappointed that no one articulated that they heard him, although I think people did, including me. And she was frustrated that nobody got on her bandwagon either. I wasn't yet clear enough about how to help that, and so I just let it go. (Wh, W, SS)

Although the instructor could understand the perspectives of both the man and woman engaged in the conflict, she chose not to intervene because she was not sure how to do so; consequently, a potentially valuable learning opportunity for the entire class was lost.

Similarly, a Latino man acknowledges that he did not take appropriate responsibility for the group dynamics when he allowed one male student to dominate a conversation about romantic relationships in a way that might have felt oppressive to the women in the room:

We have a male student who is fairly dominant and insistent in the way he presents things. He does it in a way that is not easy to confront because he presents it as this is how I think, and this is how it is. He started talking about his own issues around women and about preferring open relationships, even in intimate relationships. I see the class, the rest of the women, are kind of looking at him like, "Here he is objectifying relationships and objectifying women." So I'm seeing this happen, and I'm not sure where he's going with this. The class was sort of struggling. I have a class of about twenty people, and one man can dominate the classroom. After the class I knew I should have brought that up, about how this plays out in groups as well, and how sometimes, somehow we need to think about ways that it's disempowering and oppressive and how not to allow that to continue. I know this, I know it. And I watched it happen and didn't do anything. (L, M, SS)

The above examples illustrate a fundamental challenge for faculty in their efforts to work with student conflict and the resultant emotional tensions: faculty often lack experience to deal with conflict situations, particularly around race-, gender-, or sexuality-related topics (Kane, Sandretto, and Heath 2002; Meyers 2003). An underexplored area within the relevant literature, it is important to recognize that most faculty, even skilled faculty, occasionally struggle (or have previously struggled) with these issues. Teaching, particularly about contentious topics, can be challenging, especially at a time when diversity is forefront on the agenda at many higher educational institutions.

Although learning to engage students meaningfully with topics like race, gender, and sexuality takes time, some faculty have used these challenging moments to continue to improve their teaching throughout their professional careers. More concretely, by critically examining their past experiences and embracing student conflict as valuable learning opportunities, some faculty have been able to refine their pedagogical philosophies, practices, and skills in a manner that is attentive to intra- and intergroup tensions, across social identity markers. The following section more explicitly focuses on the successful pedagogical practices they have employed.

Successful Pedagogical Approaches to Student Conflict

To address the classroom challenges highlighted in the previous sections, some faculty intentionally utilized pedagogical strategies that led to improved classroom dynamics and interactions across various social identity markers. More concretely, they articulated their revised approach to teaching and learning with respect to three realms: (1) pedagogical philosophies, (2) pedagogical practices and techniques, and (3) pedagogical skills. We elaborate on each category, outlined in table 5.1, and in the subsequent sections. However, although this schema provides a concise way of distinguishing between the various inductively derived themes in the data, in actuality these categories are overlapping, interrelated, and not necessarily mutually exclusive. A final section discusses the pedagogical outcomes these approaches yield.

Table 5.1 Pedagogical Approaches to Student Conflict

Educational Realm	Strategies
Pedagogical Philosophies	• Engaged Pedagogy and Applied Learning (e.g., Freire model)
Pedagogical Practices and Techniques	• Create safety • Share stories • Take risks • Operate democratically • Model for students • Use small group work
Pedagogical Skills Faculty Self-Awareness Understanding of Group Dynamics	• Find voice • Increase cultural awarness • Understand the experiences of students • Expand awareness of group dynamics • Push students to learning edge
Pedagogical Outcome	• Colearning environment

Pedagogical Philosophies. Across the interviews many faculty noted that their current pedagogical philosophies emphasize engaged and/or applied learning. Engaged learning involves a student-centered approach to teaching that helps students critically examine the course material to make connections between content and lived experiences. Central to this approach is the theoretical work of Paulo Freire (1970), who argues in *Pedagogy of the Oppressed* that educators should focus on building nonhierarchical colearning environments with students; he also contends that educational systems need to embrace "liberatory" (active engagement) methods instead of relying on the traditional "banking" (passive receptor) model of teaching and learning. To that end, he states, "Those truly committed to liberation must reject the banking concept in its entirety, adopting instead a concept of women and men as conscious beings, and consciousness intent upon the world. They must abandon the educational goal of deposit-making and replace it with the posing of the problems of human beings in their relations with the world.... Liberating education consists in acts of cognition, not transferrals of information" (79). In a complementary manner, hooks (1994, 11) further elaborates on the role of teaching to promote an engaged classroom: "Teaching is a performative act....Teachers are not performers in the traditional sense of the word in that our work is not meant to be a spectacle. Yet it is meant to serve as a catalyst that calls everyone to become more and more engaged, to become active participants in learning." (For more on engaged pedagogies see chapter 1 and the discussion in Lindholm and Astin 2008).

Likewise, an Asian American man in the natural sciences discusses in depth his desire for students to develop their own critical consciousness through active, engaged learning within a context that promotes democratic ideals. The following passages exemplify many of the fundamental tenets of Freire's philosophies, including, (1) valuing the expertise and lived experiences of students, (2) modeling colearning practices that are attentive to individual learning styles, and (3) shifting from passive (e.g., test taking) to active (e.g., reflective essays) approaches to knowledge assessment:

> I've been actually very influenced by a lot of the literature in terms of active learning. So it's very important that when we're talking about things, we actually require them [students] to bring in their own perspectives. What has affected you in the past that made you approach this decision this way? Same thing about very contentious issues like race, class, gender, sexual orientation. We actually ask them to bring their own experiences, their own values. And we create these groups so that they're kind of safe learning environments. One of the things we're trying to do is model the kind of approaches that we would like the students to take. So that it becomes part of the culture, so that you can see a kind of democratic activity or democratic culture becomes part of the culture of how we behave. So going back to Freire's work—you assess the learner, the needs of the community come out of the community, and the instructor is there to assist but not to dictate and not to lecture. And the approaches must be tailored for each of these different circumstances.... We're really trying to change the paradigm of teaching. In our science this is kind of the bulwark of, you know, traditional, very conservative, top-down teaching, this is very different. So, again, instead of giving a lecture, we think of an activity that will get the students thinking about these things. Instead of having a test and having a multiple-choice answer, we have the students write reflective essays. So, you know, it's a shift from facts and behaviors and skills to attitudes. It's a shift from passive learning to more active learning. (AsAm, M, NS)

Although his approach may not be widely accepted within the sciences, through modeling and adapting to the needs of the learners he reports that he is able to effectively apply his teaching philosophies in a manner that promotes self-empowerment, critical thinking, group collaboration, and learning through doing. Moreover, he is able to articulate explicitly the pedagogical philosophies underlying his engaged or applied learning techniques—strategies that can be particularly useful when exploring contentious topics like race, gender, and sexuality.

Pedagogical Practices and Techniques. Intrinsically connected to pedagogical philosophies are the pedagogical practices, techniques, and skills employed to achieve desirable or anticipated outcomes. Faculty can support student development by applying engaged learning strategies, such as creating a safe space, sharing personal stories, naming issues of inequality in the classroom, modeling democratic ideals and risk-taking behavior, emphasizing small-group interactive activities and work, building meaningful relationships among students, and giving voice to students, particularly students from targeted identities. Two humanities professors, a white male and an African American female, for instance, believe that modeling risk-taking behavior, like sharing personal stories in a safe environment, can create new, more connected ways of interacting in the classroom.

> The class itself led to other people sharing stories. Somebody's mother died of cancer, so on. It enhanced their sense of what's possible to talk about. You can be in an alienated context, which is what a college classroom normally is, full of fear and distance, and you can still take risks. You can try something and it's okay. (Wh, M, H)
>
> I also try to be personal. I don't like saying a lot of personal stuff about who I am, but I like to give enough when it's relevant to set a tone in the classroom, that it's okay to be human. (AfAm, W, H)

For similar reasons, a white man in the natural sciences purposefully uses interactive cultural awareness activities like the social identity matrix as pedagogical tools in the classroom, thereby allowing him to share aspects of his identity to model openness and engagement while also better understanding the experiences of students in his courses.

> We've taken at some time the handout about the social identity matrix, and I do it myself and we break it down and have a couple of two-on-two, one-on-one discussions. I always pretend I'm one of the gang, and students are asking questions and whether I think of myself as heterosexual, those sorts of things.... We all sort of enjoy talking about others, our self-identities, and certainly part of that is race, and we've done some things like the privilege walk, and a lot of people talk about how they have privileges. (Wh, M, NS)
>
> *(For further explanation of the social identity matrix and similar exercises, see Adams, Bell and Griffin 2010)*

Through such pedagogical exercises, this faculty member is able to connect with students on a more personal level and demonstrate how students can connect with one another, thus providing the foundation for a reciprocal, colearning type of relationship among the students. Encouraging students to open up emotionally requires a level of established safety and trust; it also requires faculty to be attentive to the experiences and perspectives of students.

Structural factors in the classroom can also help facilitate the development of positive intergroup dynamics. The "contact hypothesis" suggests that several conditions matter in terms of increasing intergroup understanding and reducing prejudice. Specifically, four key conditions are relevant here. First is that there is equal status among participants. Small group work involving diverse peers can lead to interactions that minimize typical power dynamics and create more intimate learning environments. This leads to the second and third conditions, a common goal involving sustained personal interaction. Because students work together toward a specific task with diverse peers, this facilitates the opportunity for people to get to know one another and challenge unconscious biases. The fourth condition, support by authorities, happens when this process occurs via the instructor's initiative in the classroom. One example of the contact hypothesis in classroom practice is the jigsaw puzzle technique (Aronson et al. 1978); it is utilized in K–12 education, but its principles are applicable to higher education classrooms as well.

Dovidio and Gaertner (2004) discuss aversive racism in the United States, which refers to the conflict that most white people (and, by extension, members of any privileged group) have between embracing egalitarian values about different groups and the unconscious stereotypes, fears, and self-interest dominant groups hold at the expense of groups of people of color. Engaged pedagogy and changes to the delivery of classroom content become critical in helping students experience and perhaps resolve this internal disequilibrium (Bowman 2010; Gurin et al. 2002). Surfacing prejudice, anxiety, and fear in order to interrogate issues of systemic power and privilege can only happen when students engage affectively as well as cognitively in the class. Despite a long understanding that there is a significant connection between emotional and cognitive learning (Owen-Smith 2004), strategies for connecting these two in the classroom are relatively rare. Linking these learning strategies can be critical to resolving the "identity crisis" that dissonance can create.

Some faculty members replace previously employed lecture-based models with group-process models—using heterogeneously constructed small groups and the purposeful introduction of conflict as an opportunity for student growth. Others emphasize the importance of (1) modeling empathy and perspective taking to allow for a range of viewpoints to emerge within a discussion, and (2) supporting students in their desire to take curricular and/or pedagogical risks with group assignments.

> You have to be able to listen to a strong viewpoint and then come back and sort of be the devil's advocate about this perspective. You try and have some balance there. And I think that's hard to achieve, especially if you maybe personally really do fall

on one side or the other. You can't let that drive everything. That doesn't make for a full discussion. It becomes too one-sided. So I guess I have this ability to speak on other perspectives, or at least try to bring them out into the discussion. (NA, W)

They [white students] were pledging sororities, and they wanted to do their presentation on "Woman Is the Nigger," and I was like, oh, my goodness? What are you three sorority girls doing with this?! And, after I kind of took a deep breath, I thought, okay. I had the presentations worked out so they had time in class and I could work with each group. They did a knock-out presentation and the class didn't really bat an eye. (AfAm, W, H)

The faculty member in the first example occasionally plays devil's advocate as a means of presenting and advocating for students' acknowledgment and critical engagement with potentially conflicting perspectives; the colleague in the second passage takes a chance by allowing white students to construct an oral presentation on a racially loaded topic. In both cases the women's ability to embrace active pedagogies and practices provides space for critical engagement and learning to occur. One can anticipate conflict as a result of classroom risk taking. The above scenarios turned out well, but conversations involving identity can trigger intense emotions that do not always end productively.

Pedagogical Skills. To be effective teachers, faculty must be cognizant of both the content and process issues involved in managing a conflictual situation. Said differently, they must be able to (1) contextualize the information that is being conveyed or discussed, and (2) handle the affective dynamics related to personal and group sharing (Beale and Schoem 2001). They must also be attuned to the internal (self) and external (others) factors underlying classroom interactions; consequently, faculty must develop a critical self-awareness and adept understanding of group dynamics. A Latina faculty member learns this firsthand when two incidents early in her career caused her to reflect on her knowledge gaps around targeted religious and sexual identity groups:

When I was teaching right after my Ph.D., I was guilty, really, of presenting a stereotype in class. I had written something on the blackboard, something like, "The man who had many wives," and it alluded to multiple marriages. I had a student who was a Mormon in the class, and he felt very alluded to and very insulted by the sentence, and so he came and he told me. I apologized—I had not thought about the effect that the sentence would have had. (L, W, H)

In another class on race and ethnicity I felt very uncomfortable having to deal with issues of sexuality because I just feel like I didn't have enough familiarity with queer theory, and I had not read enough about the experience of being lesbian or gay. I felt very uneasy about how to approach it. I was so dumb I asked students,

"Who's gay and who's not?," and that was so terrible. Then, of course, I had students who later e-mailed me about how that was the wrong thing to have done. What I was trying to get at with that was to show that that identity is not fixed, and that people actually change sexual orientation sometimes throughout their lives. But it didn't work out, so I realized that I could have made that point in a different way without, you know, without putting students in such a difficult circumstance. So we make big mistakes. (L, W, H)

Albeit different, in both scenarios this faculty member unintentionally offended and/or further ostracized groups of students who are already marginalized. In the former she had not considered the impact that a seemingly benign sentence about marriage would have on students whose religious beliefs have sometimes supported polygamous unions; in the latter she not only asks students to "out" themselves but also tokenizes them by implicitly expecting LGBQ students to represent that experience in the class. A member of the dominant group in terms of sexual orientation and monogamous marital status, her own power and privilege around these social identities prevent her from imagining alternate or subordinate narratives, from recognizing the heterogeneity of these experiences, and from engaging with them in a more nuanced way. In the end, she takes ownership for her actions, apologizes, and has presumably learned from these oversights. Her lack of familiarity with these topics (academic content) and discomfort discussing them (interpersonal process) is certainly not unique.

Several other faculty discuss the importance of recognizing their own biases and the implications of doing (or not doing) so on group morale within the classroom. For example:

I guess you have to have the awareness that your bias exists. [Teachers] have to acknowledge that for themselves and to recognize that it could have an influence in my classroom setting.... Teachers could become so focused on what they're doing that they say and do things that call some students out or send a message that this class is geared toward one type of students and not other types of students. And you have to monitor yourself for that, to do that kind of thing. For example, in a class when a teacher is lecturing a lot to the minority students and not to the female students who might tend to be sitting in a group over here. I think becoming aware of that sort of thing, what you might be doing and not knowing what you're doing, people have to take the extra step to find out about themselves. (NA, W)

As this passage suggests, an important skill related to managing students' intergroup communication and interactions successfully is being self-reflective enough to understand how one's own worldview, life experiences, and implicit or explicit biases emerges in one's actions and thereby affect the classroom space.

Faculty must also be self-aware enough to understand their own strengths and weaknesses and know how to use them most effectively. Although humor might work for some and direct challenges for others, the overriding issue is to establish a comfortable environment for open and productive class discussions. The need to know oneself, reflect on identity issues in the classroom, and find one's unique and authentic voice is consistent with the literature about how both dominant and targeted racial- and gender-group faculty have been intentional in creating effective working/learning relationships in the classroom.

Together, these faculty skill sets, along with the pedagogical practices described earlier, create a foundation for helping students find and expand their learning edges—that is, those places where students are at the perimeter of their current knowledge. In doing so, these applied pedagogical techniques often facilitate a deeper and more complex understanding of course material. In somewhat abstract terms a white man describes how these learning moments can be powerful and emotionally damaging if not handled properly, or powerful and profound if done responsibly:

> She learned how she was raised and how other people might see things. In that moment, she turned, her entire body moved, and her eyes lit up, and she wasn't crushed and she didn't cry. I got lucky, you know. I timed it just so, so it was just enough pressure to really push her beyond that point without hurting her. That was the one moment in school that turned it around and made her understand the future. (Wh, M, SS)

In similar fashion, another faculty member notes that getting students engaged in productive discussions involves practice and that even with experience, the process of understanding and appropriately responding to group dynamics can still be challenging at times:

> Sometimes I would try to throw out provocative discussion questions. And I would get some people who would talk and sort of respond or ask other questions, and I liked that about teaching. I see teaching very much as a place to get a dialogue going. I mean, there's a contract in the classroom where I'm the teacher, and I have to make sure it all goes to schedule. So while I say I really like getting discussion and questions, I'm aware that being able to do that in a productive way involves a lot of experience and skill on how to make it not like a talk show but to get there. It's important for me to hear their ideas so I can then figure out how to respond to them. (AfAm, W, H)

This example articulates how a variety of classroom techniques can help students reach their learning edges, even with material that is unfamiliar or uncomfortable. Achieving pedagogical outcomes that reflect a balance between content and process, however, requires faculty to have specific pedagogical expertise and skills to adapt learning situations for their students.

Pedagogical Outcomes. Ideally, faculty using the aforementioned engaged pedagogical philosophies, practices/techniques, and skills will be able to establish and maintain productive student-to-student and teacher-student interactions and relationships within a safe colearning environment. This section focuses on self-reported pedagogical outcomes—outcomes that suggest that the pedagogical strategies some faculty have employed seem to have been successful. A white man in the humanities describes success as expanding students' learning edges by encouraging transformations in their thoughts, actions, or worldviews:

> The sparking of intellectual curiosity is even more necessary than getting a certain bit of knowledge. The sense of transformativeness, that students have let themselves be changed intellectually and see themselves being changed. Not just me seeing them go through a process, but it being mindful for them. (Wh, M, H)

And an Asian American woman explains that transformation is not necessarily a unidirectional process. In the following example she was able to truly experience both the sharing and receiving of knowledge when a student not only surpassed her expectations but also provided a new, innovative way of conceptualizing domestic violence:

> I always have a backup plan. If the student didn't connect the dots, I will, but I really didn't have to do it. They surpassed my expectation and made a connection that I personally haven't made. And I have been in this field, working in violence against women for years. I had a working definition of domestic violence, and it came from hundreds and thousands of sources, accumulated over the thirty years of battered women's movement in this country and internationally. This student provided this new dimension or different ways of framing, which really went beyond years of collective thinking. It was amazing. I was kind of trembling and was really busy writing that down. (AsAm, W, SS).

The last example exemplifies a true colearning environment in which both teacher and students learn from one another. The Freirian notion of transformation in these last quotations reinforces the pedagogical philosophies, techniques, and skills necessary to reach this important outcome. Clearly, faculty in this sample have struggled to get to this transformative space. From their own words we know they have handled some student-to-student conflicts better than others have. Through intentional self-reflection and pedagogical learning, many of these faculty are experiencing positive examples of transformation in their classrooms.

Conclusion

Faculty in our sample have found active and/or applied learning to be a useful pedagogical strategy, particularly when engaging with contentious topics like race, gender, and sexuality. Congruent with our empirical findings, Sleeter and Grant (2009) recommend four practices that they argue are central to multicultural education: (1) modeling democratic ideals in the classroom; (2) critically analyzing life experiences and circumstances; (3) developing social action skills; and (4) building coalitions with others. These four practices map to the theoretical framework presented earlier.

Our data also highlight the importance of faculty development focused on effective engagement with social justice issues in the classroom. Likewise, Anderson and Carta-Falsa (2002) and Hickcox (2002) acknowledge that for engaged, student-centered pedagogies to be successful, faculty must be willing to take personal and intellectual risks, which may require many of them to learn to apply new pedagogical practices, techniques, and skills that extend beyond the course content. In addition, Weinstein and O'Bear (1992, 41) identify common faculty fears specifically connected to discussing diversity issues (e.g., confronting the biases of self and others, doubting own competence, wrestling with intense emotions) and recommend that faculty participate in professional development workshops to help ameliorate some of these concerns.

Despite these faculty development challenges, our findings remain encouraging. With time, many of the faculty in this sample have developed the pedagogical competencies necessary to navigate difficult conflict situations among students. Moreover, these strategies are useful tools for all successful teachers, regardless of whether identity issues are central to the course content. Ultimately, engaged pedagogies, coupled with successful faculty implementation, can yield positive outcomes within diverse classroom spaces.

Chapter 6

Responding to "Hot Button Issues"

Pedagogical Approaches to Racial Conflict in the Classroom

**Penny A. Pasque, Jessica Charbeneau,
Mark A. Chesler, and Corissa Carlson**

This chapter explicitly considers the divisional differences (i.e., humanities, natural sciences, and social sciences) in how faculty interpret and address classroom-based conflict. Some core questions are what options do faculty members, who have substantial power in the classroom, have under these circumstances and how does the content and style of instruction in that classroom (referring to divisional distinctions and teaching strategies) affect such power dynamics and the recognition and response to conflict? In terms of the constitutive elements of classroom conflict identified in chapter 3, the student, instructor, and pedagogical elements are here highlighted, albeit the power of the curriculum (reflected in disciplinary foci) is reflected as well.

Our orienting questions inquired into whether and how faculty address conflict around issues of race and ethnicity, what methods faculty use to address (or avoid) such conflict, and the degree to which they are intentional about using or creating conflict to encourage discussion and learning around race and ethnicity. In addition to reading through all sixty-six transcripts, we specifically viewed responses to questions about conflict: "How do you deal with issues of racial diversity and multiculturalism in your classroom?" and "How do you deal with conflict between racial groups (or racial conflict) in the classroom? Can you remember any specific examples?" We used a constant comparative approach to this analysis of faculty members' comments on approaches to conflict situations in the classroom, from which the results emerged from the data itself. A typology of four major themes (with some variations within) emerged from the narratives of the faculty, and we then searched for these themes in extant literature, both about conflict responses broadly and then specifically in university classrooms. The total number of comments made by the sixty-six faculty members in response to these inquiries that specifically addressed issues of conflict was 161. Any individual faculty member's comments reflected different major themes described below. In recognition of this complexity, therefore, we focus in this chapter on individual comments rather than on individual faculty members themselves.

Background

The majority of faculty claim to value diversity; however, few report making many changes in their classroom practices to deal with diversity-related issues (Maruyama and Moreno 2000). Although recent research demonstrates many of the positive outcomes of campus and classroom diversity, these scenes may also become the site of conflicts between students of different racial/ethnic backgrounds. In a classic work on practical approaches to racial conflict Kochman (1981) suggests that one conflict management response is ignorance or avoidance of the situation, and this certainly can be applied to the classroom. In the context of racially diverse settings, Frankenberg (1993) refers to this as color-blindness or, given the power differentials typical of race relations, power-blindness/evasion. A second strategy often involves containment or control of both the setting and the rising conflict. And a third stance many in the field of conflict management suggest involves creative problem solving (Rubin, Pruitt, and Kim 1986). In the context of the collegiate classroom this stance can translate into treating conflicts as opportunities for learning, as "teachable moments"; this is part of the message contained in materials created by Warren (2005) as well as Schoem et al. (1993, especially section 7), and could lead faculty to consider classroom racial conflict as an opportunity to enhance student learning about diversity.

In some cases, however, faculty are encouraged to work on strategies to prevent and reduce conflict in college classrooms, as such conflict may be "distressing and disruptive" or as some faculty are just not effectively prepared to handle such situations (Meyers 2003, 94). Kardia and Sevig (2001) also note that many faculty members lack the skills to effectively address and utilize conflict in planning and dealing with classroom exchanges. And Sue and colleagues (2009) report that the white faculty members they studied expressed fear about losing control of the classroom, especially in the face of heated emotional encounters.

In the face of these concerns Meyers (2003) provides strategies for preventing classroom conflict such as communicating warmth and interpersonal sensitivity, establishing a shared course framework, and building a sense of community among students. Such a position views community and conflict as mutually exclusive, as though classroom conflict reflects negatively on the possibilities of students engaging one another fruitfully and reduces student learning.

Alternatively, Rich and Cargile (2004) use the theoretical framework of social drama as a reflection of racial conflict in society and in the classroom. In this approach faculty are encouraged to engage the conflict in the classroom in a transformative manner. They state, "we should invite conflict and the social dramas that may ensue. It may seem easier to skirt issues of race but it is at our own peril. We believe that teaching students how race and privilege are perpetuated can potentially lead to lasting transformations. For some students, the transformation may begin during class. For others, perhaps, the seeds have at least been planted" (363).

Graff (1992) also argues that instead of avoiding the conflict embedded in the tension of increased structural diversity across college campuses, faculty should incorporate the roots of the conflict by using the substance of the disagreements as content itself. Implementation of Graff's approach includes the tenets of multicultural education and conflict, whether explicitly or implicitly recognized as such, and has the potential to make significant change in classroom learning that students could then carry into their work and personal lives. Embracing classroom conflict in this manner creates a learning environment where students engage in dialogue; indeed, "Good teachers, after all, *want* their students to talk back" (Graff 1992, 9). In doing so, students and faculty are practicing democratic engagement around diversity and educational matters more broadly. Essentially, Graff argues that "conflict has to mean paralysis only as long as we fail to take positive advantage of it" (5).

In this manner, faculty in colleges and universities across the country have an opportunity to take advantage of conflict in the classroom in order to maximize teaching and learning to educate students to participate in a diverse democracy. Specifically, Howard (1999) urges white educators and educators of color to become "personally conscious" in their responsibility to address issues of race in the classroom. Effectively utilizing conflict may also increase student involvement in discussion, provide opportunity for students to change their own ideas, and help students develop more complex ideas (Nagda, Zuniga, and Sevig 1995). It may present students with challenging information and perspectives they had not considered previously, creating a situation of cognitive distance or disequilibrium that can lead to change in one's worldviews or views of others (Bowman 2010; Gurin et al. 2002; McFalls and Cobb-Roberts 2001). Thus, conflict is not only necessary to individual development but to the continuing process of democracy as well.

Appropriately utilizing conflict can help students have "breakthroughs" and encourage experience and training in the pedagogical use of conflict in order to increase students' learning. As Chesler contends, we need to shift our focus to include not only the learning of diverse students but also "the ability of faculty to teach in diverse classrooms—and what structural and cultural changes in the academy are required to support such faculty growth" (quoted in Chin 2002, 25). Further, Hurtado (2001, 29) argues that more research is needed about engaging in intergroup dialogue "to understand how conflicts arise and are resolved when 'hot button' issues are addressed in group discussions."

Findings

Four major themes emerged regarding faculty members' approaches to conflict situations around issues of race and ethnicity. The first theme is "no conflict," in which the faculty member states that there is no conflict in their classroom. Second, some faculty avoid or trivialize classroom conflict. In this case, the faculty member recognizes that there is a conflict and at times provides a specific example, yet avoids addressing it. In the third theme the faculty member seeks to gain control of the situation by stopping the conflict, often using authoritative methods of teaching to do so. Fourth, a number of faculty members use the conflict in a manner intended to be productive for the students, letting or coaching students to "play out" the conflict in the classroom or engaging proactively with the students in a transformative dialogue aimed at helping them learn from the conflict. In the next sections we describe each of these emergent themes and provide representative examples of each.

No Conflict

The first theme that emerged directly from the faculty members is "no conflict." In these examples the faculty report that they did not experience racial conflict in the classroom, even if they shared a story of a racial conflict elsewhere in the interview. In the first example the faculty member defines conflict as "anxious" or "excited" and explains that he did not experience this in the classroom:

> *Have there ever been issues or points of conflict or tension among students in your classes along racial or ethnic lines?*
>
> No. I would guess to some extent that we do eventually get to socioeconomic [issues] but nothing has come up in that context. We talk about education eventually and what they're exposed to in junior high and high school, and that's somewhat sociological. But we've never gone into any issues that have elicited—and you pick up the vibes in class—anything that gets people anxious or excited or hostile or anything like that. (Wh, M, NS).

This faculty member perceives points of conflict around race and ethnicity as negative because conflicts are defined as students becoming anxious, excited, or hostile. It is important to note that the researcher did not define conflict as a negative or positive entity; rather, it is the white faculty member who defines conflict as negative and states that this does not come up in his classroom.

In a second example the faculty member states that hard sciences stick to facts and that facts do not include any racial conflict:

> Racial event in the classroom? Hmm. I've been here almost over ten years now, and I cannot remember one racial event in the classroom.... [We deal with] facts, just the facts. Hard science. So, yeah, I can't think of anything. (AfAm, M, NS)

Here, the content of "hard science" is based on fact and is something that does not intersect with or include racial issues or conflict. But the natural sciences often do address issues of race and ethnicity—for example, in health disparities, economic inequities, representation of women and people of color in the sciences and medicine, and the like (Bowman 2010). For this African American man, however, facts within the natural sciences are mutually exclusive of "racial events" or issues.

These examples raise the question of whether there truly is no conflict in these classrooms around issues of race—or, as the first examples notes, socioeconomic differences—or if the faculty member is ignoring the subterranean racial landscape. Frankenberg (1993) talks about the latter possibility as race evasion and race noncognizance: the complexities of racial conflict are present but the faculty member may choose to ignore them.

Avoidance

In the avoidance category the faculty member recognizes that conflicts around race do exist in the classroom but consciously avoids addressing them. In the first representative example the faculty member describes how one student addressed another student who was saying something with a negative "racial connotation":

> It was a big group and you could feel this feeling, this tension, but then he [the student] kept going and nobody stopped him. And I think a few people looked at each other and then someone stopped him. I think if we're not going to say something, then people think it's okay to say it, and it's not. I would have definitely talked to the student, but then I wouldn't want to make a scene in front of everybody. (AsAm, M, NS)

In this example the faculty member clearly recognizes that issues need to be addressed, otherwise "people will think it's okay to say it, and it's not." However, he was not the person who addressed this situation as it arose because he did not "want to make a scene in front of everybody." As a result of the faculty member's conscious decision to avoid a scene, another student stepped in to deal with the situation.

In the next example the faculty member talks about wanting to avoid conflict about issues of race or to hope it would not happen again. However, she does state that she would like to figure out how to handle the situation differently in the future:

> In one class where the students were especially and wonderfully diverse in their own personal backgrounds and multicultural families, I asked them to collaborate with each other, and they paired up or were in larger groups to make projects. And one group did [it] about grandparents and the Holocaust, and another group—well, others did other things about being Filipino or being Chinese American, from India, things like that, whatever they were. And there were lots of white kids who [were exploring their heritage], I mean, there was some demand in this to kind of thing about the cultural heritage. But some black students in the class were really angry with the students who put the project together about the Holocaust and were adamant that that was way overblown. I mean, there was some denial about the importance of the Holocaust, but also a kind of competitive conversation about our miseries are worse than your miseries and slavery was worse than the Holocaust and things like that. And I really was pretty much at a loss how to deal with that. It made me very uncomfortable. I haven't avoided having such projects, but it made me hope it wouldn't happen again, and it made me kind of seek for ways to work that out differently. I think I must have said at the time I don't think we should be competing about whose—I mean, things are awful as you experience them. (Wh, W, H).

This faculty member admits that she was at a loss about how to deal with the conflict around slavery and the Holocaust that was developing among students but simply validated how awful each experience was. Although she has not discontinued such projects, she hopes that this type of conflict does not happen again. Further, it makes her "kind of seek for ways" to address the conflict in a different manner.

In each of the representative examples in this section the faculty member ignores or avoids dealing with racial and ethnic conflict or does not know how to pedagogically utilize the conflict to increase student learning on the topic of the class discussion.

Control

In the control (or recontrol) category faculty members often utilize authoritative approaches to addressing racial conflict, ones that take (or take back) control of the classroom by delivering a monologue, stopping the conversation, or changing the topic. For example, when asked how she deals with racial conflict in the classroom, this white social science faculty member says she cuts off the discussion, as she does not have time for "stupid debates" in her classroom.

> I certainly have silenced students. I've certainly just ended behavior that was inappropriate. I certainly have just engaged them in debate and shot down their arguments. But I also probably turn it in such a way that the other students do not lose a lot of energy. I mean, I'm not into having stupid debates in my classroom. So sometimes you just need to cut it off and move on so you don't lose time. (Wh, W, SS)

This faculty member provides space for students to debate with her and then shoots down students' arguments. She could have been talking about students who she perceives to say racist things in her class and does not expect students in the class to deal with these issues and expend a lot of energy. Therefore, she elects to address the conflict herself, controls the situation, and does not allot time and space for students to address each other.

In a second example a Native American faculty member addresses racial conflict by diffusing the situation and diverting students' attention to something else:

> They were going at each other verbally. I was at the other side of the classroom when it [an argument about race and welfare] started, and so all of a sudden there was this explosion and people were yelling at each other. But I walked over and sort of talked them through it. All I could do was to diffuse and so at the point of time I got them to talking about something else and we went on from that point. Then I dismissed class a bit early and I did sit down and talk with the students again. (NA, M)

In this situation the students were in conflict with each other about race and welfare. The faculty member works on diffusing the situation by redirecting the discussion or distracting the students by shifting the conversation to another topic. This strategy ended the conflict during the class, and the faculty member later met the two involved students after class to further the discussion, but not with the class as a whole.

Using the Conflict for Learning

Examples of "using the conflict" include times when faculty define conflict as a useful tool in order to deal with the topic at hand. In some of these cases the faculty let the students talk through the conflict during the class time in order to gain a deeper understanding of the material, and at other times they structured the course around the conflict and provided time for students to process through the conflict themselves. Our review and analysis in this section is intentionally in greater depth, as the section is more theoretically challenging and more pedagogically instructive for the field. Specifically, we move from examples of "using" conflict in a relatively passive style (i.e., setting up a dyadic discussion for students to talk out the areas of their disagreements) to a more intentional and transformative style (i.e., actively constructing exercises around course material that surface conflicts and enable students to focus in on points of disagreement).

In this first example the faculty member first talks about not knowing how to work with student silence and anger. Ultimately, however, she asks students to take the week to write about the conflict, and in this way, the students and faculty member could work privately on the issue and then come back to it in class the next week. Stated another way, the conflict arose, and then the faculty member altered the syllabus in order to utilize methods that would help the students address the conflict.

> With silence and anger I end up not knowing what to do about it. But I do think that by creating an atmosphere where people feel that they can speak at any point, and that they kind of own the classroom, and have a right to have debate. A lot of challenging, I don't have to do a lot if I've got the right students. They just take care of stuff that comes up and set people straight. I don't know how I had that idea that day, but of having people write meant that they could have their private thoughts and get a week away from it. (Wh, W, SS).

In a similar manner the next faculty member works to address the conflict that arises in what she sees as the most useful manner possible—through the use of fishbowls.

> Racially problematic behavior gets handled. Immediately we stop the class, we form a fishbowl, we have a discussion. What happened, why did it happen? What does it mean? What are the consequences for everybody in this room? What alternative behaviors do we have? I mean that's immediate. (AfAm, W, SS)

Fishbowls are a teaching and learning strategy by which students break up into two groups, each group consisting of students who have homogenous or similar backgrounds and/or experiences. After a short time apart, both groups of students come back together. One group creates an inner circle and the other creates an outer circle. Students in the inner circle share their perspectives with each other and students on the outside may only listen. The students then switch circles, and the students who listened now get to sit in the middle and speak, and students who spoke now get to listen. Finally, all engage in an open discussion. In this way, students must hear the entire argument of the other perspective and the multiple perspectives between students who share the same backgrounds before reacting to one another.

In the next two examples the faculty use exercises of having students write down feelings in order to talk about whiteness. This intentionally facilitates a discussion between students. The first example is one of intentional mediation between different perspectives, somewhat like the fishbowl mentioned above, but with two individuals. The second example engages the entire class.

> I asked the two people who were heatedly arguing to stop it and come into the middle of the room and everyone else to sit outside and be quiet. And then I slowly orchestrated a conversation between the two people in the middle, where I asked one person to say what was on his mind and the other person to repeat that before responding, and so forth. This controlled the level of emotionality and let people, at least those on the outside as well as those in the middle, to hear what was being said. (Wh, M, SS)
>
> I asked everybody to take a sheet of paper and not sign it, but write down what they feel is difficult about talking about whiteness. We did that, then took all the papers, exchanged them, and I said, "Now everybody really had something to say. Not only your remarks, but what others wrote." And it was really nice, I mean people really did talk about all that was going on in discussing whiteness. And some people said things that I knew were going to stir other people. White kids thought about power and nothing else. So to be honest with you, I think that a couple of people would have lied about this [if they had had to read their own words]. I could just sense the tension rising, someone would say, "I never thought of myself as the white person before, I'm not sure what to do" or "Part of me just thinks there's something about being white's a negative thing, there's got to be more than that. Help me." This one guy said, "This is some bullshit," and there was that too. But then the people that were most sincere were like, "Man, you must hear what I'm trying to say." And that's probably the most emotionally charged thirty minutes in a class. And again, falling back on that, we're not going to love one another, and it's going to be difficult, but we can learn together. And I guess it must have pretty much worked pretty well, because nothing sort of happened after that. (AfAm, M, SS)

In each of these examples the faculty member utilizes intentional teaching and learning strategies to flush out different perspectives on race and whiteness, a difficult topic for most students to discuss honestly. The faculty have different methods for teaching and learning depending on the class and perspectives. In each case the faculty member intentionally uses the conflict in conjunction with an intentional teaching method in order to facilitate a deeper discussion of the topic at hand.

In a proactive variant of "using conflict" some faculty define conflict as a good thing, intentionally create situations in which conflict will occur, and work together with students in order for the conflict to be useful—and transformative. For example, the next faculty member asks students for clarification, probing into a comment that a student made. By intentionally addressing this comment, the faculty member helps the student revisit what she had said, clarify, and learn from the situation. In addition, she also helps other students in the class learn more about where the first student was coming from.

> In my class last semester, where an Asian student, who had grown up in Hawaii, so she had grown up sort of, in terms of being very multi-ethnic but predominantly Asian and not a lot of African Americans or Latinos, used the term "colored." She talked about going to a lecture on women of color on campus, and how interesting it was, and she really learned a lot about African American women's health, and this is something that she felt she should know about, and whatever, and then she said something about colored women. I thought, well, let's see if anyone says anything. And I said, "Does anyone have any questions for so and so." So since nobody said anything, I said, "I noticed you used the term 'colored' and I was wondering if you could sort of explain what you meant by that." And so that gave her an opportunity also to realize that she had said something that might be viewed as inappropriate, especially by some members of the class, maybe more than others who may not be as aware. I knew that if I didn't say anything about it, there would be some members of the class that would be highly offended, and others who would feel uncomfortable, and then some who wouldn't even notice that it was an issue, and I wanted to make sure that that was addressed. (L, W, SS)

In this example the faculty member directly addresses the language of the student but does so in a way that lets her explain her meaning. In this way, the faculty member confronts a covert conflict situation by surfacing it directly in front of the entire class.

The next example expands beyond social science to natural science and is another representation of a proactive variant of "using conflict": the faculty member deliberately raises controversial issues to explore perspectives and promote cognitive disequilibrium:

> We deliberately try to make our classes and small groups as heterogeneous as possible, in terms of race and ethnicity, geographic origin, gender.... We'll actually introduce issues that may be so-called hot button issues and ask the students to really think

about them and reflect on their own values and then bring these things into the sessions. And part of this is really to create a sense of disequilibrium. We post questions or raise contradictions that will allow students to really kind of think about who they are and what their values are. (AsAm, M, NS)

This faculty member intentionally incorporates controversial issues into the curriculum ahead of time, knowing that students will contradict each other and explore their values as they learn of differing perspectives.

In the final example of "using conflict" the faculty member approaches conversations about race as "awkward," "normal," and "natural." In this way, he addresses the tensions around race early in the semester in order to increase interaction on the topic in the beginning of class:

I try and create situations where people have an opportunity to learn. I see awkwardness [about race] as normal and natural. I'll sometimes do an exercise asking people to think about their social identity. I often do that early in the semester so that the issue of race and gender and class identity is seen as part of our common problems. When people start to talk with one another about these issues it helps to deal with the information gap, it starts at least to put people into conversation with one another and moves people into interaction with one another in ways that don't fit with their normal styles of interaction. (Wh, M, SS)

In this example discussions of race become an expectation throughout the entire course, as they are included early in the semester. In this way, the faculty member can "use the conflict" or discussions about race to build upon for the remainder of the semester.

Disciplinary Differences in Approaches to Conflict

There are no major differences by gender in faculty members' comments about their approaches to conflict. However, faculty members of color are substantially more likely than are white faculty to make comments reflecting the use of control and less likely to report using conflict for learning. Although these findings differ somewhat from national surveys reporting faculty members' general classroom approaches (Lindholm and Astin 2008; Maruyama and Moreno 2000), these surveys do not focus on approaches to conflict and certainly not to racial conflict in particular.

It is clear, moreover, that natural science faculty are more likely than social science or humanities faculty to state that there was no conflict in their classroom and less likely to report using the conflict for learning. This finding supports research by Park and Denson (2009), who indicate that Science, Technology, Engineering, and Mathematics (STEM) faculty are less likely to be committed to diversity and to promoting racial understanding in the classroom. To be sure, subject matter concerns may make a difference in terms of the material covered or the personality and social style of people who are attracted to a particular field. And these concerns largely determine what is seen—by students and faculty—as relevant or appropriate to bring up in class. Stated another way, people who are deeply drawn to discussion of diversity issues may choose to teach or take courses in the social sciences or humanities rather than in the natural sciences. Further, epistemology may come into play: the natural sciences have not experienced the cultural turn in academic thought in the same way that has profoundly affected discussion in the social sciences. However, as Bowman (2010) points out, the natural sciences often do address issues of culture, race, and ethnicity in courses that deal with health disparities, human factors in technology, representation of women and people of color in the field, and more. Facts and epistemological perspectives within the natural sciences and engineering are not mutually exclusive of "racial events." Indeed, Riley (2003, 150) argues that "it is a cop-out to say that we as engineering professors are not capable of conducting discussions on racism and classism, and therefore are exempt from doing so. To continue to ignore race and class is to send a clear message to our students that it is not expected of them as well."

Conclusion

We identified four emergent themes from the faculty, some who never experienced or denied that there were racial conflicts in the classroom, some who saw such conflict but avoided dealing with it, some who worked to control the environment when conflict arose, and others who intentionally utilized the conflict in a way that would deepen student understanding, albeit with different approaches.

A number of faculty said that they had no idea how to deal with this type of conflict, such as the white woman from the humanities who said, "I really was pretty much at a loss how to deal with that" and hoped that it did not happen again. This raises the question about whether and how faculty can receive focused (re)training around teaching and learning, specifically with issues of diversity within their own discipline. Such training could address various pedagogical approaches to including diversity throughout the general curriculum, such as more authoritarian approaches as were found in the "control" section, and ways in which to intentionally utilize conflicts, such as mediation approaches and proactive and transformative learning approaches. A variety of active and experiential learning approaches may be successful in these situations, even within the natural sciences (Prince 2004; Riley 2003).

To be sure, race is complicated, and there often is a sense of awkwardness around the facilitation of classroom discussions about race. In these instances faculty need to find ways to go beyond their own awkwardness and help students deal with the issues at hand—failing to do so is educationally irresponsible. In addition, faculty need to recognize their own triggers in these situations in order to stay present in discussions and able to facilitate a complex and transformative exchange among students. Faculty development programs may be useful in helping colleagues examine and test their own group and pedagogical assumptions as well as in learning and practicing new classroom techniques, some of which may address issues of racial conflict. Of course, some faculty resist participation in such programs, and others who do participate must still employ lessons learned in the face of institutionally engrained patterns of race and gender inequality.

Both conflict and harmony or collaboration are normal in our society and in our collegiate classrooms. Students of varied backgrounds bring to the classroom both a desire to associate and learn with one another and, to a lesser or greater extent, confront the associated anxieties and prejudices regarding one another. Recognition of both sets of realities is essential for maintaining a stable classroom and a learning classroom. Active and effective modes of faculty response to racial conflict in the classroom probably contain elements of the following: recognition of conflict, even if it is somewhat hidden; diagnosis of the nature and focus of the conflict (e.g., is it really racially based); listening to the voices of students who are party to such conflict as well as their allies and associates; normalization of the existence of racial conflict in the context of a racially inequitable and contentious society and educational system; initiation of some creative set of exchanges and even problem solving among the contending parties; and the continuing effort to balance control of a potentially difficult situation with the commitment to student learning from and about such situations. Clearly faculty need to be alert to the prejudices—both conscious and unconscious—and discriminatory behaviors, whether intentional or not, that students bring with them. Faculty also need to be able to acknowledge and deal with their own internal states: their own prejudices, anxieties, fears, and hopes for themselves and their students.

Positive and productive responses to or use of conflict is important to democratic ideals both in the society and in the university classroom. It can promote open discourse, inclusion, and representation of multiple perspectives, and it prepares students for later experiences with such conflict. It is in the relationships among teachers and students that this can be reached (Gurin et al. 2004; Association of American Colleges and Universities 2002; Parker 2003). Not only are faculty working in more diverse classrooms and departments, but in doing so they are also met with the increasingly complex and conflicted issues inherent in a diverse democracy. Conflict is not new to educational practice, nor is it absent from democratic practice. Exploring how faculty respond when faced with conflict sheds light on how higher education can contribute to the growth of a more diverse democracy.

Part III Examinations of the Role of Identity

Chapter 7

Racial Practices in the Classroom

White Faculty's Pedagogical Enactments That Reproduce and/or Transform White Dominance

Jessica Charbeneau and Mark A. Chesler

Whiteness, like race itself, is both a social construction and a lived reality, a subjective experience and a set of objective power structures and relationships. As we focus on whiteness and white dominance, we refer to a set of social forces beyond the individual and beyond a conscious belief in white supremacy. White supremacy and racial prejudice seldom are taught explicitly, but as Bonilla-Silva (2006) argues, covert socialization into white dominance occurs rather universally. Although many white people do not hold or express prejudicial or supremacist attitudes, they nevertheless are affected by and reflect their white and privileged racial standing in their behaviors (Doane 2003; Lewis 2002). Assumptions rooted in white hegemony and privilege are acted on by individuals (consciously or unconsciously) and integrated into the policies and practices of social institutions (Feagin 2000; Feagin and Feagin 1986; Omi and Winant 1994).

In this chapter we go beyond individual attitudes and intentions in an analysis of the everyday enactments of whiteness in the teaching practices of white faculty operating within the racialized social context of an Historically White University (HWU). Identifying specific enactments of whiteness—behaviors that signify what it means to be white in our society—is vital to exposing and challenging racial hegemony and hierarchies, the mechanisms by which the structure of white dominance is reproduced or transformed.

We base this analysis on the eighteen interviews conducted with white faculty members in the larger study. This group of faculty is ideal for this analytic project because as individuals with a Euro-American cultural background, they have been conferred with the privileges of whiteness, and like most white Americans, were taught to take for granted the privileges this racial identity guarantees. At the same time, the entire sample in this study has been recognized as most likely to challenge the system of racial privilege, both personally and in the classroom. How they wrestle with this socialization and act to reproduce or transform white dominance should tell us much about the wider range of white faculty pedagogies and enactments. The portions of the protocol we use here sought information around three areas related to faculty pedagogy: (1) personal racial/ethnic and teaching biography, (2) pedagogical approaches to teaching and learning, and (3) views of the impact of their own social identities and on their approaches to teaching and their experiences with diverse groups of students. We developed the major themes through an iterative process moving between informal thematic reading and open coding of the interviews and the literature on whiteness and pedagogy. We then used focused coding of the interviews to determine the presence of these themes in the pedagogical experiences the white faculty described.

The selected themes and their associated behaviors are neither exclusive nor static: particular faculty may display several different types of enactments, and their behavior may change over time. Individual faculty members may act in a variety of ways, with or without intention, that serve either to reproduce or transform the hegemony of whiteness. Because any white faculty member could—and did—report many different behaviors, some of which fell into different categories, we categorize and comment on particular (and often situational) reports of thoughts and behaviors, not on persons.

Theoretical Framework

The reproduction of whiteness and white (and male and upper-middle-class) dominance is part of the "hidden curriculum" (Margolis and Romero 1998), evident in curricular requirements, graduation standards, the spatial structure of campuses and classrooms, residence hall arrangements, and other formal and informal policies and practices of higher education institutions. Conversations about pedagogical practices as well as teaching acts themselves take place within this organizational context, and faculty members' pedagogies are shaped by and thus reflect the larger educational institution. Pedagogical practice is the principal way white professors enact their whiteness as they work and relate in the classroom. It includes the way faculty engage in interactions with students—how they relate with white students and students of color as they select and present classroom material, conduct student assessments, utilize particular teaching approaches or tactics, make and act on assumptions about student learning styles and achievement, and formally and informally engage with students. In this way the educational institution, in the person of the faculty, makes explicit the implicit distinctions between who is privileged due to race and who is not, who has or can be expected to have talent and merit and who does not. As such, institutions of higher education are spaces where all students are taught the norms, practices, and expectations that comprise the structure of white hegemony (Zamudio and Rios 2006). It follows that they are also spaces where students of color—and all students—learn what constitutes being nonwhite within this structure. At the same time, whiteness currently is being reshaped by a growing recognition of and dialogue around the need for transforming pedagogy, how to implement it in the college classroom, and the struggles involved in racially transformative efforts (Adams, Bell, and Griffin 2010; McKinney 2002; TuSmith and Reddy 2002; Wagner 2005).

Our empirical analysis of the pedagogical practices white faculty report using in the classroom leads to the category system reflected in table 7.1. This framework is illustrated in terms of everyday enactments of whiteness (column 1) and how these same enactments may be manifest in white faculty members' classroom pedagogical practices (column 2). We identify these enactments as either *reproducing* or *transforming* depending on whether they may reinforce or challenge/change white hegemony.

Illustrations and Interpretations of Whiteness in Pedagogical Practice

Reproducing Enactments of Whiteness by Reflecting Limited Racial Awareness

One way in which white people sustain and reproduce the structure of white dominance is through behavior that reflects limited awareness about their whiteness and its implications. According to an early commentator, "The most striking

Table 7.1 Reproducing and Transforming Enactments of Whiteness*

REPRODUCING ENACTMENTS OF WHITENESS	
In general	*In pedagogical practice*

REFLECTING LIMITED RACIAL AWARENESS

1. Ignorance and obliviousness: Claiming ignorance or being unaware of difference	Remaining ignorant or resistant to recognizing white privilege, racial inequality, racial difference, and the value of diversity in the classroom
2. Minimization of difference and dominance: Minimizing or denying racial difference and inequality	Minimizing or denying race-based power differentials between professor and students and between students of different identities Adhering to a color-blind view of difference
3. Voluntary attention to difference and dominance: Turning on and off awareness of difference and inequality	Recognizing, valuing, and addressing race and racial issues only on one's own terms and timing

REFLECTING WHITE SUPREMACY

1. Acts of omission that maintain white hegemony by applying white norms to everyone: Assuming that white norms are universal standard by which lived experiences are judged	Assuming that traditional versions of knowledge production and dissemination are shared or prioritized similarly by all Assuming that their own experience and way of learning are shared by all Assuming that safety is experienced similarly by all students in the classroom
2. Acts of commission that disempower or exclude others: Disempowering others through implicit and explicit demonstrations of privilege and oppression	Employing pedagogical practices that secure and sustain the power of whiteness in the classroom

Table 7.1 continued

TRANSFORMING ENACTMENTS OF WHITENESS	
In general	*In pedagogical practice*

EXPRESSING RACIAL AWARENESS

1. Disclosing personal whiteness:
Acknowledging the presence of whiteness and articulating the impact whiteness has on social interactions and structures

Announcing and discussing their own racial identity and those of students and how that affects classroom dynamics

2. Acknowledging and attending to racial plurality:
Understanding plurality ways of believing, experiencing, and living in this society

Recognizing and including other voices in the curriculum, instructional tactics, and classroom interactions

3. Revealing patterns of white hegemony:
Recognizing that the dominant societal narrative is based on the white racial group and acknowledging one's social location within this system of white privilege

Explaining patterns of white dominance as they arise in course materials, instructional approaches, classroom dynamics, and the university itself

CHALLENGING WHITE SUPREMACY (POWER AND PRIVILEGE)

1. Creating alliances with members of other racial-ethnic groups:
Acting to bring individuals and groups of varied racial/ethnic identities together to form relationships that transcend normative racial structures

Coteaching with colleagues/students of color
Creating cross-race student workgroups
Engaging in ally behavior and creating opportunities for students to develop such behaviors

2. Acting to alter structures/cultures that promote white dominance:
Challenging patterns of white supremacy by trying to transform structures, practices, and cultural norms that directly or indirectly perpetuate the racial hierarchy and resulting inequalities/injustices

Providing opportunities for students to challenge existing racial structures through exposure to alternative ways of learning and acting/being
Altering traditional norms and practices in the classroom, the institution, and/or the community

*(Adapted from Charbeneau 2009)

characteristic of whites' consciousness of Whiteness is that most of the time we don't have any ... to be white is not to think about it" (Flagg 1993, 957). Whether intentional or not, whites' obliviousness to race-based issues and inequities, including their own privilege, serves to minimize racism and maintain dominance (Bonilla-Silva and Forman 2000; Forman and Lewis 2006; Headley 2004). The power of whiteness is also sustained when people adopt a color-blind attitude and when racial prejudice or discrimination is defined as the inappropriate actions of a few white people (Bobo, Kluegel, and Smith 1997; Bonilla-Silva 2001). Thus, the operations of systems of racial oppression and dominance are denied or trivialized, and the status quo of white dominance is interpreted as a "natural phenomenon." In fact, Mills argues that this constitutes an epistemology of ignorance whereby whites remain ignorant of the "racial contract" and thereby innocent of involvement in racially discriminatory acts or policies (Mills 1997).

In the classroom white faculty's limited racial awareness reproduces white hegemony when they fail to recognize and act on the racialized structure of the society, their own racialized privilege, and the impact of their race and pedagogy on diverse groups of students. Commenting on the invisibility of Whiteness, Lippin (2006, 110–11) suggests that while teaching courses in ethnicity "my whiteness was so 'subject' to me, that I couldn't see it.... There is greater danger that lies in unacknowledged and unexamined points of view. What we do not bring to consciousness has even greater power to influence us. Without recognition we remain in unwitting collusion with our own unconscious, unexamined perspectives." White faculty also exhibit the privilege of choice afforded them and other white people by deciding when and when not to engage in racial issues (Wagner 2005). This may be particularly common in disciplines in which a focus on race is considered secondary or unrelated.

Ignorance and Obliviousness. Limited racial awareness can also take the form of ignorance or inattentiveness to racial issues, as reflected in the following examples:

> *Do you find your race to be important?*
> I have no idea. I don't think so. (Wh, W, NS)
> It [diversity] really doesn't come up. If there is negative feeling, any significant negative feeling on campus about it, I've not picked it up. I wouldn't be surprised if there were some ... but if there is some it's held very close to the chest so to speak and I've not seen it spill over into any public discourse. (Wh, M, NS)

The first faculty member indicates a lack of awareness of the impact her racial identity may have on herself as well as others. The second white faculty member notes the possibility of negative racial feelings on campus but dismisses its likelihood, believing that he would have "picked it up" if it were present. The failure to be conscious about one's own and others' racial experience and perspectives is both an example of privilege and a way in which low awareness maintains white hegemony.

A priority on presenting scholarly material may also contribute to some faculty's inattentiveness:

> I'm certainly interested in students, but my main thing has always been the material.... I really want them to understand this material ... and that means, for me, a lot of effort has to go into explaining ideas. And I guess in those moments when you're explaining ideas the students do become kind of a blur. (Wh, M, H)

This white faculty acknowledges that his priority on delivering course material overshadows a focus on student concerns, including ones related to race/ethnicity, thus precluding the responsibility of attending to them.

Minimization of Racial Difference and Domination. Even when differences are acknowledged some faculty act in ways that overlook or discount the relevance or impact of such differences on students' lives and classroom processes. Feagin and Vera (1995) refer to this stance as the adoption of a "sincere fiction" that enables one to divorce oneself from acknowledging white privilege and the accrual of advantages thereby. Assuming a color-blind view may seem to be the most humane and egalitarian approach to interacting with students, but (1) it is not realistic because all who are sighted "see" color and most interpret color within the societal framework of racial hierarchy; (2) it negates the history and contemporary impact of racial discrimination and oppression on everyone; (3) it devalues, by making invisible or irrelevant, the different economic realities and cultural styles of students of different racial/ethnic backgrounds; and (4) it thus masks the power differentials among students or between students and faculty members of different racial/ethnic backgrounds (Bonilla-Silva 2006; Frankenberg 1993).

At a structural level the academy often keeps white privilege in place by ignoring or casting nondominant groups' uniqueness outside the realm of intellectual and practical relevance. In this way, denial of racial difference and white dominance differs from obliviousness in that the faculty member recognizes differences but elects to minimize or otherwise not deal with them, as illustrated in the following examples:

> *Do you think you can teach effectively without paying attention to issues of diversity in class?*
> I can in my field. I think as long as everyone in the classroom feels they can talk to me and ask me questions, then it doesn't matter what color they are or what gender. (Wh, W, NS)

This white faculty member does not overtly deny the presence of racial issues but instead minimizes their impact on the course and students and, thus, the importance of addressing them.

Denial and minimization may also take the form of supplanting the importance of racial difference with emphasis on other differences or issues, such as social class, religion, or intelligence. These other issues are important in their own right, but minimizing the importance of race by comparing its impact with other social identity group memberships leads to overlooking and thus reinforcing whiteness and white dominance.

Voluntary Attention to Difference and Dominance. A somewhat unique variant of denial is evident in the tendency for white people to understand and act on their own racial identity and others' racial oppression when it is convenient or safe for them to do so but to close their eyes and turn their backs when it is challenging or threatening to them. Racial awareness also is occasional and voluntary when white people construct their own ethnicity as a story of parallel oppression and struggle, often as "immigrant tales" (Gallagher 2003; Waters 1990), rather than stories of struggle simultaneous with stories of white-skin privilege. The result often is avoidance of one's membership in the privileged social category of whiteness. Such voluntary racial awareness is also evident when progressively minded white faculty cast themselves as "good white persons," ones who can transcend the structure of racial oppression in their own attitudes and behaviors and stand out from "more ordinary" whites. For instance,

> I grew up in an eastern urban area … [and] saying I work in an inner city and with people who are black or Latino gives me a lot more credibility than someone who just sort of sits and reads.… So that if I want to like call on a kid who's African American or Latino and say, "You know, what's going on. You know?" I mean not to call on them to tell me what it's like to be black but to connect to them. I think they know who I am. So it's not like I'm this foreign person. And I think students feel comfortable raising that stuff that they might not feel comfortable [raising] in other classes. (Wh, M, NS)

This faculty member argues that his background and involvements with students and communities of color give him credibility as not a "foreign person," not like other white faculty. However, the assumption that one's individual history or actions can override the structural impact of white identity and dominance in interracial dynamics is questionable at best and a further example of white privilege. People of color, and certainly students of color, who experience power differentials based on both their racial and student status cannot voluntarily or safely make these assumptions.

Reproducing Enactments of Whiteness by Reflecting White Supremacy

Whiteness also is reproduced, both in and out of the classroom, by ensuring white supremacy through acts of omission and commission. Racism often is reflected in acts of omission when faculty members use texts written only by white scholars, validate only traditional disciplinary knowledge and methods, or simply overlook racial concerns or events/incidents in class. Acts of omission implicitly exclude people, ideas, and events that do not conform to apparently universal white norms and expectations. In acts of commission white professors may disparage or "put down" students of color, cut them off, exclude them by using examples that are not familiar to them, and/or dismiss their concerns regarding a particular content issue or the course in general. As one example, Scheurich and Young (2002) argue that " if a college professor makes a racial slur during a class lecture, this is seen as overt racism … a public, conscious and intended act." But they also draw attention to the operation of covert racism, wherein " a professor may consciously choose not to mentor a Mexican American doctoral student … because of racial biases" (223). The latter bias is not readily apparent and may be disguised by provision of an "acceptable" reason for the behavior, such as a concern about English language proficiency, different areas of interest, and so forth.

Acts of Omission That Maintain White Hegemony by Applying White-Based Norms to Everyone. This stance is distinguished from ignorance/obliviousness and denial of difference/domination in that it recognizes or admits difference but valorizes and prioritizes the values and practices embedded in whiteness. White faculty may assume that all students should behave and learn in normative ways that are part of their own and white students' experiences and approaches. Such a monocultural approach to classroom content and process defines curricular content and examples, methods of evaluation, and pedagogical methods likely to be drawn from and centered on the dominant white experience (Chesler, Lewis, and Crowfoot 2005). The following excerpt illustrates the operation of the myth of normalcy and universality in the assumption that no special knowledge or skill may be necessary to deal with a diverse classroom environment:

> *What kind of knowledge, skills, and temperament do you think a faculty member needs in order to do a good job in a racially diverse classroom?*
> You think they need different skills [than] for a nonracially diverse classroom? I don't know. (Wh, W, NS)

White faculty also may take their accustomed ways of teaching and relating with students for granted and assume that comfort, safety, and learning opportunities are experienced similarly by all students. One example of how this behavior can take shape is by applying dominant white norms to classroom discussions that include racial conflict:

How do you deal with conflict between racial groups in the classroom?
    Well, in all kinds of ways. Some of them [students of color] don't do anything, because they're just getting through, you know. Some of them raise the issues rather repeatedly and annoyingly because it's about emotion, and so they don't quite know how to raise it in a way that the people can hear it, you know, someone bringing up their own color or issues of racism or prejudice in an angry repetitive, annoying fashion. Instead they [should] bring it up in a more thoughtful [way] ... you know, it's okay to bring it up. You don't have to get angry about it. (Wh, M, SS)

In the above example the white faculty member focuses on the students of color as instigators of conflict and is prepared to deal with it and appear comfortable with the presence of racial conflict in the classroom as long as these conversations stay within parameters that are acceptable to him. Directing a nonemotional or nonangry dialogue that is constructed "in a way that the [white] people can hear it" may or may not be intentional, but it results in keeping the white faculty and white students safe. As Kendall (2006, 153) points out, "My experience is that when white people ask for safety they [mean that they] don't ... want to be yelled at by people of color" (see also Sue et al.'s 2009 report of white faculty members' fears of dealing with "emotionally charged" conversations). When white faculty do not recognize potential differences in how students from varying racial (and socioeconomic class and gender) backgrounds experience the classroom and enact their concerns, they cannot take action to ensure that all students can take advantage of educational opportunities and resources.

Acts of Commission That Disempower Others through Exclusion or Demonstrations of White Privilege and Oppression. White faculty may also assume that access to educational resources is shared equally among all students and that most differences in students' success navigating institutions of higher learning are due to individual skills or cultural backgrounds and not strongly influenced by institutionalized racial privilege or disadvantage. Faculty who do not attend to the structural concerns or barriers experienced by students of color (or of white students engaging in learning with students of color) may fail to address the challenges they face. For example,

Minority students, black students, will often in recitations, often they'll come in late. And you have to be patient and understand that that's their way, I think, of expressing "I'm in control of the situation. I'm going to come late to this class and it's going to be fine. I don't have to be in this class." They'll make appointments with you for help and then not keep them. And again, I always think that that's because they really feel like they have to be in control and feel so lost. And so I just take off points. (Wh, W, SS)

This faculty member interprets students of color as trying to protect themselves or assert power in their relationships with her and the class by meeting course expectations on their own terms, by coming late to class or not coming to appointments at all with her. Her response to these underlying power/control issues—her role in the dynamic—is to assert her own power and control by penalizing the students for their behavior. She demonstrates empathy for the students of color but judges their behavior solely according to her cultural or professional standards.

White people can enact whiteness through acts of commission because they have both power and a secure position within the racial hierarchy. Demonstrations of oppressive behavior are often evident in acts that blame others for their disadvantaged or painful situations. This is captured in the posture the same white faculty member reports taking in another difficult situation:

[In the class] there was this Muslim young woman. People would say things about Saddam and Pakistan ... and she just kind of stood there or stopped and she wouldn't turn around. And she looked troubled but she wouldn't speak. So perhaps it's just her and this type of thing of being a Muslim in this atmosphere. (Wh, W, NS)

This time the white faculty member recognizes white students' problematic behavior and also recognizes the Muslim woman's distress but does not intervene. Moreover, she places the primary explanation for the Muslim student's response—or lack thereof—on her identity instead of on the identities of and treatment she received from other students or on the surrounding classroom culture of racial privilege.

Transforming Enactments of Whiteness by Expressing Racial Awareness

Some scholars and activists (Johnson 2006; Kendall 2006; Thompson 2001) argue that it is possible and important for white people to transcend the various forms of racial unawareness and oppressive behaviors that maintain white dominance. For example, instead of reproducing white hegemony through racial unawareness, they have suggested ways to disclose their racial identity privately and publicly, acknowledging and attending to diversity and plurality, and revealing white hegemony and their own location in a system of white privilege. Behaviorally such awareness may take the form of acknowledging occasional prejudice or deliberately using the term "white" in self-descriptions and in references to others (as contrasted with only using racial identifiers when describing others, as in "my black friend" or "his Mexican cook"). Public acknowledgments and disclosures of whiteness also can reveal the overarching nature of white hegemony and privilege within which all racial interactions and systems take place, including in their own course materials, classroom dynamics, and instructional approaches. Deconstructing whiteness by recognizing and disclosing it challenges its universalization. Moreover, and openness about the dynamic tension between "being white and benefiting from privilege on the one hand, and opposing the ideology of whiteness in education, on the other" (Mathieson 2004, 238) is in itself a potentially liberating experience for white faculty and for students of all races/ethnicities.

Disclosing Personal Whiteness. A classroom example of disclosing whiteness comes from Maxwell (2004, 163), who deliberately and straightforwardly acknowledged her whiteness and shared this information with her classes: "I generally do this by telling my story—my story of coming out as white." Naming one's whiteness is one way to make race and its societal implications visible in everyday interactions in the classroom. Given the relatively rare nature of such self-disclosures and the potential vulnerability implied thereby, disclosures of race and its implications can lead to temporary defensiveness and caution on the part of white students—and not coincidentally, both caution/distrust and greater comfort/participation from students of color. A white colleague reports below how he publicly shared his racial identity in the classroom as a model for students' own exploration of the issues:

> We've taken at some times the self-identity matrix. And I do it myself and we break it down and have a couple of two-on-one discussions. I always pretend I am one of the gang and students are asking me questions and whether I think of myself as white and heterosexual, those sorts of things. (Wh, M, NS)

He further reports that such exercises help students explore privilege and whiteness in the context of a range of social group memberships, including race, gender, socioeconomic class, and sexual orientation.

In most cases students of color need to test how safe it is to engage in honest conversation about race or any other topic with white faculty and students. One colleague notes how she aids this process:

> I feel like my race is read. You know, they read my race. My commitments around antiracism I'm very open and direct about it. I'm very conscious that students of color are judging, evaluating, interpreting how safe they are with me, what I'm going to do if white students say, as they do, painful and hurtful things. So I know that I am being read, I should be read. I'm putting things out so that I will be read. (Wh, W, SS)

This faculty member understands that although she is unique, she also may be "ordinary" and that we "who are white walk into a conversation carrying all of the people of our race with us, whether we want to or know that we're doing it" (Kendall 2006, 129).

Acknowledging and Attending to Racial Plurality. Several authors suggest broadening the subject matter of their courses or at least introducing multiple voices and views in their curricula and reading lists. In addition, Law, Phillips, and Turney (2004, 100) urge institutions and their faculty to "include considerations about delivery as well as course content and resources.... The process of learning should be inclusive and take into account the needs of all learners." This means focusing on pedagogical alternatives that generate a variety of course activities and approaches that permit students with different individually—or culturally—based learning styles to find their own best way of working/learning.

In addition to diversifying course material, several white faculty members discuss drawing students' attention to the interactive social arrangements of the classroom, such as the way people of different races/ethnicities sit together or communicate and relate with one another.

> So I think about it [diversity] ahead of time. I think about the structuring of the curriculum, about watching out for classroom seating patterns, about watching out for who I talk with, and a whole bunch of things like that ahead of time.... So that I will sometimes early on, first day, second day of class, ask students to meet in groups of people who don't look like them. (Wh, M, SS)

By challenging students to examine their own classroom—or out-of-classroom—behaviors, faculty can help students gain an understanding that they are not only observers but also participants in racialized patterns. The following quote is an example of how some white faculty address plurality by reaching out to students and guiding their progress in the course:

> What I've tried to build in my courses is a menu of opportunities and to try to educate the students in class about the nature of different options. There are twenty different ways to get here. You can take one-on-one tutoring approaches. You can come to class and use groups that are informally structured through the course pack. You can go to the science learning center and do this. You can be part of a living-learning community. You can be part of the honors community. You can read advice that's here and come and meet with me about these things. You can write out stuff that I look at. And how do I make the decision about which of these things is good for me and bad for me? Well, my answer is "Let's talk about your ability to understand what these differences are and how you might enter into this." (Wh, M, SS)

By going beyond the dominant and traditional instructional set of practices and tools, this white faculty is making space for—and as a result affirming—alternative (and perhaps culturally preferred) ways of learning.

Revealing White Hegemony and One's Location in a System of White Privilege. The kinds of acknowledgments and disclosures noted above can in addition reveal the overarching nature of white hegemony and privilege within which all racial interactions and systems take place. Some faculty members report structuring classroom exercises or reflecting on classroom dynamics in ways that deliberately draw students' attention to patterns of white dominance.

> One of the things I do in my classes for students who are going to be service providers is I have them do a self-reflection to recognize how they're a tool in that service provision. And that includes looking at privilege and oppression and prejudice and discrimination, not only the experience that they're going to give to other people but what that's about. (Wh, M, SS)

Creating opportunities for self-examination can incorporate examination of structures of racial oppression. White faculty who can link such academic and social structures to students' own lives can help students recognize these patterns in their future roles and careers.

Transforming Enactments of Whiteness by Challenging White Supremacy (Power and Privilege)

In addition to revealing the nature of white dominance, white people can challenge it in more or less overt and vigorous ways. One strategy involves creating alliances with people of color and with other whites working for racial change. Indeed, both Thompson, Schaefer, and Brod (2003) and Thompson (2001) have published multiple case studies of the activities and struggles reported by white activists working for racial change. Faculty members seeking to create effective and lasting alliances between themselves and students of color, between white students and students of color, or between themselves and progressive or antiracist white students must create reciprocal relationships, common agendas, understanding of each party's self-interest, mutual caring and concern, and significant sharing of status and power. This is quite unlikely in the classroom without major challenge to the dominant ways in which university education follows a pattern of "banking" rather than "liberationist" education. Freire likens banking education to the lecture or lecture-and-discussion method of instruction, whereby faculty "deposit" knowledge into the heads of students. A more liberationist approach would involve students in defining their own learning agendas, interacting dialogically with the material and one another and focusing on solving real life issues that matter to them (see Freire 1970).

Creating Alliances with Members of Other Racial/Ethnic Groups on Diversity Matters/ Issues. Building alliances between members of different racial groups is bound to encounter difficulties rooted in the history of white supremacy and differences in power, resources, and values, both among student groups and between students and faculty. Nevertheless, some faculty members try to create new kinds of connections by paying special attention to or challenging the ways in which white students act out patterns of dominance—perhaps in order to ease the burden on students of color to engage in such challenges—and in other cases attending to the needs and problems that students of color often encounter in a white-dominated educational and social environment.

> I generally try to challenge it [white students' inappropriate behavior] before the students of color have to challenge it. That's part of what I see as my responsibility as a white person and as a teacher ... not let the entire burden be on the students of color. (Wh, M, SS)
>
> One of the situations that comes up in classrooms, if you look at research or read a book that involves people of an African American heritage, or whatever ... often the white students will discuss it while the people who are most directly represented probably are feeling resentful and feeling the naiveté of the others as they try to discuss the book.... Generally what I'll do there is I'll try to say things that I feel are representational or in the ball park of what the silent students of color would say as a way of encouraging them to feel represented and to bring their voices in. I also watch closely for them to indicate that they're ready to speak, and if they are silenced by the white appropriation of their issue in the classroom, not that whites shouldn't talk about it but not in a way that appropriates the issue in the classroom, I will get with that student afterwards. I will call or talk to them before the next session, or whatever, to make sure that they know I know it's going on and encourage them to not feel damaged or isolated by it, or encourage them to speak the next time. (Wh, M, H)

The above quotes illustrate how being an ally on diversity issues can involve challenging white students' racially inappropriate behavior, checking in after a potentially damaging racial exchange in class, and encouraging all students to have a voice in class. Alliance building between white faculty and students—whether students of color or white students—requires a willingness to acknowledge that past and current experiences of racism will inform these relationships, reflections on how their comments may be interpreted, and a willingness to engage students on their own grounds.

Acting to Alter Structures/Cultures that Promote White Dominance. White people can also take steps to change the very structures that uphold white hegemony by altering the systemic conditions that support and maintain white privilege. Such action may be incremental or radical, collaborative or coercive, focusing on personal relationships, classroom situations, or out-of-the-classroom policies and events (see extended examples of this approach in chapter 11 in this volume).

Some faculty members who see patterns of white dominance in their own teaching or in classroom dynamics organize their courses or specific lessons/lectures to challenge overtly the typical ways race operates in a university classroom. Others alter their ways of instructing and interacting with students and their approaches to student learning.

> I can give a straight lecture where I don't ask for any participation. For me, diversity really comes into play when you're encouraging active learning and participation. I certainly have times when I need to rush [through] the material. For me, I think that [what] is really important is the mode of authority, the style of authority, the [classroom] structure. Diversity is about drawing out multiple voices in the classroom and getting people, allowing them to speak. And you can teach race and give a whole course on race and never hear a single voice. (Wh, W, SS)

This white faculty member argues for an interactive approach to teaching that may more successfully serve all students' learning. She implements a pedagogical practice that consciously incorporates multiple voices instead of merely that of the white professor. As a result, the normative practice of (white) professor as expert is diminished in order to encourage a more inclusive dialogue.

For some white colleagues, challenging traditional patterns of white dominance in the classroom involves anticipating or surfacing the conflicts that underlie so much of polite racial interactions:

> I had everybody in the class split [in half] and each half take on the role of being a member of a group that wasn't their group and then gave them a controversial topic. What happened is that the people who were no longer playing themselves but were playing a member of some other group said some outrageous things that hadn't been said in class before. Then we stopped it and the other half of the class was to be an analyst. The first thing I did was to say, "What I want you to do is to tell me if things were being said here that we haven't heard before?" And then they did get it and they saw that there were sentiments that the person of color assumed the white person they were now playing would say [and vice versa]…. And it was the closest we came to people shouting at each other. And I just kept saying, "Alright this sure brought out a lot of anger didn't it? Okay, why do we have so much anger at this point?" (Wh, W, SS)

In the above example above the faculty member deliberately designs an activity that surfaces covert conflict and permits racial phenomena to be discussed and analyzed openly. Conflict is not avoided or suppressed but instead is used as a pedagogical tool with which to explore and analyze both the intellect and emotions that often surround beliefs and assumptions around race and racial conversations.

The Struggles of Implementing Transformative Pedagogy in Practice

It is not surprising that many faculty talk about the ways in which they struggle as they negotiate whiteness in their pedagogical practices. Whether in the classroom or in other instructional exchanges with students, these spaces of teaching are located within a larger context of institutional, disciplinary, and gender as well as racial norms. When white faculty members try to adopt transformative pedagogy, they often enter into new territory that departs from many core instructional and institutional norms. Conflict, tension, and unease may result. The struggles described by the white faculty in this study surface in the spaces between the analytic dichotomy of reproducing and transforming pedagogies and in the effort to articulate and act upon racially transformative ideals and ideas.

The following quote describes how a relatively self-conscious faculty member discovered, upon reflection, how much her pedagogical practice departs from her values as well as the knowledge and courage it will take to match it up to her values:

> Well, I think number one is the faculty needs to talk about race and ethnicity, they need to talk about it openly. I think a lot of instructors don't do that because their course may not be on that. Like in one of my classes for semester after semester I never talked about race. For me that class was about [socioeconomic] class and unfairness, but we talked about topics without mentioning race. It was incredible. First of all realizing that you are doing that, and secondly having the courage to do it and then getting comfortable with the kinds of things that can come up. (Wh, W, H)

Without a comprehensive awareness of the way whiteness shapes racial dynamics, white faculty can find it difficult to recognize difference in the classroom and, as a result, struggle in their interactions with students of color.

> We've had a couple of Native American students who had just challenged everybody on the faculty to figure out how on earth to grade the kinds of products they turned in. They were actually Native American cultural productions. And they were quite wonderful in a whole lot of ways, but they don't fit your ordinary grading criteria. I think most people have dealt with them by trying to figure out how to ... teach them

to write case reports and to learn how to participate in some means of communication that isn't intrinsically their own. But how do you help them learn to do that without devaluing what they bring to it is a struggle.... How do you kind of value where they're coming from without stereotyping, without stigmatizing, but adapting what you do in a way that allow people to play to their strengths? (Wh, W, SS)

In this example the inadequacy and lack of pluralism or diversity in traditional and normative pedagogical practices, evaluation standards, and explanations of course material are exposed as a group of Native American students challenge the grading criteria. This white faculty recounts her particular struggles around, on the one hand, racially conscious interaction with the support of the Native American students and, on the other, the reality of preparing them to enter a profession that maintains culturally normative (e.g., white-oriented) standards of evaluation.

One of the most striking elements woven into the struggles of negotiating whiteness is fear and risk. Many white faculty express concern and fear of offending someone, fear of being accused of racist behavior, uncertainty around how to handle a racial situation, wariness of losing control of the class's dynamics, discomfort around emotionally tense situations, and sometimes the acceptance of all of the above as part of the dynamic of teaching in diverse classrooms (Sue et al. 2009; Weinstein and O'Bear 1992). As the following quote illustrates, the skill and (relative) comfort to act in transformative ways does not necessarily come easily:

I needed to be some kind of peacekeeper and I had my own allegiances, or something like that, and that I was unprepared for that moment. The students who were angry were the students of color and they were very strident, and it was very hard for me to make the class comfortable, which probably wasn't a very good idea anyway. It probably was important to not be comfortable. But I was uncomfortable and didn't really know what to do, and I thought the [white] students were very alarmed and abashed and maybe not very educated by the experience. I don't think that it had a lot of useful meaning. It was just a very tense time and not a good time. (Wh, W, H)

Making this transition to a transformative pedagogy entails internal and external growth with respect to racial awareness, walking the fine line between empowering all voices and behaving in a biased manner, finding the courage to take risks, and recognizing strategic ways to challenge white hegemony and supremacy.

Conclusion

The analysis presented here supports the argument that everyday enactments of the larger social structure of whiteness are manifest in the pedagogical practices of these faculty members. It is to be expected that white faculty would serve as conveyors of corresponding racialized practices and may well unintentionally act in ways that reproduce whiteness. Even if they do recognize the impact of these practices, they may be at a loss to know how to do things differently.

There are several reasons why transformative approaches are difficult to implement, even by faculty such as these who are known by their colleagues to be committed to dealing effectively with diverse classrooms. As one informant said, working on these issues means "You have to embrace conflict and not be scared of it, not be scared of emotion." Implicit is the requirement for white faculty to gain greater clarity about their own racial identity, their understanding of racial issues, and the role they themselves play in maintaining the racial structure, even as they may work to alter it. O'Brien (2006, 84–85) reports her response to being challenged by students of color for overlooking them, thus outing her own implicit racism. She writes that "My response was to tell the class this was another excellent example of how well-intentioned people may not realize how their behavior is being perceived, and that we must be ever-vigilant and mindful of falling into patterns of injustice that require great effort to struggle against." Thus, the value of engaging in transformative pedagogy is not simply to help students of color, nor merely to reeducate white students, but rather to act on one's own self-interest in being a better teacher and in creating a more just and effective educational environment for everyone.

Although we know that white people and, thus, white faculty have in common a privileged social location and styles of enactment based on race, we also know that whiteness is differentiated and stratified by gender, rank/status, age, sexual orientation, physical appearance and ability, socioeconomic class, and—in the academy—discipline. Among the reports of reproductive pedagogies there is a tendency for faculty to pose themselves as external to diversity-related issues in the classroom, as being out of sight and out of mind. In the reports of transformative pedagogical practices, faculty assume a more internal positioning on the issues and assume a responsibility to address them. Generally, the white men do so by acting proactively to directly address situations, sometimes in relatively abstract and discursive ways. The white women more often address the issues in a more personal and emotionally vulnerable manner, encouraging dialogue and exposing themselves and their students to discomfort or conflict. Disciplinary differences show up in the strong tendency for reproducing practices to be reported more often by white faculty in the natural sciences and transforming practices to more often be reported by white faculty in the humanities and social sciences. This is not surprising given the subject-matter differences and disciplinary norms that underlie the curricular and pedagogical practices in these groups. However, it also means that professional and disciplinary norms must be considered for effective faculty development around transformative pedagogical practices. The examples of transformative pedagogy presented here must be considered within the organizational context of institutional racism and the constraining factors of higher education in Primarily White Institutions—reward structures, disciplinary norms, and so forth—that keep these transformative practices on the margins or as optional elements of faculty development.

Chapter 8

Race, Gender, and Bodily (Mis)Recognitions

Women of Color Faculty Experiences with White Students

Kristie A. Ford

Identities are shaped not only by self-perception but also by others' perceptions of self. More pointedly, one's bodily self can be perceived differently depending on the viewer. The power of the viewer to recognize (render visible), misrecognize (render selectively visible), or not recognize (render invisible) a body has profound affects on both micro- and macrolevel processes. As misrecognized raced and gendered bodies, "outsiders-within" the academy (Collins 1986), women of color (WOC) faculty are one site at which bodily negotiations occur. To that end, Turner (2002, 74) notes, "Faculty women of color experience multiple marginality, characterized by lived contradiction and ambiguous empowerment. Their lives are often invisible, hidden within studies that either examine experiences of women faculty or faculty of color." This chapter seeks to *recognize*—and thus render visible—some of the unique challenges that WOC faculty encounter within the classroom space of Historically White Colleges and Universities (HWCU). In so doing it explores the interaction between the student and instructor elements of classroom conflict outlined in chapter 3.

WOC faculty have had to navigate a particular set of interpersonal and structural challenges in the academy. In particular, the experiences of WOC as both raced and gendered bodies in academe and, more specifically, in the academic classroom have been largely overlooked in the relevant literature (Harlow 2003; Myers 2002). To advance the discourse on the bodily experiences of WOC faculty, the literature must expand beyond individual narratives to study more systematically the sociocultural patterns and collective experiences of this group of women. Further, the experience of being a racially "othered" gendered body in academia must be more fully understood. And finally, we must engage the classroom as an underexplored site of bodily negotiation.

This chapter addresses these gaps by empirically examining the raced and gendered bodily dynamics that WOC faculty encounter when interacting with white students in the classroom. The data base is the twenty-three self-identified WOC (ten African Americans, seven Asian Americans, four Latinas, and two Native Americans) in the sample, representing a diverse range of backgrounds, perspectives, social identities, disciplines, and academic statuses. Analyses of the interviews proceeded inductively, resulting in the various themes presented below. The subsequent results section focuses on these women's accounts of bodily (mis)recognition. More specifically, the following questions are explored: In what ways do white students recognize (or misrecognize) the bodies of WOC faculty? How do these bodily misrecognitions affect faculty-student interactions? And what body management strategies are involved in WOC faculty efforts to navigate these raced and gendered bodily assumptions effectively? This chapter systematically documents and theoretically frames the experiences of WOC faculty in the academy via an exclusive focus on the faculty members' understandings of how they negotiate the classroom space based on their observation of student perceptions of their raced and gendered bodies.

Beyond Hegemony

Hegemony, defined by Gramsci (1971) as a process in which dominant groups maintain power through a combination of coercion and consent, is reproduced in higher education through institutional structures of power and privilege that normalize certain social identity groups as characteristic of teachers and administrators. Hegemonic reproduction is evident in microlevel interactions (e.g., students disregarding the expertise of WOC faculty, students "putting down" students of other races/ethnicities, white male faculty telling racist or sexist jokes) and in the macrolevel policies of departments and HWCUs. Connecting institutional hegemony to the recognition, misrecognition, or nonrecognition of bodies, Patton (2004, 193) notes, "The power to mark the body comes from those who have the power to represent. Groups who are able to retain and maintain the hegemonic order have the power to mark, classify, assign, and represent those 'others.' ... Thus, the politics of domination and representation become played out on the body in favor of retaining the current hegemonic order."

Disrupting the hegemonic classroom space, the presence of WOC faculty challenges white students' constructed understandings of effective pedagogical practices, curricular topics of importance, and noteworthy scholarship. Not only are WOC faculty challenging white students' hegemonic worldviews (e.g., Latino/as are lazy, blacks are intellectually inferior, Asians are passive) in raced and gendered ways, WOC faculty now have evaluative authority over student learning in the classroom. According to Grahame (2004), such challenges to hegemony result in student resistance; the resistance is a response to the (real or perceived) attention given to diversity issues within HWCUs. In the face of this resistance WOC have to learn strategies to effectively manage their bodies within the academic classroom.

Body Management in the Academy

Body management is not a new area of academic inquiry; within feminist scholarship a great deal of attention has been devoted to how women physically (e.g., beauty routines) and behaviorally (e.g., use of space) negotiate their bodies through frameworks such as "body management" (Bordo 1993) and "body projects" (Ong 2005). Feminism has been instrumental in exposing the gendered nature of social life and in reworking male-normative theoretical approaches to the body; it has also been remiss in fully acknowledging the raced and classed intragroup differences that shape a woman's experience with her body (Bordo 1993). The term "bodily recognition work" signifies the physical, behavioral, and emotional work or meaning-making process that WOC faculty engage in (both individually and collectively) to counter hegemonic narratives of bodily misrecognition within white, privileged academic spaces. Harlow (2003, 349) notes that "these performances [or bodily negotiations] are affected by the degree to which students and teachers begin their relationship with a mutual acceptance of the professor's status and identity." "Bodily misrecognition," then, refers to a range of false perceptions, linked to raced and gendered stereotypes about WOC faculty, that inform certain types of actions (or inactions) in the classroom (e.g., assuming incompetence, reducing identities to monolithic categories, failing to acknowledge the complexity of their personal, social, and professional identities). It is important to note that perceptions of bodily recognition (or misrecognition) are socially constructed and determined largely by the viewer and the person being viewed: the ability to "see" oneself or others in an authentic way is a function of power relations (Grazian 2005).

Bodily Misrecognition

WOC identities are indeed fluid, yet their lived reality reflects how they are categorized as visibly othered bodies within the academy. The process of interpreting bodies according to certain criteria often results in misrecognitions among both parties; for the WOC faculty, students' false presumptions about their relationship to knowledge and intellectual pursuits are directly linked to raced and gendered bodily stereotypes. Although the consequences of misrecognition may sometimes be negligible or even advantageous, without exception, the women interviewed highlighted the painful experiences they have endured as raced and gendered bodies in academia. Using the analogy of the "hall of mirrors," an Asian American professor speaks about her experience of negotiating the "odd perceptions" she encounters from students:

> It's like being in a hall of mirrors kind of thing, you know. There's all these odd perceptions that you think they have of you, which you don't know if they really do. It seems like they do. And you don't know where it's actually coming from. And you can't distinguish the real perception from the variety of other ones that others have, you know. So it's like, you always feel like ... you have to explain yourself to somebody. And that's such a hard thing to do all the time.... I don't say much about who I am.... I mean, there's so much that they're already reading on the body that I can't control ... that I feel like I want to kind of send the message to them that I don't want them to read me like physically. So if I identify as Asian American, they'll always kind of read me. It'll legitimize what their perceptions, whatever they are, you know. (AsAm, W, H)

Similarly, many of the women spoke directly or indirectly about the racialization of their gendered bodies (and/or the gendering of their raced bodies) by students generally and by white students more specifically. Even though students of color may also engage in bodily misrecognitions of WOC faculty, in accordance with the predominant themes in these data, this chapter privileges reported interactions with white students because these intergroup interactions emerged with much more saliency and emotionality than did those with students of color. In addition, the ways in which race and gender intersect are often difficult to untangle fully. Although one identity may be more or less prominent depending on the social context, the women of color recognize that their bodily experiences are markedly different from those of their white women and white and nonwhite men colleagues. Significantly, this pattern was unique to the interviews with the WOC; although men of color and white faculty may encounter similar experiences, the theme of bodily (mis)readings or (mis)recognitions inductively emerged with this subsample with a level of consistency that was not reflected in the data from the other social identity groups (for more, see Harlow 2003, and chapter 4 in this volume).

Speaking specifically about the experiences of black women, Crenshaw (1995, 358) acknowledges that "The intersection of racism and sexism factors into black women's lives in ways that cannot be captured wholly by looking separately at race or gender dimensions of those experiences." The subsequent results sections of this chapter are informed by three primary themes that emerged inductively from the data: (1) how white students misrecognize the bodies of WOC faculty based on physical appearance and speech patterns, (2) how such bodily misrecognition affects faculty-student interactions, and (3) how WOC negotiate their perceptions of the raced and gendered assumptions placed on their bodies within academic social spaces.

White Students Misrecognizing WOC Faculty Bodies: Hegemonic Narratives of Difference

Brekhus (1998) discusses both the theoretical and pragmatic implications of being visibly "marked" or "unmarked" in society. Although the marked item is always more narrowly specified and heavily articulated, the unmarked generally remains unnamed: "it presents the vast expanse of social reality that is passively defined as unremarkable, *socially generic,* and profane" (35–36). As a result, unmarked or nonstigmatized groups remain virtually unnoticed as they are deemed normal, mundane, and, thus, taken for granted.

Omi and Winant (1994, 59) state, "One of the first things we notice about people when we first meet them (along with their sex) is their race. We utilize race to provide clues about *who* a person is." Gender is also culturally and socially constructed in a binary manner. Women and men learn how to perform their roles in accordance with cultural expectations; those who fail to "do" gender correctly suffer the societally enforced punitive consequences within misogynist systems of power (Butler 1990; Fenstermaker and West 2002). Consequently, constructed gendered roles and behaviors produce relationships of dominance and subordinance that appear natural or innate. Like race, the arbitrary coding of gendered markers (e.g., level of emotionality, bodily adornment practices, style of speech) conflate "doing" (fluid identity) with "being" (outwardly stable identity) and ignore the social constructedness of raced and gendered bodies. Together, the intersections of race and gender create complicated systems of oppression that WOC navigate, both interpersonally and structurally, within institutions of higher education.

Socially inscribed in narratives of difference are implicit racist and sexist notions about WOC faculty (e.g., narratives of incompetence, nonrigorous mother figures, reverse discrimination). The following report by a Latina faculty underscores this point:

> I'm still trying to figure out ... it's really hard knowing what kind of impression or impact you as a body, you know, are making and as a body that's in a certain kind of relation to the students. I do know that, and I think this happens with everyone, you know, the whole question of what they're supposed to call me—Professor X, my first name, you know, has everything to do with how old I am—my gender—my race, possibly. Although I think my gender, my age, kind of play a bigger role there.... I still don't know what is appropriate or right in terms of title. And students will often ask me, "What do you expect us to call you?" And I ... you know, I always end up with like, "Well, whatever feels comfortable." But the reality is I'd prefer if they'd call me Professor X. But they don't usually.
>
> *What do they call you?*
>
> By my first name. It's kind of unbelievable to me.... And I've sort of gone back and forth on that, like do I need to kind of create this distance or what? And I still haven't decided what's right for me. I guess I'm still figuring that out. I do know that, you know, with women faculty, students feel, or want to ... a lot of times women students want to make women faculty into their mothers or maternity figures. And so I know that impulse is there. I feel that, you know, that has benefits, and it has drawbacks.
>
> *Do you feel in some ways that that undermines your ability to teach?*
>
> It changes how I teach.... Teaching as a woman, and as a woman of color, it's definitely a different experience than teaching as a man. Or a white man, or a man of color. We all occupy these roles in very different ways. And we have to develop strategies that respond to how we embody that role of teacher in the room. (L, W, H)

Failing to look like the average white man, two humanities faculty describe instances in which they are assumed to be administrative assistants or graduate students:

> One of the graduate students asked me to bring her these copies, because she thought I was a work study [assistant]. She saw me in the lounge and she said, "Will you make me these copies?" I wasn't angry at all, because this is common. I thought to myself, I'm going to talk to her, but the secretary saw it and said, "She has not learned that every black person, you know, in the hallway is not a janitor or a copy-maker." You constantly have to define yourself. (AfAm, W, H)
>
> Also race connected with gender, the fact that sometimes people do not identify me as a faculty member—they have confused me as a graduate student. I still

remember, actually, going into the classroom, and the students didn't know that I was the teacher ... And, so there are these issues about not only phenotype but also assumptions about what a professor is supposed to look like that obviously, you know, affect how people see you and how people construct you. (L, W, H)

In both instances their bodies were misrecognized precisely because they did not physically resemble the prototype of a typical instructor. Likewise, the following colleague uses the imagery of the black Mammy or maid to highlight how race and gender affect her interactions with white students:

> Because people do assume, particularly with African American women, that we are "da mamas" and some of them go so far as to say things like that. And I say, "I'm not your mother. I'm a warm person, I'm a kind person, but I'm not your mother and I don't want to be. And I have no interest. And, yes, this may come as a shock to you?" ... Or, as one of my colleagues put it, "I know this may be the first black woman you've interacted with except your maid, but I'm not your maid." (AfAm, W, SS)

As these quotations suggest, some white students are reportedly confused about how to read the bodies of women who look or sound "ethnic." In particular, bodily misrecognitions often emerged based on their (1) physical appearance (e.g., skin color, hairstyle, body shape/size, facial features, dress), and (2) accent and/or speech patterns.

Physical Appearance. Physical appearance is one way that WOC are identified as different from the hegemonic norm. Some WOC are hard to categorize, and others are readily lumped into the seemingly appropriate racial boxes—they are nevertheless misrecognized. Their nonwhite status allows for one-dimensional, monolithic stereotypes of blacks, Asians, and Latinas to persist, thus obscuring the historical and cultural differences between and within various racial/ethnic groups. To that end, a visibly identifiable black woman in the social sciences concedes, "You cannot get away from it. You are always a black professor."

In some circumstances the socially constructed identities of other WOC faculty are perceived incorrectly by students, even if they are unmistakably WOC. According to a humanities professor, the students are "totally puzzled" by her Asian American racial identity, reacting to her like an unfamiliar "Martian who drops in":

> They're puzzled. They're totally puzzled because they can't figure me out. I fall into every crack. I'm clearly not white but I'm clearly not black, so therefore what am I? I don't speak Spanish. I don't look Asian. What am I? And then where can they then place me? (AsAm, W, H)

Interacting with a visible WOC from a seemingly unidentifiable racial group can be disconcerting to students, precisely because they cannot employ a race-specific narrative of difference to her. Her body is "othered," different from the hegemonic norm, but unable to be readily placed into a particular racial category.

In addition to being racialized, the bodies of WOC faculty are also gendered based on physicality. Unsure about how students perceive her ambiguous racial identity, an Asian American colleague notes that gender also has a significant impact in the classroom because women are often seen as mother figures:

> I've had female students tell me they're very gratified to see that there is a female professor. I'm a mother. These kids are all children of mothers. You know, socially, it's much more acceptable for females to feel nurturing and act more interested, so socially that's more acceptable. I think because of homophobia in society, in most instances, it's uncomfortable for males to express caring or concern, so I think it's easier for me to do that, so I look at what's going on. Why are your grades falling? I send e-mails out after the first four weeks of the semester to students who aren't doing well in their homework, for example. I send an e-mail out to any student who receives below a fifty on any one of my exams. And I'm comfortable doing things like that, and that may be associated with my gender. Probably it's socially easier for me to do that and for the students to take it the right way. (AsAm, W, NS)

This passage highlights societally imposed constructions of "doing" gender that faculty may directly or indirectly reinforce by assuming a mothering or caretaking role with their students. In sum, this section highlights how the "unfamiliar," or narrative of difference, is often identified by both visible physical (e.g., skin color) and behavioral (e.g., nurturing personality) attributes.

Although most of the WOC faculty report instances of being disrespected based on their appearance or mannerisms, the reasons why the women are marginalized differ from race to race: black women focus primarily on bodily adornment practices such as hairstyle choice and style of dress; Asian American and Latina women focus largely on speech patterns and voice. Given the sociohistorical context of racist and sexist bodily denigration from slavery onward, it is not surprising that black women faculty overwhelmingly discuss hair and ethnic attire as potential impediments to being respected as qualified professionals within academia. At the margins of society, black women have been historically depicted in contradictory ways—as domineering and nurturing, sexually voracious and asexual, passive and aggressive (Bordo 1993; Collins 2004; Harris-Lacewell 2001). Used as a form of social and sexual control of the ethnic other's body, demeaning, minstrel-type caricatures that developed during slavery of the Mammy, Matriarch, Jezebel, and Sapphire persist and continue to affect how black women's bodies are portrayed. In addition, more modernized images of black women have also emerged. As Harris-Lacewell (2001, 2) notes, "Reduced by a racist and patriarchal society to caricatures of their true selves, African American women have consistently fought to define their actual existences within the constraints imposed by these external images." For black women faculty, these external images profoundly affect their lived experiences in the academy. One of several African American women scientists reveals how her hair and attire are markers of difference, characteristics that are not recognized as attributes of a credible professor.

> Someone's made me a beautiful outfit that is business attire, that I have actually seen women in other countries wear ... that I have seen women wear here somewhere other than the great old university and it's not an issue. If I put it on here, it's an issue. Like, "Why are you dressed like that?" or "I'm looking for the professor." "Well, here I am." "You can't possibly be the professor because your hair looks like this, or you're wearing that kind of an outfit." "Yeah, I can. I am." (AfAm, W, SS)

As these examples illustrate, black women's physical presence in the academy, particularly when their presence contradicts stereotypical raced and gendered appearance norms, reinforces institutional hegemony through narratives of difference.

Speech Patterns. Latina and Asian American women, however, talk more often about accents, use of language, tone of voice, and surnames as biocultural markers of difference. Language itself joins with other imagery of these WOC to create narratives of teacher competence and effectiveness. This heterogeneous group, characterized by various national origins, ethnic identifications, geographic locations, social contexts, socioeconomic class backgrounds, and immigration/ citizenship statuses (Pedraza 2000), is nonetheless associated with stereotypical constructions of the Latina as working class, loud, lazy, hypersexual teen mother, or maid. Asian American women are also depicted in monolithic terms; in contrast, however, they are more readily characterized as middle class, diligent, compliant, soft spoken "lotus blossoms," "dragon ladies," or "model minorities" (Pike and Johnson 2003). Indeed, within academia black, Asian American, and Latina women are likely to be inscribed with a range of negative bodily stereotypes (e.g., "educated black bitch," "China doll," "illegal immigrant") that are created and maintained to normalize whiteness (Harlow 2003; Ong 2005).

WOC Faculty Bodily Interactions with White Students: Hegemonic Narratives of Confronting Difference

> Sometimes I just think that it's hard for people to let go of some of their stereotypes; they work on it, but it gets in the way sometimes. (AfAm, W, NS)

As indicated in the previous section, some students reportedly make assumptions about the level of competence of a faculty member based on attributes such as hairstyle, choice of attire, and manner of speech. These bodily stereotypes affect faculty-student relationships and interactions in two distinct ways: (1) the bodies of WOC faculty are politicized through course content, and (2) the bodies of WOC faculty are threatened and/or disrespected by white students.

Bodies Politicized. Instead of being legitimized as intelligent and capable scholars, WOC bodies are often labeled and subsequently politicized based on course content (see other examples in chapter 4). For some, this leads to student resistance in class because they are assumed to have a "political agenda"; for others, this results in them being pigeonholed into a very narrow area of expertise. A black woman in the social sciences, for instance, notes that topics like race become politicized rather than seen as legitimate areas of academic inquiry:

> Some of those who are just on the border I kind of tipped over a little bit, but those who came in resistant I think after they leave the class they are even more resistant because they read me, particularly the white males who are conservative, read me as having a political agenda. So now it no longer becomes an academic subject; it becomes a political agenda. And I'll say, "Well I don't know any person who doesn't have a political agenda." But they only see politics when it's you presenting [an] idea that's not theirs. Somehow no other course has a political agenda. (AfAm, W, SS)

According to Baszile (2006, 200), black women's social position as the ontoepistemological in-between allows them to challenge "the reification of Blackness around maleness, the reification of gender around whiteness, and the reification of intellectualism around white maleness." This social position, however, is disconcerting to many privileged students who rarely if ever encounter curricular content and pedagogical approaches to teaching and learning that challenge the hegemonic norm. As a result, discourse around WOC faculty having a political (i.e., less scholarly) agenda pervades.

Not only are WOC faculty assumed to have a political agenda, but their areas of expertise are also thought to be limited to scholarship that focuses on people of color or other marginalized groups (Antonio 2002; Grahame 2004; Turner 2002). Moreover, because WOC faculty are more likely to link theory and praxis through a social justice lens, this type of work is often deemed less scholarly. The following statement illuminates this point:

> My evaluations for this course will have someone who writes, "Well, I thought this was going to be a course about race, and instead it was a course about how the white man keeps people of color down." ... Because I'm a person of color, they see me talking about different intellectuals, and they map those people's opinions onto me,

and then they say I am biased in the classroom or I am presenting a biased point of view. Well, yes, it's a biased point of view. It's counter-hegemonic. It speaks against power. So I try to foreground that so that they understand, at least coming in ... that what they are hearing is a biased point of view. So they can't like, you know, kill the messenger. (L, W, H)

As she suggests, by creating "social and intellectual distance from the Eurocentric masculinist professorial center" (Segura 2003, 34), WOC faculty directly and indirectly challenge the institutional structure of power and privilege within the academy. In response, racist and sexist resistance to WOC faculty emerge through hegemonic narratives of "self-serving political agendas," "anti-intellectual multiculturalism," or "watered down" scholarship.

Bodies Threatened and/or Disrespected. Uncomfortable with this seemingly racialized agenda in the classroom, in some cases white students physically or verbally threaten and/or disrespect the bodies of WOC faculty. The following excerpt is consistent with this theme:

I've had incidents with two white males ... we were reading texts that weren't very accessible ... so I told him [one of the white men], trying to be a decent teacher, "come to my office" because they were supposed to lead discussion and I will help work through and make sense of the text. He comes to my office and I ask if he went through the kind of guiding questions I gave and he said yes he did, and I ask, "How far did you get"? And he picked up the paper and he threw it in front of me and I almost had a conniption. I said, "You did not just do that? You did not just walk in my office and throw some papers at me like I'm somebody's child. I'm sitting there helping you and you are going to disrespect me like that?" So then he starts apologizing for that. (AfAm, W, SS)

This white man student's resistance is direct; frustrated with the assignment and likely unused to receiving academic guidance from a black woman instructor in and outside of the classroom, this student reacts to shifts in his worldview by trying to put her in her "place." This physical display of bodily aggression is more potent than the noted micro-interactions between this professor and student. On a macrolevel the incident is indicative of white students' struggles to reclaim a raced and gendered sense of entitlement and authority over the knowledge process in increasingly diverse and pluralistic institutions of higher education.

In addition to direct rudeness and disrespect, passive-aggressive engagements (e.g., eye rolling, inattentive gazes, silence) enable white man students to indirectly challenge the presence of WOC faculty in the classroom through a series of "microtransgressions" that, according to Grahame (2004, 7), "reinforce for faculty of color the sense that their presence is unwanted, unwelcome, and undeserved." Speaking to this point, a social science faculty member similarly notes that white students are unconsciously socialized to disrespect WOC faculty physically or verbally:

> I think students are very, very careful not to reveal their source of domination. I mean, otherwise they may not be aware that they're feeling more comfortable attacking me because I'm, say, Asian or immigrant or a woman. But I definitely feel it [although] I can't empirically show it because students are not going to come to you and say, "Hey, you know, I'm attacking you because you're Asian or you're a woman." I think women as a whole, in women faculty, and women of color faculty are easier targets. And I think a lot of times it's very unconscious on the part of the students. It's a socialization process. (AsAm, W, SS)

As her statement suggests, white students often confront difference in ways that subtly maintain racist and sexist structures of power and privilege; their entitlement is not always overt, but it underlies many of their conscious and unconscious interactions with WOC faculty. Aware of how these bodily misrecognitions affect faculty-student interactions, WOC employ a variety of body management strategies so that they will be recognized as embodied intellectuals rather than simply as raced and gendered bodies. The following section elaborates on some of these counter-hegemonic narratives of resistance.

Negotiating Bodily Misrecognition: Counter-Hegemonic Narratives of Resistance

Previous research (e.g., Aguirre 2000; Grahame 2004; Turner 2002) and several chapters in this volume reveal that the experiences of WOC faculty are markedly different from that of white faculty; WOC thus learn to manage their bodies based upon *their* perception of how white students misrecognize them within academic social spaces. Historically and systematically marginalized from academia through narratives of difference, WOC faculty must employ strategies of resistance—strategies that challenge normative raced and gendered behaviors and practices within institutions of higher education (Alfred 2001). Ong (2005) theorizes and empirically documents two such strategies—strategies of fragmentation (e.g., gendered or racial passing) and multiplicity (e.g., stereotype manipulation)—as means of explaining how WOC students cope with and/ or resist raced and gendered stereotypes. She argues that the students employ these strategies so that their bodies will be read as (1) community members or nonmembers, and (2) competent. Like the students, WOC faculty also engage in an institutional context in which their bodies are delegitimized. The interplay between raced and gendered categorization and WOC faculty's resistance to it can take many forms, among them are (1) assimilative, (2) pluralistic, and (3) transformative strategies. Although this schema provides a concise way of distinguishing between various approaches; in actuality, however, these categories are not necessarily mutually exclusive or so clear-cut.

Assimilative. WOC reacting to narratives of difference often adopt strategies that allow them, through adornment and self-presentation practices, to assimilate into mainstream academia in order to be recognized as the professor. An Asian American woman, for instance, notes that in order to gain legitimacy in the classroom, a historically white- and male-dominated space, she dresses more formally:

> How can a nonwhite woman assert an authoritativeness in a classroom dominated by white males for whom authority figures have been largely other white males? And so attire is a big part of it unconsciously. I'm always conscious how I dress on teaching days.... If I'm dressed casually on a nonteaching day and I go into someplace like the library, I frequently get the feeling that people don't ... people have absolutely no expectation that I can be a faculty member. (AsAm, W, H)

Likewise, a black humanities professor ensures that her physical appearance conforms to her classroom deportment: "I always dress formally.... I almost always wear skirts or dresses that are tailored. My hair is, you know, together or at least I try to ... and I have a formal demeanor in the classroom. I put things in writing. I have my students call me professor." For many WOC faculty, the intersections of race and gender (and sometimes age) significantly affect how their bodies are read in the academy. Adornment practices, such as professional attire, can thus enable some WOC faculty to diminish narratives of difference by attempting to conform to and fit into Eurocentric standards of dress.

In addition to their physical appearance, WOC also talk about the need to behaviorally manage their bodies in particular ways in order to assimilate into the academy and establish authority within the classroom space. Aware of the possibility of being sexually or verbally harassed by male students, one colleague reports that she is very cognizant of how she interacts with them:

> I think that, as a woman of color, I have to also be very careful about how I behave in the classroom, and I think, because of the issues of authority and so on, I cannot be too friendly.... I can be sensitive as a human being, but I can't open up totally.... I need to keep some distance with students, particularly male students, I would say. (L, W, H)

Although these physical and behavioral body management strategies may be effective for some, they can also be oppressive if they require WOC to fragment or conceal parts of their bodily self in order to adapt or assimilate into the white hegemonic system. Moreover, WOC faculty are unintentionally reinforcing hegemony when engaging in practices (e.g., dressing in Westernized clothing when they prefer to wear more culturally relevant attire, enforcing an authoritarian teaching pedagogy rather than exploring alternatives pedagogies) that do not challenge structures of whiteness and maleness in institutions of higher education. Unfortunately, but realistically, as Patton (2004, 195) notes, "Belongingness necessitates maintenance of the hegemonic order."

Pluralistic. In contrast to assimilative strategies, pluralistic and transformative strategies seemingly allow for more proactive modes of institutional resistance. By challenging common raced and gendered stereotypes through a pluralistic framework, WOC faculty can find new ways of engaging with hegemony. To that end, many WOC recognize that they are seen as exoticized bodies in the classroom and strive to disrupt this dominant narrative so that they will be respected as intellectual beings:

> I think that [race] is a very dominant factor in my life since I came to the United States. And I guess having had my first experience with prejudice or racism in college when people called me a spic, and also when people exoticized me.... So, and I would say that in some ways that has also had a big impact on how I try to present myself in the classroom. I try to be friendly. I try to be a human being, but I am not willing to allow students to exoticize me or to think, you know, that I'm a Carmen Miranda, or some kind of Caribbean Latina ... it's interesting, I've had conversations with colleagues about how important it is to bring the body in the classroom and to get away from this kind of idea of disembodied learning where we just use our minds. And I have actually responded to some of my colleagues saying, "Well, that may be a privilege that you can afford to do, but I don't want my students to think of me as a body, because that's already the dominant narrative out there." And I want them to think of me as an intellectual being, because that's where my authority lies, you know, it's in what I know and what I can do as a professor for them. So I think that that's an interesting way that racialization impacts the way you present yourself in the classroom. (L, W, H)

As this faculty member points out, stereotypical constructions of Latina women lead to significant assumptions being placed on her body. Based on her social location within the traditional structure of academia, she recognizes that she does not have the privilege to engage in disembodied learning nor is she comfortable overtly bringing her body into the learning process. Her desire to challenge the dominant narrative that portrays WOC faculty as anti-intellectual represents one pluralistic approach not only to integrating the academy but also to idealized notions of decentering hegemony within the academy.

Transformative. Transformative strategies of resistance seek to dramatically disrupt or destabilize the hegemonic power structure by fundamentally changing interpersonal and institutional values, expectations, and behaviors. Although none of the participants successfully achieved this goal, one faculty member in particular discusses several innovative pedagogical practices, including appearance and stereotype manipulation:

> I've thought about changing my appearance completely, like dyeing my hair blond or something. And just looking totally unnatural so that they would become aware of what the expectations are of me. But I just don't think I could carry it off. I'd just look silly, and that'd be even worse. (AsAm W, H)
>
> There's some ways I can say more about texts that are not about Asian Americans.... I guess I have to be more aware of what the potential response is, how they read me. And try to kind of directly go against what they perceive me to be, like to kind of shock them in a way to not see me how they think they've pegged me or whatever, right? Or to kind of be a little bit sneaky about it, and kind of go around the topic and end up back where I wanted them to kind of think about.... I'm kind of skirting the issue and not asking them to address it. But it may destabilize some of the perceptions without them consciously knowing it, you know. (AsAm, W, H)

By challenging one-dimensional characterizations of how Asian American women are supposed to look, act, or think, she hopes to destabilize the status quo, to create a counter-hegemonic narrative, a narrative of dissonance within the academy. However, the pluralistic and transformative strategies offered by the WOC are more abstract than the assimilative examples; instead of providing tangible, definitive ideas for how to implement change within the academy, they represent idealized projections of bodily recognition. Although in some cases largely symbolic (e.g., altering hair color) or seemingly inconsequential or vague, they nonetheless represent methods of subtly challenging the system rather than reproducing it. The inability of these WOC to articulate clear-cut proposals for institutional change is in many ways expected; the magnitude and insidiousness of racism and sexism within any system does not always lend itself to concrete solutions. Moreover, as the ensuing quotations illustrate, the pain and frustration of constantly engaging in this process of body management can lead to a range of coping methods that are focused on survival, not activism:

- I've learned to wear the mask damn well. (AfAm, W, SS)
- In a very practical way, pragmatic way ... it forces me to use this healthy dose of suspicion. I always approach every social, professional, and personal situation very guarded.... Yeah, and that kind of pain and emotional toll, I have not discussed that much. It just is difficult. (AsAm, W, SS)

- Well, you get angry, but you can't spend a lot of time with anger because that's self-destructive. So you try to, you know, all the strategies that you can have to kind of figure ways to survival. Like any other, it's a survival mode mentally and, you know, emotionally, so that you personally can be at ... at peace with your place in the environment. (AfAm, W, NS)

In an effort to be "at peace," these three categories of bodily resistance—assimilative, pluralistic, and transformative—represent basic typologies of how WOC faculty members navigate (or strive to navigate) HWCUs. bell hooks (1990, 149) states, "marginality is much more than a site of deprivation; in fact ... it is also the site of radical possibility, a space of resistance." In response to hegemonic narratives of difference, these WOC have created agentic sites of resistance, narratives of possibility, as they work toward bodily recognition within the academy. An extended discussion of how faculty members of various identities advocate for diversity and generate counter-hegemonic practices can be found in chapter 11.

Toward Bodily Recognition

We all suffer from the effects of, you know, the ideology of white male supremacy....
We are critiquing a system, not a person or a body.... You're talking about a system that consistently promotes certain people, right? Who probably are white males. (L, W, H)

Required to navigate a hegemonic educational system of power and privilege that was created for white men, it is not surprising that WOC faculty frequently encounter student resistance. The bodies of WOC faculty are anomalies; they represent a series of raced and gendered contradictions in academia. Overlapping and mutually reinforcing narratives of difference, incompetence, and anti-intellectual multiculturalism are so ingrained in our institutional fabric that WOC must constantly work to counter such negative bodily misrecognitions that further marginalize them within the academy. As Patton (2004, 197) notes, "The body has become the site of gender and race struggle in the academy." Indeed, WOC are the site of bodily struggle and resistance because they embody unfamiliar pedagogies and worldviews to privileged white students; their teaching and scholarship are more likely to embrace conceptual approaches, including duality, subjectivity, and marginalized voices (Baszile 2006), that disrupt the established hegemonic transmission of knowledge.

At some level we all engage in bodily recognitions or misrecognitions on a daily basis—some of which may be innocuous and others which may be more detrimental. These women experience the latter; student perceptions of them as different from the norm result in misperceptions that directly affect the amount of respect they can garner in the professional realm. This chapter demonstrates how bodily constructions of WOC faculty, specifically in relation to hairstyle, skin color, modes of dress, and use of language, affect classroom interactions. More concretely, these data suggest that WOC faculty learn to present, manage, and negotiate their bodies differently in order to gain comparable authority that is automatically granted to white men faculty. Further, student resistance often emerges in the form of politicizing and/or threatening the bodies of WOC faculty. Although these women have adopted various pedagogical and body management strategies (e.g., assimilative, pluralistic, and transformative) that have enabled them to become successful teachers, the emotional costs are nonetheless great. Moreover, as previous literature suggests, navigating isolating work environments, raced and gendered stereotypes, tokenization, and cultural taxation can also affect the performance, retention, promotion, and tenure of WOC faculty (see chapters 1 and 10 in this volume).

These stories are told through the lens of WOC faculty rather than from the perspective of white faculty or students because the voices of WOC are often discounted within academia. However, exclusive reliance on the perceptions of WOC faculty introduces the following complexities: (1) other unidentified factors, like "stereotype threat"—or defensive responses to anticipatory discrimination (Aronson and Steele 2005; Steele 2007)—could provide alternative interpretations to the faculty members' reports; (2) the fluidity of social identities can obscure bodily recognition processes; (3) the social constructedness of race and gender presumes that bodily (mis)recognition may be a reciprocal phenomenon (e.g., WOC can be misrecognized by white students and WOC can also misrecognize white students); and finally, (4) the implications of misrecognition can vary, both individually and institutionally.

The consistent patterns in these data, however, indicate that the experiences of WOC faculty can be challenging when race and gender are inscribed onto their bodies in ways that limit expectations of them. Bodily misrecognition allows for hegemony to prevail and to be reproduced at both the micro- (racist/sexist social interactions) and macrolevels (oppressive institutional climate). Ideally, bodily recognition can be more fully realized when members of the academy take collective responsibility for making the invisible visible, for valuing a multiplicity of voices, and for embracing more inclusive, nonhegemonic ways of thinking, teaching, and writing.

Chapter 9

Putting Their Bodies Off the Line

The Response of Men Faculty of Color to Classroom-Based Conflict

Alford A. Young Jr.

Men faculty of color are uniquely situated with regard to conflict in the higher education classroom. As men and as people of color, they simultaneously occupy superior and subordinate statuses. That simultaneity allows them to enact varied forms of agency in generating and reacting to classroom conflict, and they can do so more comfortably and seamlessly (and possibly with less severe social ramifications) than can women faculty of color. However, men faculty of color encounter the same kinds of conflicts experienced by other faculty of color that have been documented in this volume. Moreover, and similar to the case of women of color faculty, a considerable number of the conflicts occurring in the classrooms of men faculty of color directly involve matters pertaining to race and ethnicity. As has been documented in other chapters, this is because students are more likely to question or challenge the authority or scholarly expertise of faculty of color in general.

Such questioning and challenging often emerges because these faculty may teach on matters pertaining to race and ethnicity, which may be a source of anxiety for some students, or because these faculty publicly acknowledge, intentionally foster, or become points of focus for social interactions and dynamics in the classroom that involve race or ethnicity in some way (e.g., the occurrence of explicitly racist acts, the criticism by some students of other students' learning styles or manner of engaging course material given their racial/ethnic background, or the visible expression of consternation about some aspect of the course material that the instructor has selected). Otherwise, and again like women faculty of color, these men may experience conflict just by their presence, by the fact that their presence runs counter to the norms of white men hegemony in the academy and in the classroom. Students of color may expect what these faculty may determine to be an unwarranted degree of additional support, understanding, or awareness of their concerns given their shared identity status. Alternatively, they may experience conflict resulting from the perceptions of students from majority racial backgrounds that such faculty provide unwarranted degrees of support, understanding, or awareness of the concerns of students of color or that such faculty hold biases or prejudices against students from majority backgrounds. Not surprisingly, then, as men faculty of color possess racial and ethnic identities that are subordinate, they often bear the same kinds of challenges that women faculty of color encounter (see especially chapters 4 and 8 for examples).

Despite all that has been said, however, there also is an obvious difference between men and women faculty of color. As men, they stand in positions of considerable power and, in critical ways, literally do so when in the front of their classrooms. These men benefit from simply being men, which is the gender category that is attributed more legitimacy in the professoriate (Collinson and Hearn 1994; Harlow 2003; Hubbard and Stage 2009; Li and Beckett 2006; Vargas 2002). Furthermore, there are ways in which their actions in regard to classroom-based conflict reflect this socially privileged status. Hence, taking into account the unique position that they stand in, the objective of this chapter is to explore how men faculty of color discuss conflict as a property of classroom experience. The emphasis here is on how they situate themselves as factors in these conflicts. This includes how they position themselves as conflict provocateurs, victims, bystanders, or in other manners in the course of discussing conflict. In doing so, this chapter especially considers how these efforts of self-situating emerge in both conscientious and unreflexive manners.

Each of these efforts reflects what sociologists Schrock and Schwalbe identify as "manhood acts" (Schrock and Schwalbe 2009; Schwalbe 2005), or, in other words acting as men: appearing emotionally detached, competitive, and willing to objectify women and others (Bird 1996). In the case of how men faculty of color discuss classroom conflict, these manhood acts often appear as subtle, nonaggressive, or not overtly threatening to others. Hence, although they do not take the form of what may be regarded as more traditional manhood acts, they do reflect patterns of self-representation and explanation that distinctively pertain to the men faculty included in the study sample.

The data for this chapter come from interviews with the twenty-five men faculty of color included in the study sample. Ten of these individuals are African American, seven are Asian American or self-classify as Asian Pacific Islanders, four are Latino, and four are of other racial categories.* Ten of the men are in social science fields, nine are in natural sciences, and six are in the humanities.

To be clear, this analysis centers not so much on what they say about classroom-based conflict but rather on how they tell their stories. This point of emphasis is especially revealing because, unlike the case with many of the women who were investigated in other chapters in this volume (see especially chapter 8), the men express significantly less anxiety or frustration with conflicts occurring in their classrooms. Perhaps most importantly, they almost never implicate their own (racialized) bodies as being relevant for conflicts that they discuss nor do they seem to personalize conflicts in any extensive manner. They almost always refer to conflicts that take the form of student-versus-student or otherwise explain how emerging classroom-based conflict is (or should be) a property of the student community to resolve or reconcile. Hence, rather than discussing themselves as participants in such conflicts (and what is especially absent here is their discussion of having been interpolated by the students as critical factors in creating any such conflicts), these faculty discuss their roles almost exclusively as mediators, arbitrators, or referees who direct the students toward resolving, managing, or reconciling with the conflicts. Hence, rather than explaining themselves as victims, heroes, or direct sources of conflict for students, these faculty speak in ways that take their racialized bodies out of the scenarios of conflict that they present.

Importantly, only three men faculty of color report that they do not experience classroom-based conflict, and all three are natural scientists. The inability of natural scientists to document such conflict as it pertains to race or ethnicity as well as their assertion that the nature of their course material denies this kind of conflict from emerging has been discussed in chapter 6. Yet, as this chapter

---

*As the categories that each of these final four men belong to are quite small, they are grouped together in such a generic depiction in order to preserve their anonymity.

illustrates, even those who argue that such conflict did not emerge still offered commentary about how some students (even mildly) questioned their legitimacy as instructors or seemed surprised or unusually curious about them being the course instructors. As one natural scientist put it,

> I hate to say it. I mean, that's the way my department is. It's sort of bland in some ways ... nonemotional or nonethnic. It's just—that's the one thing about science. Science, the laws of nature are the laws of nature. I mean, there's no disputing them. I mean, you could dispute them, but really it's not a matter of race. It's a matter of intellect or something else other than race. (AfAm, M, NS)

Another simply said,

> I don't have any racial conflict in my classroom.... No, no, never. Either it's now habit, or I'm just so totally blind that you have to hit me over the head [to see it]. (AfAm, M, NS)

The Expression of Social Power by Men Faculty of Color in the Classroom

Sociologists have often argued that agency is understood to be the capacity to act on one's behalf or on the behalf of others in order to acquire or achieve some desired ends (Bourdieu 1990; Coleman 1990, Dawe 1978; Emirbayer and Goodwin 1994; Emirbayer and Mische 1998; Fuchs 2001; Giddens 1984). Indeed, a significant point of attention in the preceding chapters has been on the extent to which certain faculty identify with and enact agency in regard to conflict (see chapters 5, 6, and 7). These chapters have argued that instructors sometime initiate or encourage conflict in order to foster certain learning objectives (see chapters 5, 6, and 7). In other cases faculty question why they do not engage conflicts in ways that seem to them, at least at the time that they are interviewed, as the most appropriate or effective for desired learning outcomes. In still other cases conflicts that directly involve some aspect of a faculty member's identity result in that instructor feeling some degree of seemingly inescapable entrapment or victimization, and this mostly occurs for women faculty, white as well as of color (see chapters 4 and 8).

What is striking about the men faculty of color is that there is virtually no conversation about their identities being invoked in the classroom in ways that reflect any inner turmoil, tension, or anxiety. If this ever was the case, the men either do not recall or discuss any such occurrences (and if they did occur and are suppressed by the men during the interviews, then this speaks of a form of self-presentation that resembles a traditionally masculine form of face saving). It is the assertion of agency in these ways that reflects what was labeled earlier in this chapter as manhood acts. Sociologists Schrock and Schwalbe (2009) state that manhood acts are "aimed at claiming privilege, eliciting deference, and resisting exploitation." They also make clear that the body type of a male is not relevant to enacting such acts, as the male body in any form is a symbolic asset in comparison to the female body being a liability in efforts to "signify possession of a masculine self" and "put on a convincing manhood act" (281). The accounts the men faculty of color provide—and especially how they position themselves in the reporting of emerging classroom conflict—reflect particular acts of manhood in that they explain their capacity to enact agency in ways that are vacant in the previous chapter's commentaries from women of color.

For example, as an African American social scientist says in discussing a class that he offers that contains an extensive amount of race-specific course material,

> The second time I taught the class at the large level … they came close to rebellion. (AfAm, M, SS)

He explains that the students were not interested in investing as much attention to race as he expected them to do in this particular course. Although this is not an uncommon way for students to respond to courses that do not appear in the course title to be about race or ethnicity, what is unique is how the professor responds to the students.

> My response was, "You know, I … those of you who are pissed off, go away." You know, I just didn't want anything to do with them…. I stepped away from it after that for a little while [meaning he refused to acknowledge the complaints of the students]. (AfAm, M, SS)

And in reporting to how he addresses conflicts between racial groups in his classroom, another African American social scientist says in a matter-of-fact tone,

> I don't get involved. I try to create conflict. (AfAm, M, SS).

Although at a surface level this comment may appear to be self-contradictory (i.e., one's effort to create conflict presumably immediately involves oneself in it), the point of this faculty member is to state that once the conflict is generated—and in his case, referring to students experiencing pedagogically healthy conflicts with the material and with students having to deal with each others' reactions to that material—he distances himself from the discussion and directs students to challenge each other.

Employing Conflict in the Classroom

Like many of the instructors in this study, a significant number of the men of color discuss conflict as an important pedagogical resource (in fact, about three-fourths of them make references to this). However, these men's discussions of conflict as an educational resource lack any overt emotional pitch. Their remarks also reflect a lack of feeling on their part that there is much personal stake in employing conflict in this way. As a Latino social scientist explains,

> What I've noticed is it's more in what they [students] don't say and what they don't do. And when I see it, when I see, for example, the silence, you know, on controversial issues, and when I see sort of body language and such that says, "I don't really want to talk about this" or "Could we just go on?," then those are my cues to sort of like say, we need to deal with this, you know. (L, M, SS)

In clarifying his approach he goes on to say,

> I don't say I'm seeing body language and all this other stuff, but I'll say, "You know, I want to talk more about this," or somehow I'll pick on it. I don't know if it's intuitive or not. I don't know what it is. (L, M, SS)

Along similar lines a natural scientist says,

> We deliberately try to make our classes and our small groups as heterogeneous as possible in terms of race and ethnicity, geographic origin, gender. We'll actually deliberately introduce issues that may be so-called hot-button issues, and we ask the students to really think about them and reflect on their own values and then bring those things into the sessions. And part of this is to create a certain sense of disequilibrium.... We post questions or raise contradictions that will allow the students to really kind of think about who they are, and what their values are. (AsAm, M, NS)

And an Asian American social scientist says,

> Part of it is diffusing conflict, you know, before it elevates to a level, before it is unmanageable. So part of it is managing the conflict. I can feel the tension in the air, and I want to make sure that people feel safe. You know, you want the tension, but you want safety as well. It's trying to balance that out. I think that's the challenge, that's what it also comes down. It comes down to one, validating and empowering on this end. And two, maintaining this level of safety where people don't feel necessarily attacked, yet keeping the level of tension high enough that we all feel challenged, but not to the point where it spills all over the place and outside of the classroom and where I'm able to facilitate. It's making that balance and I need to, I think I need to

or I think I can allow for a little more tension. I'm starting to feel a little more of a comfort level and a confidence in myself as a facilitator to allow for the level of tension to get a little bit higher. To make it slightly less safe for the white students and slightly more empowering and validating for the students of color, that's my goal. I'm not there yet. (AsAm, M, SS)

Finally, another social scientist says,

> Like when I see it [conflict], I try to think of also how can we learn from this. If it's conflict that I immediately see people are arguing, I think for example, we've got—had—gotten into some discussions about affirmative action, you know, prior to the Supreme Court decision, where students will talk about, you know, it's about quotas and tokens and things like this, and all others we'll talk about it being not like that, you know. It suggests to me that maybe there wasn't like the kind of info—access to information or they didn't have the information that was needed. (L, M, SS)

Evident in the prior comments is a lack tension, anxiety, or sense of challenge to each faculty member's status as the facilitator of the learning experience in the classroom. None of the remarks include any faculty member commenting about feelings of vulnerability or experiencing emotional turbulence or challenge as these conflicts ensued. Hence, the absence of certain kinds of commentary about their experience with classroom-based conflict is as revealing as what they say.

Keeping the Students' Bodies in Play

Otherwise, the men faculty of color discuss conflict as wholly belonging with the domain of the student experience. Accordingly, their reporting of these occasions involves sharing little anxiety or tension about these developments. A selection of examples makes this point.

In the first example a natural scientist discusses a racial incident that occurred in his classroom. He indicates that the incident was provoked when a white student from a rural background expressed criticism about people who received government benefits. As the professor states,

> [The student] ended up making the comment that nobody is on welfare unless they want to be. (M, NS)

He goes on to explain,

> The student across from him was a young black woman whose parents were on welfare and had no choice. They were trying to find jobs, so she knew better. And

immediately everybody reacted to what each other had said and it became quite a teachable moment for all of us. (M, NS)

As the professor continues, it is clear that this moment is far from stress-free. He says,

They were going at each other verbally. I was at the other side of the classroom when it started and so all of the sudden there was this sort of explosion and people were yelling at each other. But I walked over and sort of talked them through it. I did not—it's difficult to know what to do precisely in that situation, I admit that I'm not trained to ... I'm not in a position where I want to talk to valuing everybody's opinion because of that idiotic statement about welfare. I don't value that statement—it's idiotic. I couldn't. Or there was no good way to convince that student in thirty seconds that the statement was idiotic because of the interaction that occurred, everybody became entrenched. About all I could do was diffuse and so at that point in time I got them to talking about something else and we went on from that point. (M, NS)

What is quite evident in this account is that an explosive moment unfolded. A black student feels insulted by another student's remark, and the instructor immediately empathizes with the black student and unambiguously indicts the white student for creating the charged moment (at least in his own mind if not in the classroom). Yet, rather than discuss any sense of inner angst or emotional unrest, the professor ends his comment by emphasizing his efforts at diffusion. The integration of empathy, understanding, and willful deactivation of the moment is consistent with the ways in which nearly all of the men of color present a relatively dispassionate approach to classroom-based conflict.

Another means of placing oneself outside of the emerging conflict is to decidedly take oneself out of the parameters for discussing or resolving a conflict. For example, some men of color conscientiously direct any apparent conflict back to the students in a way that makes it seem that the professor is not to be the sole active participant in its resolution. In other words, such conflicts become "teachable moments" rather than problematic situations in need of resolution. The capacity for these men to turn these episodes into explicitly teachable moments rather than have them stand as problematic distractions to the educational process illustrates the particular agency afforded to them. An example of this appears in the remarks of professor who explains,

So when issues of inter-racial ignorance or awkwardness, separation, that kind of stuff comes up, you just make it everybody's issue, then [meaning every student in the class]. (AfAm, M, SS)

In virtually every one of his recollections of episodes of conflict that occur in his classroom, this professor consistently mentions how he encourages the students to take ownership of each developing conflict and make themselves agents for finding a resolution or reconciliation.

An African American humanities professor reports that he allows great latitude for his students to speak their minds in his classroom, especially when it comes to contentious or controversial issues. He says,

> I am very generous. I will let a student ramble in ignorance for three or four minutes, which is a long time in a classroom." (AfAm, M, H)

Rather than feel that he is at any risk or threat in allowing this activity, he says that after students express their views, no matter how problematic others may find them,

> I will come back with some very difficult questions for that student, or I will allow other students to ask that student questions. It comes from my belief that most, most students have a sense of when they're ignorant, even when they're posing, they have a sense of when they're speaking out of ignorance. And, eventually, if not in that moment, at some point later in the course, if they continue to do it, they're going to catch themselves. (AfAm, M, H)

And putting it most directly and without elaboration, another African American social scientist says the following after being asked how he deals with white students' resistance to the classroom:

> I don't deal with it at all. The rest of the class does. (AfAm, M, SS)

Repositioning the Conflict to Nonclassroom Space

One of the more pragmatic efforts of men of color to handle classroom-based conflict is to relocate the combatants or redirect the conflict to social spaces other than the classroom. Nearly half of the men mention utilizing this approach in some manner. In what becomes one of the more elaborate explanations of how the students were encouraged to embrace conflicts, a humanities professor says that he tells his students the following:

> We have to respect each other, no matter that we are different from each other. We have to have this respect. Now, we can argue, differences are there, so let's talk about these differences. And I want you to have your full freedom, but in a very decent and academic manner. (M, H)

In order to control or minimize conflict that can interfere with the learning experience, this professor holds meetings with groups of students outside the classroom to reflect on particularly difficult conflicts that have occurred or sometimes to address unresolved ones. He says,

> I say to them, "Can I make a suggestion?" One, I'm going to record this, and then, I—you know, each month, we have a coffee hour, you know, two hours—and I put them in a very nice room here, a meeting room, and we get them sweets and coffee, and I make them tea, and I make them all kinds of things, and I say "Now, this is the time to talk about these issues," and let's do it again in a very, you know, academically oriented manner, and then I let each person talk. (M, H)

If the conversation itself does not lead to an appropriate resolution, the professor appoints a committee to provide some adjudication. As he explains,

> I appoint like a court—a committee, there, like a debate—and I say let's debate these issues. Why not? And, then we have judges there. You know, I don't want to be a judge. I just want to be an observer.... I select, by the way, people who are really, you know, very understanding, and you see we end up the discussion sometimes in a very harmonious, you know, manner where there's some kind of reconciliation. (M, H)

He also sees his office as a valuable nonclassroom space for resolving conflict. In fact, he explains that one way in which he takes his body off the line in regard to students of color who he says are particularly observant of how he handles conflicts is to invite the students directly implicated in a conflict into his office. He says,

> Students look at me ... maybe because of my color ... not the, you know, the white group, the other group, to see how I am going to handle situations.... That's why sometimes I'm talking about getting the students into my office, and I say, "Please, you know, I want to know—not—I don't want to convince you or you convince me, but let's talk about the issues." I want to discuss this openly. (M, H)

In another example an African American social scientist says,

> A male student just assumes the leadership of a group and just starts talking, you know what I mean? Most of the men doing most of the talking. And, I say, "Hey, you know, what's going on here? Why is it that most of the guys are carrying most of the conversation? What's going on here? Let's look at this. Um, why aren't more women speaking up?" And then some of them get uptight because I point it out.... How I dealt with [such a student] was to make it very clear in a sort of semijoking but semiserious way that he was ... he should say what he wanted to say, he had a right to say it. But there was one time when it was like everybody jumped, and I said,

"Wait a minute, now," you know, be respectful. He then said, "I don't care. It's okay...."
But of course we weren't ... you know, we did have to be respectful. (AfAm, M, SS)

In explaining the resolution to the matter the professor says,

> I took the students aside and I just said, "You know, I know that you're not trying to offend anybody, you're not even trying to be mean, you're just ... you know, this is how we'd have a conversation is that we argue about that stuff. Can you just cool it down.... Some folks are uncomfortable." (AfAm, M, SS)

Repositioning conflict outside the classroom is a technique also employed to address students of color who behave as if the man professor of color should be an uncritical advocate for them. As this same professor says,

> They sometimes try to identify with me in a way that says to the nonblack students, "I have a special relationship," and immediately I nip that in the bud. I do not allow that. Every student is a student equal, and I think, if they try that, I indicate very quickly that it's not going to work. And I usually do it, again, very gently. I don't believe in, you know, putting a student on the spot. But if it were to continue, I would have a discussion with the student outside of the class. (AfAm, M, SS)

Unlike primary or secondary schooling environments, the classroom in higher education is a neutral space. Higher education faculty cannot take ownership of their classrooms in the ways that instructors in other educational sectors can. In primary and secondary educational institutions the classroom is often office space for faculty. Such faculty often decorate and arrange the classroom space precisely as they desire, and these are overt acts of spatial control. In higher education, however, faculty usually have to leave their offices, research laboratories, and other private domains in order to go to classrooms and teach. Once in the classroom, the faculty can rarely, if ever, demonstrate dominance over the physical space other than to move some chairs or furniture and then prepare for a colleague to teach the next class. Consequently, the higher educational classroom is much more of public space than is the classroom in other educational settings. The capacity to relocate students from the classroom and into a faculty member's private space (or, as we have seen, to a more intimate setting that is selected by and adorned— with snacks and beverages—by the faculty member), then, demonstrates both agency and the power to minimize the significance of neutral and public space in dealing with conflict. Women faculty, whether of color or not, certainly are not denied opportunities to function in these ways. The absence of commentary on their part about doing so, however, does indicate that men are particularly committed to act in these ways, all of which allow them to elicit deference (if the most successful outcomes results) and resist exploitation (at bare minimum).

The Rare Cases of Men Faculty of Color Putting Their Bodies on the Line

Despite all that has been said about the capacity of men faculty of color to voluntarily withdraw from or otherwise highly regulate or minimize the attention drawn to them in classroom-based conflicts, there are some examples in which their bodies are unavoidably at front and center of conflicts. Not surprisingly, race or ethnicity is the crucial factor in these occurrences.

Indeed, the only case in the data in which a man of color faculty member shares considerable emotional angst about race occurs during a moment when his identity claim is challenged by students who claim that same identity. Here we return to the case of the Native American professor who speaks about how he was challenged (discussion of this instance is first presented in chapter 4):

> There was a woman who called me out in class for not being Native enough. They say, "You're not Native enough." There is always this thing between Natives: "You're not brown enough." She really unleashed her anger at me. (NA, M)

He does not give specific information about how he reacts to this challenge, but in discussing how he would respond differently if given the chance, he does say the following:

> I wish I wasn't so emotional. But I just don't know how else I could handle that.... I would not have been so reactionary. I have a visceral reaction and wish that I would just slow down. I wish I would have slowed down to really address what was going on. She was not really mad at me, but seventeen to eighteen years old and very angry. She was releasing that anger, and at me. I wish I wasn't so reactionary at the time. But that was when I was a new faculty member. (NA, M)

This kind of challenge may appear similar to those shared by women faculty of color, and by women more generally. However, it represents the only case shared by a man faculty of color that involves a high degree of emotional reaction. Others are much milder in tone or else involve the faculty member being much more dismissive of the challenge made to him.

An example of this style of reaction comes from a faculty member who showed to his class a documentary entitled *The Color of Fear*, which is based on a dialogue involving eight men of various race and ethnic groups about the state of race relations in America. As the professor explained,

> It was a real heavy movie. A number of the white students in my class were in tears, having come to this realization suddenly that they are contributors to the cycle or dynamics of oppression. Students who never ever thought before that they

were. So we were having this very emotional discussion, and one of our female students of color raised her hand and said, "You know all of you folks here crying think that you know what it's all about now, well you don't. This movie was the G-rated version of reality, and this was nothing." She was very much giving voice to her own frustration while minimizing the experiences of everyone else in the classroom. (AsAm, M, SS)

The professor goes on to say that this expression was the spark for a conflict that ultimately moved from student-to-student to student-to-faculty. Rather than let the students engage each other, the professor says that he became more directive of the conversation and, in doing so, ultimately makes what he believes is a failed effort to advance the classroom conversation. He says further that

I got into this one-on-one discussion with her and I said, "Well tell us the R-rated version. Don't pull any punches here—tell us the R-rated version. We want to hear it." And I don't think that this person was ready to articulate that and instead came back at me with "Well, in this course we're really not getting into the real issues." (AsAm, M, SS)

In a rarely used statement by the men faculty of color, the professor says that he "started to take it a little bit personally," such that he was compelled to say, "Well you know, everybody is at different levels. Some people are here and some people are here, and we got to learn to teach other folks." In reflecting on his action during that encounter he says,

It didn't even sound right to me when I was saying it. I didn't do a good job. I didn't handle it well. It almost sounded like I was being defensive. The students of color are so disempowered in the class as it is, especially because there are so few of them in our classes. I really should've done a better job validating what she had said and just leaving it at that, as opposed to try to take it personally, like, "Are you saying I'm not pushing our class far enough or not providing the class with enough challenging material?" (AsAm, M, SS)

Although this situation does not reflect the intensity of the previous one, both reflect moments when faculty feel that they are perceived as failing to deliver in a racially or ethnically appropriate way. For faculty of color who have won awards for teaching or achieved institutional identities as good teachers, these encounters understandably become ones in which faculty put their racialized bodies on the line, irrespective of their gender.

However, gender does become an important distinguishing factor in how the men faculty of color respond to what they perceive as challenges to their authority. Rather than expressing overt anger at such occurrences, the men who speak of these occurrences instead emphasize the apparent inadequacies of the students to be more responsibly aware of the kinds of people who serve in the professoriate. Essentially, this is a classic portrait of the male externalization of responsibility in comparison to a common tendency of women to internalize or engage in self-blame.

In discussing whether there are students who implicitly or explicitly question his legitimacy as their instructor, the following faculty member says,

> This is the white students.... They just tend to resist towards you.... I think there's a racial component to what's going on in that situation. If I were white and older, and came in ... they wouldn't experience it as I don't know my white stuff ... [if the students did not agree with my perspectives] they might experience it as, you know, he's so out there I don't want to pay attention, but they wouldn't, I wouldn't get challenged on the sense of, you know, you really don't know what you're talking about. I don't mean to make too much out of it, but I am aware of it.... [It is a] new experience for me, to feel like I have to prove myself as an intellectual. (AfAm, M, SS)

He then provides a particular example:

> In the midst of one my freshman seminars, sort of about ten weeks into the semester, for some reason it came out, I said that I went to an Ivy League college. And they all said to me, "You went there! Wow!" (AfAm, M, SS)

Rather than express hostility or anger, the professor says,

> You know, I burst out laughing. Sounds like, "Oh, now you think I'm smart." (AfAm, M, SS)

This kind of response, itself, is not inherently gendered. Where gender difference matters is that it is only the men who offer responses to challenges to authority in a manner that either reflect no emotional vulnerability or effectively mask it.

A similar example was offered by a humanities professor who says,

> As I mentioned, some of them say, "I don't' want to say something that would be offending," you know, and not upset me, not upset the other members, and they—as I mentioned, some of them don't want to say something because they think I belong to the other group, so they don't want to say something that they think might make me feel a little bit uncomfortable. (M, H)

In discussing his students' reaction to his approach he says, "I keep after them to, to open up and some of them do—some of them do."

Of course, some of the body work done in the classroom by the men faculty of color is deliberate. In these cases the faculty explain that they take careful note of the behavioral choices that they make and how they might play out in the classroom, especially as people of color doing so. As one African American professor says in discussing challenges to his authority:

> I respond to that, you know, with whip in hand. I don't allow somebody to come at me like that because I don't come at people like that. It's just personal. But no, if someone comes at me for any reason, you know, be it, you know, my race, my height, my … you know, anything like that, they come at me, I go at them…. I call that my Malcolm X philosophy of life. (AfAm, M, H)

He goes on to say,

> From the first day [of class] I have to establish the context that makes them very aware of how the dialogue is to be structured…. When they see the way I listen, when they see the way I listen to a student, who may be saying something that's offensive—African American students are constantly looking. I mean, they are self-conscious about modeling themselves, I mean, and that's one thing I learned very quickly—when they see the way that I listen. So the first time it [an offensive remark is made] happens, I respond. I don't allow them [the students] to respond. I respond, I respond very respectively, I do not label. I don't say, "That's racist. That's ignorant." I don't do that. I say, "Explain to me why you say this? What, what enables you to know this?" or I bring it back to the text frequently, that we're discussing because one of the things that happens is they're speaking from something that someone has told them that they've heard or that they've experienced and they are sort of forcing. So I say, "What in this passage that we're discussing, um, leads you to this conclusion?" (AfAm, M, H)

And in evaluating the success of this approach he says,

> And, when they start engaging the material, I think it forces them to try to be more coherent about the relationship of their experience to the material. And the African American students see that, and I have, um, I have observed the ways in which they think. They respond very, um, calmly and respectfully, um, in virtually every situation. I can't actually think of a single situation in which that experience was repeated. I think it has a lot to do with the context of—that's set from the first day. (AfAm, M, H)

In one case a Latino faculty member shares sentiments that reflect a similar level of security about managing classroom conflict:

> It's just this being aware that you have different people in your classroom, you know, and that different people have been socialized differently, have different life experiences, and it's going to affect how they think about what you're saying or discussing in your class. So I think the first thing is just sort of being ready to know that, you know, some people will think about this differently…. Many times we're very hesitant to say, "Yeah, there are stereotypes out there," and you know, you can sort

of use the knowledge or some of the knowledge in these stereotypes to maybe more smoothly coordinate how you interact with people from different groups. I think the important message there is that at least, not necessarily relying on that knowledge, but just relying on the possibility that somebody's going to be different, and you've got to be ready to respond, you know, and just be more careful about how they're responding to things, and they may have a different take on it. So just sort of being a little more open-minded and ready for different reactions, I would say. (L, M, SS)

Aside from the singular case in which a man of color was challenged about him appropriately belonging to the racial category in which he held membership, oc-currences in which the men faculty of color experienced their bodies being put on the line reflected extreme agency on their part. If they did not freely choose to do so, then once the students called their racialized bodies into a conflict or else responded to them in a conflicting manner, the men assertively acted to minimize or challenge the students' legitimacy in doing so. As has been argued, these acts elicit deference and/or resist exploitation so that the faculty member can focus on pursuing his desired pedagogical and educational goals.

Conclusion

Essentially, the nature of much of the commentary of the men faculty of color takes one of three forms. In one case the men articulate much less of a sense of feeling victimized or entrapped by conflict. In part, this is due to the fact that they do not regard their own racialized bodies as central to the conflict that they recognize in their classrooms. The first response set is markedly different from the experience and stance of female faculty of color, discussed in chapter 8. Sec-ond, they more easily dismiss or minimize the conflict as a critical or significant part of the classroom experience. The second response set is also discussed in greater detail in chapter 6. Third, they respond to conflict by stating how they either relocate or desire to relocate the conflicted students to spaces outside of the classroom, which in many cases means the faculty member's office (an obvious place of faculty power). A consistent theme here is the extent to which men find their private office space particularly appealing as a site to deal with students who they determine are not functioning as the faculty desire in the classroom.

Taking these three patterns into account, it is clear that in a very basic sense the men faculty of color demonstrate a social power that has been traditionally at-tributed to men in professional employment spheres and in society more generally (Bird 1996; Carrigan, Connell, and Lee 1985; Clatterbaugh 1996; Connell 1995, 2000; Kimmel 1996; Kimmel, Hearn, and Connell 2005; Kimmel and Messner 2007; Pleck and Sawyer 1974; Whitehead 2006). The men faculty of color act upon and benefit from their status as men. However, there is a very different yet highly telling aspect of how these faculty discuss classroom-based conflict that emphasizes their distinction from white men faculty. This is evident in the way that their stories are replete with commentary about being sympathetic, understanding, or especially insightful about how race and ethnicity operate in these conflicts.

Often, the men of color faculty emphasize how race or ethnicity is operating in ways that do not surface in the comments of the involved students but instead appear evident to such faculty, or else they express a social solidarity with the students of color or otherwise demonstrate intimate understanding of the actions of those students, all without implicating themselves as ever feeling particularly threatened or implicated in these conflicts. As reported in chapter 6 and 7, many of the white men faculty, even in this unique sample, do not see or discuss the operation of race/ethnicity in the classroom conflicts they report. Hence, the men faculty of color engage in manhood acts while possessing the emotional dispositions of many women faculty of color, although to a much less extensive degree. In doing so, the men faculty of color represent a unique form of intersectionality that blends the behavior (especially agency) associated with traditional masculinity with the critical consciousness associated with subordinate categories of race and ethnicity. Hence, the men faculty of color are uniquely positioned to recognize and experience constraints in their social relations in the classroom but also to act upon them in ways that help them preserve a desired sense of self.

Of course, the interview-based data can only allow insight into how these faculty construct accounts of past events and circumstances concerning classroom-based conflict. The faculty have the freedom to tell their stories as they desire. Consequently, this means great potential to deny, deemphasize, or diminish the extent to which emotional angst or turbulence emerged for them when moments of conflict surfaced in their classrooms. There is no secure means of certifying whether such reactions actually occurred. However, an important finding—made evident in earlier chapters—is that many women of color and white women reported these emotionally laden reactions. Hence, the interview settings themselves may be sites for the proliferation of manhood acts that, as has been discussed throughout this chapter, allow them to protect and preserve images of secure confident masculinity (Schwalbe and Wolkomir 2001, 2002). The unique situation of men faculty of color in regard to classroom-based conflict, then, is revealed not only by the stories that they tell about their experiences in the classroom but also what might not be told in such stories. Although interviews may not reveal complete portraits of what transpired at points in time, the very act of creating a story or account of the past is, itself, quite revealing of what it means to be a man faculty of color in the higher educational classroom.

Chapter 10

"Why Don't You Get Somebody New to Do It?"

Race, Gender, and Identity Taxation in the Academy

Tiffany Joseph and Laura Hirshfield

Many studies document the challenges faculty of color and white women faculty experience in predominantly white- and male-dominated higher educational institutions (see chapters 1, 4, 8, and 9 in this volume). Some of these challenges, which include marginalization, discrimination, and invisibility, are related to the problematic behavior and attitudes of colleagues and students as well as institutionalized campus cultures and operations that do not effectively promote an egalitarian or multicultural community. This chapter examines and extends one particular cultural practice, the cultural taxation of certain groups of faculty members in academic departments.

Cultural taxation is the expectation placed on faculty members of particular identity groups to address minority-related departmental and institutional affairs. Here we introduce the term "identity taxation" to encompass classic experiences of cultural taxation as well as to refer to the extra pressure or burdens that faculty members experience either as a result of their invested interest in and dedication to departmental and campus diversity issues or simply due to their race, gender, or other marginalized social identity. We begin with an analysis of identity taxation in practice, exploring diversity-related teaching and service expectations of faculty of color and white women faculty as well as the problematic behavior of colleagues. We also comment on how white faculty who are committed to diversity issues experience identity taxation, although in a different manner and to a different degree. We argue that legitimacy—or the sense of belonging or feeling qualified to be in academic departments—can be considered another form of identity taxation that affects the social and professional lifestyles of faculty of color and white women faculty. Finally, we discuss the ways in which intersecting identities create additional burdens for professors in multiple marginalized groups.

We conducted our analyses using open and focused coding with the transcripts of the entire set of sixty-six faculty informants. We read through each transcript, noted patterns of recurring themes, and used a qualitative software program (NVIVO) to code each transcript line by line. We focused on the responses to questions about interviewees' experiences with their colleagues, departments, and the culture of the university. However, we also examined other interview sections that seemed relevant for identifying experiences of identity taxation. Finally, we chose a fairly conservative coding strategy, only identifying peer-to-peer conflicts or additional work expectations as raced or gendered if the informants identified them as such. This strategy meant that rather than coding identity taxation within groups (i.e., women vs. men or faculty of color vs. white faculty), we coded identity taxation only when the informant somehow marked the event as gendered or raced or a combination of the two. When we reviewed our findings and noticed that identity taxation and legitimacy were dominant themes in the interview narratives, we organized our work around the themes of racial taxation, gender taxation, and the intersection between the two.

Theoretical Background of Cultural Taxation

The phrase "cultural taxation" was first coined by Padilla (1994) to describe the increased expectations for faculty of color to address minority-related departmental and institutional affairs. He defined cultural taxation as "the obligation to show good citizenship toward the [academic] institution by serving its needs for ethnic representation on committees, or to demonstrate knowledge and commitment to a cultural group, which may even bring accolades to the institution but which is not usually rewarded by the institution on whose behalf the service was performed" (26). The literature on cultural taxation suggests that faculty of color often have more departmental and university obligations to fulfill because they are expected to teach the same load and achieve the same research standards as their white peers in addition to serving on various diversity-related committees and advising and mentoring students and faculty of color (see chapter 1). Such expectations often lead faculty of color to become overburdened and overcommitted. These extra burdens, often combined with a lack of collegiality and the marginalization of their research interests, contribute to invisibility, solo status, and occupational stress (Delgado-Romero et al. 2003; Essien 2003; Segura 2003; Smith and Witt 1993; Stanley et al. 2003).

Some women faculty members, of various racial/ethnic backgrounds, experience a similar phenomenon of taxation that negatively impacts their bid for promotion and success in academia. Qualitative studies have consistently cited this issue in discussions of differential tenure promotion rates and have suggested that some academic institutions and departments even pressure women to take on a larger share of service commitments (Porter 2007; Turner 2002). Women faculty also often feel a more personally motivated sense of duty or desire to increase diversity, so the impetus to accept service invitations is especially high for them. Conversely, quantitative results using more representative samples have found mixed results regarding gender discrepancies in the service load at universities and colleges. Although studies conducted in the 1980s found that women were on more university-wide committees than their male peers, more recent studies have found less divergence (Bellas and Toutkoushian 1999; Porter 2007; Turk 1981). These findings may mask two important phenomena that influence the women faculty in our sample. First, although there is not a consensus about whether women faculty have increased committee/service responsibilities, there is some evidence that they are disproportionately asked to sit on diversity-related committees, which may involve more "invisible" work than do other committee memberships (Seifert and Umbach 2008; Trower and Chait 2002). In addition, most of the research on women faculty members' service load neglects a central feature of the academic environment: discipline (Seifert and Umbach 2007). Especially because women are numeric minorities in the natural science disciplines, it follows that women in science would more likely be asked to attend faculty and committee meetings to increase diversity (Winkler 2000).

Identity Taxation

The concept of cultural taxation is not complete enough to encompass the entire series of phenomena that members of marginalized groups of faculty experience. We call this broader concept "identity taxation," referring to patterns whereby faculty members shoulder any labor—physical, mental, or emotional—due to their social identity, their membership in an underrepresented minority group within their department, school, or society, beyond that which is expected of other faculty members in the department.

Findings

"Classic" Cultural Taxation

Unequal Expectations for Faculty of Color and Women Faculty. In many of the interviews faculty of color report their colleagues' stereotypical assumptions that they are expected to focus their work on issues of race or diversity. This is often implied when colleagues ask minority faculty to serve on diversity committees, teach race-related courses, and be the departmental advocate for students of color:

> So they'll [colleagues] send students to me and I'm like, that's not my area, I can't help you. I mean I'm trying to incorporate some more of that in my class, but that's not my area of expertise. But anything dealing with black people or people of color, they just send all those students to me. It could be not anywhere in my area, so there's a kind of sweeping interpretation of what you do. (AfAm, W, SS)

This experience is but one of many examples in which faculty of color face cultural taxation: being expected to perform in certain social and academic capacities because of their racial or ethnic group membership. Even though her research expertise originally does not incorporate racial or diversity issues, her colleagues assume that she is most qualified to address such issues in her courses and to mentor students of color.

Women faculty in the sciences also mention being expected to advise female students and to be more sympathetic to diversity issues. A white faculty member in the natural sciences explains that her male peers neglect the women students, exclaiming,

> They say they don't like talking to the female students and they'll send female faculty to talk to them. I'm always supposed to be serving them [women students] because we're women. (Wh, W, NS)

Another white woman natural scientist describes the additional pressures of mentorship with a bit more humor, saying,

> The one thing I can say is many of my colleagues who aren't willing or are less willing to deal with many issues of diversity, be it gender or racial or socioeconomic ...

will send those issues to me. I've dealt with a number of them. And I would rather have that happen than to have them either totally dismiss them offhand ... or not deal with them. Be nice if they try a little bit on their own, but ... at least ... they do know that there are people around who can help. (Wh, W, NS)

This faculty member is more concerned that issues of diversity be dealt with than focusing on how the burden of dealing with such issues falls unequally on her shoulders. In addition, though she is white and does not study race or diversity herself, she is expected to act as a diversity advocate simply because, as a woman in the natural sciences, she is a minority. The assumption that she must therefore be sympathetic to and knowledgeable about the experiences of students in other minority groups because of her one minority group membership is curious and perhaps unfounded, yet this is reported quite commonly.

Faculty of color and women faculty also share a perception that their white and men colleagues are not asked to participate in similar activities, which leaves white men faculty more time to focus on research. Furthermore, the assumption that only faculty of color and women faculty are capable of effectively mentoring students of color and women students removes this task or responsibility from white men faculty who should also be invested in students' of color and women students' academic success. Informants often perceive that their colleagues share an assumption that minority and women faculty have more experience with such issues because they deal with being members of marginalized race and/or gender groups on a daily basis in ways that white and/or men faculty do not. Being stereotyped as the voice of diversity marginalizes minority and women faculty and belittles their contributions in faculty and departmental dialogues because, often, if a minority faculty member says something that is not related to race, it may not be given serious consideration. However, as the designated experts on race in their departments, minority faculty are sometimes viewed as overly sensitive to such issues and concerns and, thus, their opinions may be somewhat disregarded.

Some of the white men faculty in this sample also experience a mild form of racial identity taxation. Because all of the faculty in this sample are considered to be diversity advocates by colleagues and/or the university, and as such it is assumed that they have a stronger awareness about issues of race and diversity than do their other white colleagues, they are often asked to serve on diversity-related committees and feel the brunt of the responsibility among white colleagues to serve in this capacity. Thus, white faculty members who are committed to diversity issues also report feeling unequal expectations by colleagues for similar reasons to faculty of color, though not to the same extent. As one white colleague explains, "There was like four of us and that's all. We're the only people who always do this stuff [diversity committees]. And why don't you get somebody new to do it?" (Wh, M, SS). White informants explain that many of their white peers do not want to "deal with many issues of diversity" because they have the privilege of not being as directly affected by these issues as are faculty of color. In this way, the participation of white faculty in diversity-related activities is different from minority faculty participation and demonstrates the white privilege involved in making a choice to be concerned about race and diversity issues. Faculty of color usually feel they have little or no choice. Therefore, although certain white faculty are expected to be departmental diversity advocates, the burden of being overcommitted is not enforced on them as regularly and intensely as it is for faculty of color.

Feeling Overcommitted. Many faculty of color and white women faculty experience racial and/or gender identity taxation from being overcommitted or feeling overburdened, mention making personal sacrifices (i.e., lack of free time, loss of sleep, depression) to complete all their regular as well as diversity-related tasks. Given that they teach in a research-oriented university and have seen other faculty of color denied tenure, minority faculty feel pressure to live up to and beyond the expectations of their colleagues if they are to survive in academia. As an African American professor explains,

> I'm a full professor, you know, that's real. I'm tenured, that's real. Was it an easy path? Was it the path that was given to other people? I came in the same year as some guy who, they told, "Don't worry about it, just do your work." Me, they said, "You're on this committee, this committee, this committee." You know, I had a very different path to tenure than someone else did. It didn't mean I didn't succeed … but it kept me up at night working harder than other people had to work to get the same thing. (AfAm, M, H)

This is also the case for an Asian American woman in the natural sciences, where the numbers of women and faculty of color are small:

> All female faculty are asked more than male faculty to participate on things like panels, service and things of this nature. MLK Day for example. So the female faculty are asked disproportionately to do these things. And by and large, most of us agree to do it every time asked as schedules allow. (AsAm, W, NS)

Many faculty of color specifically use the term "overburdened" to describe how they experience their lives as faculty members. Just as faculty of color face different expectations for committee representation compared with their white peers, women in the natural sciences are similarly overburdened by a departmental need to appear to have sufficient gender representation. Faculty members in the natural sciences are much more likely to bring up women's increased departmental service or committee burdens than are faculty in other departments. In one instance, a white man natural scientist describes a long, fruitless search for a woman who could be present at a meeting with a provost and explains that they eventually "settled" on having a female secretary represent women at the meeting.

Although serving on extra committees and engaging in recruitment show goodwill toward one's department and the institution, such activities usually do not earn faculty points in tenure and promotion evaluations. Therefore, the more time faculty of color and women faculty are asked to commit to diversity-related departmental and university activities, the less time they have to work on their own research. Despite their narratives of inequality and an unbalanced system of tenure expectations, very few faculty members in this sample express anger. Most appear resigned to the "facts of the situation" and, if anything, express stress or anxiety rather than frustration. For example, a Native American professor says,

> I think that early on when I was a lot a more stressed about tenure and things [laughs], I'd ... I sometimes felt that there was a real expectation that I should work, you know, in a "save us" capacity about those [diversity/race] issues.... And, which I did. But you know they're not asking other white male faculty to do this. They [the department] think that they [white men faculty] should spend time focusing on their research rather than going around the country giving recruitment talks.... It just made me anxious and nervous about getting everything done. (NA, W)

This quote also suggests an unequal system of expectations for minority and women faculty than for white men faculty. Although she is asked to travel on behalf of the department and give recruitment talks, she notices that the department does not hold the same expectations for her white men counterparts. Such conversations with the faculty of color and women faculty in our sample reveal the physical and mental toll that these extra activities take on them.

Colleagues' Prejudicial and Problematic Behavior. Another type of identity taxation that faculty of color and women faculty frequently cite involves dealing with the problematic behavior of their departmental colleagues. According to them, this behavior exists in various forms, including colleagues ignoring the issue of race completely in departmental dealings and implying that minority faculty do not belong in the department. In fact, one of the biggest problems faculty in the sample face is their colleagues' denial of racism and discrimination:

> They [colleagues] say there's no discrimination. I ask my colleagues and they discuss it and they all agree there's no discrimination. And the work continuously goes back to me. [Makes me feel] Disappointed, disgusted, and morale is totally diminished. I don't know maybe ... it's really bad. So bad. (AsAm, W, NS)

This Asian American woman argues that a substantial number of faculty members believe that issues regarding racial diversity—and particularly manifestations of racism—are no longer present within department settings. These narratives also emphasize that minority faculty feel a responsibility to place race on—or back on—departmental agendas. This is an additional form of cultural taxation, because without their work, the lack of racial diversity and the incidence of racism within departments would remain invisible. White colleagues' lack of awareness is problematic because the invisibility or denial of discrimination ensures that racial and diversity issues cannot be properly addressed.

Although they state that many of their peers deny the existence of racism or any disparities in treatment due to race, faculty of color also feel that at times their white colleagues and departments market their racial difference to the department's advantage, as when they are sought out to be the minority representative on departmental or divisional committees:

> I think that I've been a beneficiary of affirmative action and all that stuff, so in many respects race has been a benefit to me. But I think it also creates an enormous amount of work for the same reasons. People want some woman of color or some person of color to be sitting on every committee, being everywhere, and that includes the students.... And I feel bad, but I couldn't, I mean I couldn't physically go to all of the things that I get invited to, between the student organizations and the faculty things that I have to do, and whatever. Just not possible. (L, W, SS)

A white faculty member identifies another type of problematic behavior—that many white colleagues do not censor their racial (or even racist) remarks when minority faculty are not present.

> The worst situation is if you have a group of white faculty by themselves in a room and they are talking about students, including students of color, in a class context. Um, or you've got a group of white faculty who are in a room and they are trying to think about who they would invite for a speaker. Those are very dangerous situations, they say things they would not otherwise say and shouldn't say. In an organization they shouldn't say them—those are very tough. (Wh, W, SS)

Although these "dangerous situations" may not directly cause cultural taxation for faculty of color (because these things may not be said in their presence), they can produce discomfort for white faculty who are open about their advocacy of diversity issues and may cause them to experience the added burden of "policing" their colleagues' inappropriate or disrespectful comments.

Some women faculty mention experiencing a more overt form of gender identity taxation in the form of prejudice they face from their older men peers. Interestingly, this prejudice also is identified by some men describing their women colleagues' experiences, mainly in the natural sciences. A white man faculty member discusses this prejudice in terms of his role as a mentor, explaining that he spends a fair amount of time talking to one of his more conservative colleagues about what he perceives as their insensitivity to their women peers. A white woman natural scientist explains that although she does not feel like her authority is purposely undermined, "If a male colleague says the same thing [as I do], the student or the colleague will certainly believe it more from the male" (Wh, W, NS).

Some of the faculty members also describe snide comments about women, as in the following response to a question about what brings up racial issues among her colleagues:

> Gender issues [come up] more than racial issues, I would say. A female is characterized in a much more hysterical or emotional fashion than a male, when in fact our department has a history of a few male professors actually coming to fisticuffs after a faculty meeting. This was years ago, but the point in my telling you the story is that the behavior on the male side has been historically much more extreme than the female side, and yet, very often, there's a strong gender identification. (AsAm, W, NS)

Unfortunately, these beliefs about women appear to be fairly widespread. As a white man explains,

> We're talking about a discipline that has been white, male, and in the country, also white male.... And we aren't isolated. [Another university in the Midwest] tenured one of their first women to come through the ranks a couple years ago for the first time in the history of the university. And so, for the record, I have certainly been part of very uncomfortable conversations in my department, given attitudes and prejudices that I have to say mostly my older colleagues have. And not just in my department. I mean, within the natural science community. (Wh, M, NS)

Although women in natural science departments may not always have to deal with prejudice and discrimination face to face, dealing with colleagues' negative attitudes and the subtle comments or harsher evaluations that often are the by-product of such beliefs create an additional burden of time and emotional energy beyond that expended by their man peers.

The Challenge to Legitimacy as a Form of Identity Taxation

We now expand the definition of classical cultural taxation to include "differential legitimacy," referring to faculty of color and women faculty's extra burden of legitimating their academic and/or research qualifications in their departments and universities. Because many faculty of color have benefited from affirmative action policies, white colleagues frequently assume that faculty of color are less qualified (Balderrama, Texiera, and Valdez 2006; Delgado-Romero et al. 2003; Gunning 2000; Laden and Hagedorn 2000; Turner and Myers 2000; and see the discussion in chapter 4 concerning students' assumptions regarding the qualifications of faculty of color).

In addition, some faculty of color conduct research with communities of color using "socially conscious" methodologies, research styles that are considered by some to be both less rigorous and more political. White colleagues sometimes believe that research on communities of color is irrelevant and illegitimate because it cannot be done "objectively." Like faculty of color, women, especially those in the natural sciences, experience their work quite differently from their men peers (Winkler 2000). They often lack the complex networks that their men counterparts enjoy and struggle to gain legitimacy and authority in their field, sometimes causing discomfort in discussing issues of gender in the department or the classroom:

> *Do you talk about being a woman in your classroom?*
> I try not to because I've had so many people come and say, "Gee, what is it like to be a woman natural scientist?" And I don't do woman natural science, I do general science. There's no such thing as woman natural science. I try to stay out of that. I'm happy to talk to women and minorities. And we do talk about what it's like to be a scientist, but it's one on one. (Wh, W, NS)

What is interesting about her reaction is the obvious desire to keep gender and the particular experiences of women in science out of her classroom, perhaps in an attempt to keep her teaching style and classroom as "objective" and "neutral" as possible.

In this sample the legitimacy of minority and women faculty is primarily challenged in four ways: (1) not feeling a sense of belonging in their departments; (2) colleagues questioning their qualifications; (3) colleagues not valuing their research; and (4) feeling the need to prove themselves.

Lacking of a Sense of Belonging in Their Department. Faculty of color often report that colleagues at times highlight their minority status to suggest that, as "outsiders" in terms of race, they do not belong in the department. Thus, they feel that their presence sometimes is used as a benefit for the department (e.g., additional funding, serving on diversity committees) and at other times is considered a deficit. For example, an African American social scientist explains,

> It [race] is a big part of my everyday life in a very frustrating way. You can't get away from it because they [colleagues] market your blackness so much, because they need to use it for some reason. I think there's a real focus on trying to make sure that you always understand that you are not desired here. So—or, that your presence here is

mostly about your blackness in one way or another. But you cannot get away from it. You are always a black professor. (AfAm, W, SS)

Although she feels that her presence is unwelcome, some other women of color experience a much more hostile environment—they have been told directly they do not belong!

> I think this department has shifted tremendously since I came here and they are very supportive, because they have to. I mean, when I first came here, no way. When I first came here I was kind of this eccentric figure in the department. In faculty meetings I had senior professors scream at me and tell me I didn't belong here. (L, W, H)

This colleague feels that although her departmental climate is quite supportive presently, historically it was acutely unreceptive to her because of her racial identity. Faculty members of color must cope with an additional burden of cultural taxation that their white peers do not encounter—that of keeping face and fighting to stay in a space that often feels hostile or inhospitable.

Questioning Minority Faculty's Qualifications. Many faculty of color state that some of their colleagues believe minorities receive certain privileges (e.g., research grants, professional appointments) because of their protected status. Both faculty of color and white faculty mentioned circumstances in which white colleagues suggested minority faculty are hired using lower standards. In this view, because of the implementation of federal affirmative action policies, some colleagues assume that being a minority or a woman is synonymous with being academically or professionally less qualified:

> For one of my colleagues to say that I deserve tenure because I'm a victim, I'm a black person, uhhh. I've heard references many times from my colleagues who I respect a lot and I like a lot, things like, "Well, you get everything because you're black. Black people are special. You get everything because you're a woman of color. You get everything. You get tenure." So the question is, am I going to get tenure because I'm black? What about all the work I've done? (AfAm, W, H)

A related and equivalently problematic issue is colleagues' concerns that if women or minorities are hired, the department's quality will be at risk. A man of color recounts hearing just such a view expressed in a meeting:

> Like we talk about hiring faculty, for example. And, you know, a lot of us bring up the fact that we should be looking for women and underrepresented minorities. And a lot of times white faculty will say, "Yeah, we need to ... we really need to make sure that our quality is maintained." And I always say, "If you look at the minority faculty in our department in the natural sciences, certainly this department, you know, the

women faculty, you'll find that we probably outperform the average. We [minority faculty] are not the problem in terms of quality." (AfAm, M, NS)

Colleagues' perceptions that affirmative action policies have given white women faculty and men and women faculty of color unfair advantages creates a dynamic in which their qualifications are constantly questioned, resulting in an extra burden of emotional labor.

Colleagues Not Valuing Minority Faculty's Teaching or Pedagogy. Several of the faculty (both white faculty and faculty of color) who study and teach about race and diversity issues report that their colleagues often either misunderstand, question the importance of, or ignore such work.

> A lot of them [my colleagues] won't engage me around the content stuff. They won't ask me to, like, see the syllabus or to talk about any issues except if they're black issues, but they only want to talk about it long enough for us to get to the coffee room together and that's it. So I don't think they necessarily take what I do all that seriously.... So that brings special challenges for me, being taken seriously. (AfAm, W, SS)

Other faculty members of color express similar frustrations that their contributions to their departments in terms of teaching are neither appreciated nor respected. Furthermore, when such faculty incorporate multicultural and diverse perspectives into core disciplinary courses, they are sometimes met with resistance because it is presumed that alternative perspectives will mean less teaching of disciplinary fundamentals. One faculty man of color describes a faculty meeting as follows:

> The other week they [the department] came up with some revisions to the course syllabi, to the course outlines for our required courses, and interestingly they gave us an edited copy where they were able to strike out words. You could see the words that were going to be deleted out, they had lines through them, and the words they were going to put in had brackets around them. I noticed in the outline that almost everything that referred to multiculturalism, that referred to oppression, that referred to diversity, any of those words had a mark through them. And I sat there and people were going on and on about everything else about this and no one saw it. No one even saw it. (AsAm, M, SS)

Colleagues' negative or passive responses to diversity issues and to minority faculty members' work also suggest a desire to maintain the culturally white hegemonic tone of academic departments.

Feeling the Need to Prove Oneself. The perception that one's colleagues assume that faculty of color are less qualified causes some to believe that they must work twice as hard to receive equal respect as do white colleagues. Explaining what he does to try to prove his academic legitimacy, a faculty member reports,

> I strive to be an example that we're [blacks] not that different, you know, that I can do anything that you can do and probably do it better if I set my mind to it.... I want people to understand that just because I'm African American you shouldn't have any preconceived notions about what I'm capable of doing, what I like to do, any of that.... I teach and I do research and we get grants, and if I can amass more money, I can amass more papers and journals than you, if I have more graduate students than you, then I beat you. That's not my goal necessarily, but I beat you. You can't say that I didn't. I'm trying to live up to my own fullest potential, but in doing that, I think you'll see that I can do everything that you can, maybe better. (AfAm, M, NS)

Even though faculty of color mention receiving research grants, publications in flagship journals, and discipline-associated leadership positions and awards, many still feel they are not granted the legitimacy they deserve from departmental colleagues. This can take a toll on their well-being, as one woman of color describes her reaction in a situation in which her white colleagues indirectly challenged her legitimacy:

> I have been known for being very assertive and outspoken in committees and in discussions with colleagues. And when racist comments come up, I discuss them right away, and I say, you know, "That's very racist," um, or "That's very sexist." I do remind colleagues about that. I still remember, too, that a colleague said in a meeting once that minority professors who had been tenured in this department had been tenured with lower criteria, you know, and I was sitting right there in front of him. And I have to say that sometimes, you get paralyzed, like you get this feeling inside your body that you freeze, and you just don't know how to react. (L, W, H)

In these situations faculty members of color often feel that their hard work is not only overlooked and undervalued but also that they have to struggle constantly to prove that they are worthy of their accomplishments.

Faculty of color are not alone in seeing such collegial disrespect; several white faculty in the sample also argue that minority faculty seem to have to work twice as hard as white faculty to earn the respect of their academic peers and to be seen as a legitimate scholar.

Identity Taxation in the Intersection of Race and Gender

In recent years the development of theory on intersectionality has allowed for more thorough discussions of how being female and of color create nuanced experiences and interpretations of the social world (Collins 1998; hooks 1990). Women of color who are "double minorities" in departmental settings face issues that white women and men faculty of color do not have to confront, including but not limited to: pressures to be a symbolic role model for women minority students, increased visibility and bodily/presentational concerns, dealing with (negative) stereotypes portraying them as maternal or nurturing, having to choose which status group to align with, and isolation from collegial networks and departmental/institutional support. Rather than having additive or multiplicative effects, race and gender are "simultaneous and intersecting systems of relationship and meaning" (Andersen and Collins 1992, xiii; see also chapter 8 in this volume) that lead to additional identity taxation beyond that of either women faculty or faculty of color.

Because they represent two underrepresented groups in the academy as well as the even rarer combination of the two, women faculty of color feel especially overburdened by service demands on their time. When asked how her race was important in her experience as a professor in her department, a humanities professor replies,

> They want a black face, or a woman face of any kind. I mean, I've had people say to me things like, "Could you have dinner with this job applicant? We need a woman, we need a black woman." That's from a particularly insensitive secretary. (AfAm, W, H)

Although colleagues are not generally this explicit in their categorizations and expectations of women faculty of color, these women are often expected to represent and advocate for minority groups that they may or may not be members of. It is as if departmental colleagues assume that knowledge of one disadvantaged group translates into knowledge of all minority groups. This is frustrating for women of color, who mentor and support not only members of the two (or more) disadvantaged groups they belong to but additional disadvantaged students as well. Although women of color in the sample frequently cite their desire to support and advise students, they sometimes feel that this commitment to advocacy and mentorship is overly taxing, and the further burden of being the "expert" on minority groups is an additional responsibility that they are uncomfortable taking on.

The responsibility to represent and advocate for diversity is not always characterized as negative, however. In fact, several female faculty members describe the excess travel and work required of them because of their visibility as role models to younger women of color as a matter of course and, at times, a source of pride. As one colleague explains,

> I do think that other people think that my race is important and the other people I [laughter] am thinking of are sort of senior people in the field and some of them are also termed underrepresented minorities. And they really feel that is very important

being an African American woman and being a rarity in the scientific community that I go out and do my share of recruiting and, you know, be a role model and I agree with them. I think there is a certain responsibility for that. And I definitely get the sense that there are other people out there who, you know, sort of have their eye on me because I am African American and a female and want to make sure that, you know, there are young girls who know that. There's somebody [at this university] who looks like you who's doing this job. (AfAm, W, NS)

Although the extra mentoring and recruitment associated with these identities is considerable, some faculty members seem to feel that it is their responsibility to continue in the fight for diversity, despite possible adverse effects on their productivity and/or qualifications for promotion.

Women of color in this sample are also much more likely than others to talk about being burdened by expectations to nurture or "mommy" their students. However, some women faculty members embrace the gendered and racial norms that they believe allow them the freedom to be nurturing to their students. As an example of the former stance, an Asian American professor describes her frustration with the demands that she felt her Asian American students placed on her:

What the Asian American students expect from me is very different. It's almost opposite from what the white students want. The Asian American students want kind of … they see you as kind of like a big sister or a mother or some kind of maternal figure who's going to kind of allow them to explore their ethnic identity. So they want affirmation from you, yeah. And they may not want you to challenge them on their sexual politics or on their politics in general or their conception of themselves or their relation to other Asian American groups. They may not want that. Which is what I kind of perceive to be my goal [laughs]. So sometimes I feel like I'm betraying them in a way because I want to get them to see things in a broader perspective. (AsAm, W, H)

In this instance she feels uncomfortable with the expectations of her Asian American students, who she thinks ask for emotional support rather than the intellectual and critical stimulation she wants to provide. These students turn to her as an assumed "sympathetic" professor who they believe understands their background and viewpoint, yet her gender is obviously a part of this expectation; as a woman she is placed into a nurturing familial role beyond that of normal advising and mentorship.

Race Versus Gender. When asked about how their race affected them, many of the white women natural science faculty describe their gender as much more important than their race. The question of gender's effect on professors' lives is a more complex one for women faculty of color, however. Many of the women of color in the sample discuss their race and gender as having a combined effect, as in the experience of being a "black woman" rather than simply being black or being a woman. However, in some cases informants' discussions of disadvantage seem to emphasize one minority experience over another as the force most prominent in their lives or as the issue most salient in their experience of disadvantage.

For example, one faculty member argues that mentorship is easier to attain for men than it is for women, regardless of their racial background:

> Again and again I've seen that men, whether it be men of color or white men, are more likely to be mentored. [It's easier for them to] find people that are going to take them under their wing and help them out. I see that in my department among the men of color in comparison with women of color. It may not be a mentorship thing, but at least people who might be able to help you figure out how you write a grant … this is not a really supportive environment for people of my race or ethnicity or gender. I think that this is probably one of the most male-dominated places I've ever worked in my life. I see many men of color, for example, of my race or ethnicity, or of other races and ethnicity who seem to be more accepted into the mainstream. So I think certainly if it was someone of my gender [who I was advising], I would say, you need to find a support system. (L, W, SS)

A lack of networking and mentorship is a frequent issue for many women in academia, especially for women of color. Whether race or gender has the largest impact on their lives in the academy, these women often face demands to align themselves with one minority group, often to the detriment of the other. This places an additional burden on women of color that most of their peers do not experience—not only are they members of two underrepresented groups that they feel they must support, but they are also at times faced with pressure to choose which identity they wish to prioritize.

Conclusion

As argued in chapter 1, the academy is designed to reward competition and individual achievement and is based on a system in which each participant supposedly is given a fair chance to meet the goals and requirements to be productive, get promoted, and achieve tenure. Unfortunately, in practice there are many barriers to this equality for all, in the form of explicit and implicit discrimination. For women faculty, these may include isolation in subdisciplines and work-groups, lack of networks, and perceived lack of authority. An additional barrier is identity taxation. Acknowledging that identity taxation exists and creates inequality in the time pressures that people experience in terms of mentorship, departmental service, and emotional labor may lead colleagues to be more sensitive about these issues and subsequently fairer in making tenure and promotion decisions.

Our informants' experiences within their departments and the larger university show that racial and gender inequality and institutionalized racism and sexism are alive and well, even among well-educated academic scholars and colleagues. Therefore, although the numbers of minority and white women faculty have increased at most postsecondary institutions, most campuses have not effectively dismantled the hierarchical and oppressive structures that once overtly prohibited the admission of people of color and white women into these sacred halls and spaces.

White faculty committed to issues of race and gender diversity also experience cultural taxation. But men and women faculty members of color are more likely to report experiences of cultural taxation than are white women faculty, and they are much more likely than white men faculty. Informants often speak candidly about how this cultural taxation affects their academic work and progress as well as their emotional health and mood. Whereas other studies have focused on how cultural taxation is manifest in dealing with colleagues' problematic behavior and expectations for departmental service and overcommittment, identity taxation—having to prove one's legitimacy and one's right and qualifications to be in an academic space—is an additional burden for faculty of color.

Even though faculty of color and women faculty report experiencing identity taxation, they often are also active agents within their departments. Despite recognizing that colleagues constantly expect them to be the "stereotyped voice of diversity" on various committees, teach or bring up diversity-related issues and issues of inequality or discrimination in the classroom or departmental meetings, and mentor students of color, many women and minority faculty seem to accept these responsibilities rather willingly. Some of these faculty mention using their positions as professors (at various levels) to give back to their respective communities and advocate on behalf of marginalized groups (see chapter 11 in this volume). Therefore, while dealing with the "extra burdens" attached to their identity group status, they also speak excitedly about the rewards of imparting knowledge to the next generation of students and some of the joys involved in working with students and disciplinary peers.

Chapter 11

Advocates for Diversity ... Or Not

Faculty Members as Change-Agents?

Ruby Beale, Mark A. Chesler, and Elizabeth Ramus

The prior chapters indicate that most faculty interviewed are not passive in deal-ing with diversity-related concerns and find ways to exert critical agency on these issues. This chapter focuses centrally and quite explicitly on faculty members' approaches to activism in meeting these ideological, cultural, structural, and pedagogical challenges. Clearly, post–affirmative action thinking has focused on diversity as a catchphrase for trying to go beyond a concern for increases in the numbers of members of historically disadvantaged groups/subordinated groups in the industrial/educational workforce and workplace/classroom. But diversity means different things to different people, and advocating for diversity may take varied forms. Consequently, in this chapter we explore the ways in which the sample of university faculty members respond to interview ques-tions asking them whether they are diversity advocates, what the term diversity means to them, and what kinds of actions they undertake when they advocate for diversity (if they do).

The Background of Diversity Discussions

Thomas and Ely (2002, 38) articulate three paradigms or definitional outlines for diversity that emerge from their work in the corporate sectors and they apply quite broadly. One paradigm, focusing on "discrimination and fairness," argues that because of a history of prejudice and exclusion, "we need managerial processes that ensure that all our employees are treated equally and with respect and that some are not given unfair advantage over others." This view parallels Roosevelt Thomas's (2002, 14) articulation and critique of a "coexistence-compromise" approach in which we "agree to recognize minorities and women as equals" (see also the discussions of color blindness in chapters 1 and 7 of this volume). Although this view reflects essential elements of the American cultural commitment to fair play and equal rights, its color-blind commitment assumes that racial and gender differences are relatively important and thus permits the systemic nature of prejudice and unequal or unfair treatment to remain unexplored ... and unchallenged. As Darder argues with particular relevance for educators: "Inherent in this perspective of fair-and-equal is the ... consequence ... that students from the dominant culture who enter with major social and economic advantages receive as much—and at times more—than students from subordinate cultures who arrive with far fewer social advantages" (Darder 1991, 111).

Thomas and Ely (2002, 39) also draw attention to what they call an "access and legitimacy" paradigm, a view "predicated on the acceptance and celebration of differences," paralleling what has been called the valuing differences approach to incorporating members of previously excluded racial/ethnic and gender groups. Thomas (2002) and Miller (1994) critique diversity efforts that call for but may be limited to this sort of heightened sensitivity and respect for differences and individuality. In the field of higher education Park and Denson's (2009) investigation of faculty members' "diversity advocacy" rests on examining their attitudes regarding the value of diversity for students' educational experiences, knowledge and appreciation of others, promotion of understanding, and inclusion of diversity in the curriculum. Chesler, Lewis, and Crowfoot (2005) argue that such approaches to education and to teaching focus overmuch on individual experiences and attitudes and underemphasize structural and cultural factors. Thus, these approaches tend to overlook the overarching hegemony of a culture based on white, male, and Eurocentric traditions, whose dominance (and thus the subordination, even in the face of tolerance and celebration, of other cultural traditions) is maintained by the exercise of societal and institutional power.

The third paradigm noted (and favored) by Thomas and Ely (2002, 49) focuses on a "learning and efficiency" model of organizations and organizational change, in which "companies have developed an outlook on diversity that enables them to ... enhance work by rethinking primary tasks and redefining markets, products, strategies, missions, business practices and even cultures." Miller (1994, xxvii) extends this organizational change approach to diversity, arguing that what is needed is a social justice perspective that is "addressing discrimination and oppression head on." Chesler, Lewis, and Crowfoot (2005, 21) mirror this view in the higher education arena, calling for a "critical multiculturalism" that carries a concern for issues of social justice and requires "redistributing power and resources and reevaluating the rules and practices ... of the institution and the classroom" (see also Giroux 1997, among others). Their view of a truly multicultural classroom involves the management of classroom content and dynamics in a way that "attends deliberately and proactively to patterns of interaction among diverse groups of students, ensuring equity in student participation by challenging appearances of masculine bias, racial/ethnic privilege, or dominance of interaction by any group" (Chesler, Lewis, and Crowfoot 2005, 237–38).

Our strategy for understanding how this sample of faculty members' approaches to diversity might fit with these varied interpretations began with open coding of all sixty-six faculty informants' responses to questions and probes asking about their approach to issues of diversity and its advocacy. The questions included, "Are you (do you consider yourself to be) a diversity advocate? If yes, what does that mean to you? What kinds of things do you do as an advocate?" We did not begin the interview process asking informants directly if they were diversity advocates, but after several informants voluntarily discussed their active efforts in altering classroom, departmental, and university conditions, we did ask about these concerns directly. Therefore, in subsequent coding we examined all sixty-six informants' answers to these questions as well as other comments in their interviews in order to more fully understand the range and context of given examples or situations.

The sixty-six faculty members made a total of 182 comments related to the meaning of diversity and 203 comments related to acts of advocacy. Because many faculty members responded in multiple and complex ways to these questions and are not easily categorized as totally falling into one of the aforementioned paradigms, for the most part the results and discussion below concentrates on an analysis of comments rather than an analysis of persons. We used a constant comparative approach to this constructivist analysis, in which the results emerged from the data itself (Charmaz 2005; Strauss and Corbin 1998). Our emergent categories included three different ways of conceptualizing diversity, and once these three themes were identified and pursued, we organized the above relevant literature.

Results and Discussion

As one might expect in a population selected on the basis of their prior involvement in diversity-related issues, 89 percent of the sample state that they feel they are diversity advocates, although faculty members differ in the meanings and actions associated with both "diversity" and "advocacy."

What Does Diversity Mean?

Treating Everyone Equally/Fairly. Six of the sixty-six faculty members queried (13 percent of the comments) refer to diversity as treating students fairly or equally. There is a subtle distinction between the terms "fair" and "equal" that can be extrapolated from the data. Whereas to treat each student equally is to give each student the same opportunities, treating students fairly means giving each student the opportunities best suited to support their performance/needs, which may mean not treating all students the same. Either way, faculty members' comments in this category tend to focus on individuals and tend to downplay or reject the relevance of group-related diversity in their classroom and teaching styles, also often citing the importance of focusing on the subject matter of their classes.

Faculty who refer to equality as a template reflect the underlying claim that by giving everyone the same treatment, students' identities will not matter in their interactions with the professor or with student peers in the classroom. For instance,

> I give lots of praise to everybody across the board, "Oh wonderful, Johnny," who's white, "Wonderful Joanie," who's black. I make sure that I call on all students equally. (AfAm, W, H)

Colleagues with this approach generally do not attend to how the apparently same or equal treatment may have disparate effects on students of different backgrounds. Indeed, some faculty members expressing this general perspective implicitly argue that it was possible for them to take a color-blind approach to diversity and behave as if everyone is the same.

Other faculty speak about treating students fairly, which has a slightly different connotation than treating students equally. Fairness refers to treating someone on their own terms, without bias or avoiding bias and without prejudice.

> Make sure that all students are treated fairly and encourage diversity in the classroom and outside. (Wh, W, NS)

This faculty member takes an active stance on diversity in the classroom but does not acknowledge either the ways in which students of color may perceive their treatment regardless of the faculty member's intent or the constraints on fairness in the context of a society riven by inequality. By limiting the vision underlying this approach, faculty may see their focus on fairness as a complete and appropriate way to address diversity concerns.

Many faculty who define diversity as treating students fairly or equally are in the natural sciences. Some in particular express the view that "science is science" and that students' identities or racial/ethnic backgrounds do not matter in the classroom or that issues of race do not exist or are invisible in the classroom.

> To be honest with you, science is kind of—as I see science there is no race. I mean, science is science. I guess you could engineer things ergonomically for certain types of people, but that's not part of what I do. (AfAm, M, NS)

All these responses—treating students fairly, equally, or denying the relevance of diversity—can result in ignoring issues of diversity in the classroom. This general view is expressed by faculty of color as well as by white faculty.

Appreciating Difference. Ten of the faculty members interviewed (24 percent of the comments) view diversity as something to enjoy and appreciate. Some faculty cite diversity as differences they celebrate in the classroom, whereas others attend to or highlight them in order to create learning opportunities. Faculty with either perspective recognize that different cultures exist, that diversity is important in the classroom, and that it needs to be acknowledged.

Some believe that a diverse group of people is made of multiple perspectives and experiences and that these experiences need to be celebrated or enjoyed. In this context a faculty responsibility might be to "draw out" such experiences:

> I think diversity ... I do believe diversity is a richness. So I try and sort of draw out from the students their experiences and their understandings of things. (AfAm, M, H)

Such examples focus on including all groups of students in classroom discussions. They do not go further to examine the ways in which such participation may or may not be equal or how they may be conditioned by different groups of students' sense of entitlement and power—or the lack thereof.

A few faculty expressing this general view say that beyond understanding and appreciating these differences, a concern for diversity means using differences as opportunities or tools to facilitate students' understanding. These colleagues often cite the need for students to be in classrooms with students of different backgrounds so students can learn from one another's life experiences and viewpoints.

> Diversity to me is something distinct from the idea of a melting pot. Diversity to me means that people of different backgrounds or schools of thought, or whatever, can

come together, respect their differences, and not be expected to homogenize. In the racial context it simply means that people who look different, either skin color or ethnic identity, can come to the table and be accepted as you are and not expected to homogenize. (AsAm, W, NS)

By referring to diversity as a group of different experiences and as a source of richness, these faculty members acknowledge and appreciate diversity's importance to the learning process. As with the first major theme, this is expressed by faculty of color as well as by white faculty.

Working Toward Social Justice. The majority of faculty members in this sample (43/66, 60 percent of the total number of comments) identify diversity in relation to changing the classroom or university in order to approach a more egalitarian and just educational environment. Instead of either a melting pot or salad bowl analogy, here the focus often is on changing the shape or nature of the classroom environment itself. Faculty comments in this category often suggest that diversity is not simply a matter of having different identities exist together or having the elements join in some appreciation or even accommodation of one another but rather of creating a more just environment in the face of differences in social identity and access to key resources, power, and privilege.

> That is to promote social justice or contribute toward a more just society, in case we cannot achieve a just society in our lifetime. (AsAm, W, SS)
> I don't think diversity is enough. I think that diversity often cannot deal with justice issues, so when I say I'm a diversity advocate, access is not the end of it.... [It's] being conscious of being white and being involved with other people to bring greater accessibility, equity, justice, or however you want to put it, to the institution. Those are somewhat different things. (Wh, W, SS)

In this view diversity is most meaningful when it helps challenge students' or the organization's previously taken-for-granted ideas or policies in order to work toward "a just society."

> I fought for doing things about racism and sexism and ageism and able-ism, and I continue to fight those fights, regularly, anywhere I go. I raise them. Sometimes I'm the first one to raise them. But because I am privileged, I can yell and scream louder than almost everybody. (Wh, M, SS)

This white man quite explicitly draws attention to how his race and gender (and probably age and academic rank) all give him enough status and privilege that he can take a strong advocacy stance without fearing recrimination. Obviously white women faculty and men and women faculty of color do not carry those privileges and may need to advocate in different ways.

There are no major differences between the groups of white faculty and faculty of color in the way they define diversity. However, women faculty are much less likely than men faculty to make comments that define diversity advocacy as *treating fairly* and substantially more likely than men faculty to make comments that define diversity advocacy as *working toward social justice*. These findings support other research about gender and sociopolitical attitudes as well as other chapters' reports of the views and experiences of female faculty members (e.g., Lindholm et al. 2005). Perhaps women faculty members' own experiences with gender discrimination in the academy have made some of them more likely to adopt a social justice orientation. With regard to disciplinary location, faculty members in the natural sciences are much more likely than faculty in either the social sciences or humanities to define diversity advocacy as *treating fairly* and much less likely to make comments that define diversity advocacy as *working toward social justice*. These disciplinary differences may reflect subject matter differences and the ways in which diversity-related issues are more likely to appear overtly in the work and teaching of social scientists and humanities faculty as well as the lack of prior exposure many natural scientists have had with these issues in their own research and teaching. It may also be related to the different sociopolitical attitudes and orientations common in different disciplines.

Actions Associated with Diversity Advocacy

When it comes to the consideration of taking action, Stassen (1995, 363) raises the question of "why faculty, often seen as more ideologically liberal and egalitarian, are often peripheral or resistant to anti-racist efforts on campus." This ambivalence or internal conflict is illustrated by Maruyama and Moreno's (2000, 16) report from a large survey of faculty members that states that by and large "faculty respondents said they did not change their practices much in response to student diversity." Thus, we note here the reports of colleagues who indicated that they are *not* diversity advocates as well as those who describe specific actions they take as diversity advocates. We also identify three different arenas in which faculty members advocate for diversity: the classroom, the department or larger university context, and the external environment of their professional interests/associations or local community.

Not a Diversity Advocate. Seventeen faculty members, including white faculty and faculty of color, say they do not view themselves as diversity advocates. For some, this is an outright statement that they do not agree with the diversity agenda or with the way in which it has been implemented. Others see diversity as a nonissue in their classroom, their teaching approaches, their field of study, or higher education in general. Some do not advocate in some particular arenas, especially where they feel it would be inappropriate (e.g., in the classroom), but are active in other arenas and ways. Still others express feelings of apathy, tiredness, lack of energy, or indicate that their primary focus is on their academic work and/or roles.

> I don't have the time, you know, to, like, caucus politically or to, like, strategize with colleagues to be honest, um, because I'm so busy. (L, W, H)

Chapter 1 addresses the high priority universities of this sort place on research productivity and the resultant lower priority on teaching and institutional service or citizenship. Given the unfortunate sense of overload with which many faculty struggle, this response is in and of itself a cause for concern—diversity related or not.

Some colleagues who articulate principled or pedagogical reasons for not being diversity advocates while in the classroom distinguish between a nonadvocate role in the classroom and advocacy in other arenas of their life/work:

> I don't see myself as trying to change minds in a kind of direct way. I don't see the classroom as an [arena for this] ... partly because I think that pedagogically it may be unethical, it's certainly ineffective. (AfAm, M, SS)
>
> Not within the classroom. I think it's very important for me not to be an advocate in the classroom. In the classroom I'm a scholar and a teacher. Because they will assume I'm an advocate, so I don't even have to play that. (AfAm, M, H)

The latter African American colleague clearly anticipates that because of his race, students will automatically think he is a diversity advocate. He reflects on a classic double-bind: as a faculty of color, whether he advocates for diversity or not, he is likely to be seen as doing so.

Other faculty members, typically in the natural sciences, believe that not only does diversity advocacy not have a place in the classroom but that it does not have a place in the sciences. Reminiscent of an earlier quote from a natural scientist, one faculty member states,

> I don't do anything other than just operate as a faculty member. I don't reach out and offer myself in advance for these things. I think scientists.... I am a scientist, and so I just should do science, teach science. And do that and that's about it. And I do that. (Wh, W, NS)

For the most part this *no advocacy* category reflects that regardless of what one thinks of as the meaning of diversity, it does not necessarily lead to advocacy efforts.

However, some faculty members who say they are not diversity advocates explicitly indicate that the issue for them is the quite limited notion of diversity that does not include a focus on inequality and justice. These colleagues clearly are advocates of the justice theme discussed previously.

No, I don't care at all about diversity because plantations were very diverse. (F, NA)

We know the intent of the above ironic statement, because elsewhere this colleague states that "affirmative action serves to maintain the status quo," that she is an active organizer of women of color, and that her "first priority is ending global oppression."

Diversity Advocacy in the Classroom. Some faculty members' educational or pedagogical advocacy of diversity is quite purposeful, in that they make an attempt to do something different in the classroom. There are, however, several different approaches to dealing with diversity issues in the classroom: actively or passively, gently or vigorously, proactively or reactively, and so forth (see examples of racially transformative practices in chapter 7 and some pedagogical approaches to classroom conflicts in chapters 5 and 6).

Many informants express their desire to be more attentive and emotionally supportive of minority students. In the same vein, many try to create a welcoming environment for minority students, using language like "reaching out":

> Well, because students of color and women have a distinct minority in engineering, I try to reach out more to such students. I let them know of research opportunities during the summer. I encourage them to come to my office hours. I try to really create an environment that they'll feel that they are welcomed, and they can speak out, and that by being a minority their voices aren't any less important. So I'm aware that I'm trying to reach out. (AfAm, M, NS)

As noted earlier, some define their advocacy not as some organized activity in the classroom but rather as an active effort to treat every person with respect and to be aware of their concerns.

There also are instances in which faculty indicate that they do advocacy as part of what a liberal arts education should ordinarily provide. This is an easier stance for those whose subject matter or department occasionally deals overtly with such issues of race and gender equity (e.g., some of the social sciences or humanities):

> Teaching ethnic studies in the humanities is already centrally dealing with issues of racial diversity and multiculturalism. I try to incorporate racial diversity not only in the content and the material of the courses but also in the kinds of questions that I ask and the kinds of thinking that I ask students to do in terms of critical thinking about themselves and about their subject position in society, issues about privilege in particular. I use discussion time a lot to tease out some of those differences of power among the students and also between different cultural groups in the United States. (Wh, W, H)

Several faculty members proactively address diversity issues in the classroom and/or in smaller group settings where they feel they have a greater opportunity to be heard and be effective. Their actions often take the form of identifying issues of privilege and oppression in the classroom and putting extra effort into classes with minority students. One prevalent form of explicitly and purposefully addressing diversity in the classroom involves making the curriculum more diverse and creating opportunities for students to interact with one another. Some of these efforts are reflected in the following excerpt:

> I put them into small-group discussions so that they would talk more about it. And then slowly but surely the African American students spoke up a little differently, a little more. The women spoke up a little differently, a little more. And then rather than asking to share it with the whole class or anything, I went around and listened and then went up front and shared what I'd heard. And then we began to talk about it a little bit more, and every week in class issues come up like, not just race, obviously, but gender is another huge one. (Wh, M, SS)

These last two excerpts appear to fit quite well with the emphasis in Gurin and colleagues (2002, 2004) on classroom diversity and informal interactional diversity. Efforts to make the curriculum more diverse and to utilize pedagogical approaches that create specific interactional opportunities or conversations about race and gender in the classroom exemplify the ways some faculty members try to educate students about issues of diversity and to challenge them to examine themselves and their views more critically.

In Their Departments ... with Colleagues ... and the Larger University Context. In addition to or instead of advocating in the classroom, some diversity advocates talk with colleagues about diversity issues and take the lead in challenging graduate student admissions policies that do not lead to departmental diversity:

> For me, it means I work very hard trying to get in my recruitment efforts, when I'm recruiting grad students, when I'm recruiting undergrads, when I go to these campus-day panels with incoming freshmen....I try to be very supportive of diversity in general, and pointing out that that's a strength here, and if you don't want that, don't come here ... maybe not quite like that. But I really do want to increase the number of talented and well-prepared minority students in our graduate program, especially. (Wh, W, NS)

In addition to advocating for increased representation of students of color, some faculty advocate within their departments for increased hiring and support for white women faculty and men and women faculty of color:

> We've been having some faculty searches recently and looking for a new junior faculty member, and we got a whole bunch of applications. And looking through them, I

have to say there was a number of women, and I looked at them first. Because I felt that it would be good for us to diversify our faculty. (L, M, NS)

I was upset because what was so obvious to me, there's no fully tenured woman or man of color in my department. And that's a big deal because we've got a lot of women, white women, who are full professors, who are powerful women in the university, and they're doing great things in setting the agenda, and yet there was no person of color in that world. (AfAm, W, H)

Another faculty member describes his approach with his colleagues as having been "a battering ram" on these issues, especially at the level of work for institution-wide change:

I've definitely been an advocate, especially in the department I was sort of like a battering ram on this issue from 1975 through the '90s. I was involved in many organizations of faculty members, some basically antiracist groups. I am now in a situation where that is being expressed mainly through committee work [affecting reviews of] a lot of faculty of color. That's mainly the way it gets expressed. But it was always my role. (Wh, M, H)

The time period this faculty member refers to saw numerous student and faculty protests about various issues of racial inequality and injustice on campus. Currently, he continues his involvement and commitment to a campus social justice agenda, now working within the critical arena of advocacy for the promotion and retention of colleagues of color.

Some faculty members take the lead to help others learn new teaching techniques that might be most useful in diverse classrooms and/or with controversial subject matter:

We're really trying to infuse and incorporate social justice issues into the social science curricula. So as part of this curricular enhancement, curricular transformation, we're doing a multilevel, multiphased evaluation. We're interviewing faculty and students, either individually or in focus-group settings, and we're soon administering some written surveys for students, tracking their leadership of this group. We have about five faculty and numerous student volunteers. I am part of the leadership of this group. And this is really in response to a direct result of a faculty vote. (AfAm, W, SS)

We formally organized about instruction and diverse classrooms. And even now there's an informal group of us who are connected as much by our ideology about research in an activist frame as we are about teaching. This group got together on a regular basis for a while, with about fifteen faculty working on particular issues. (Wh, M, SS)

These reports indicate that some advocates are able to play significant roles in reaching out to and organizing others in their departments and professional or social networks. The diversity advocacy reported above is not likely to change the core culture and pedagogy of local departments, but it does involve a broader set of colleagues acting on pedagogical issues and approaches.

Advocating Externally ... in the Local Community and/or Professional Associations. In addition to advocating in the classroom or with department and institutional colleagues, some faculty advocate for diversity outside the university itself:

> I got financial support to go into the local public schools and try to help them [with their science teaching]. I got a lot of support from upper administration and from the college. (Wh, M, NS)
>
> I'm an academic who's done experimental community-based work that, through a different route, engaged issues of race and ethnicity. I think I do a lot better job of that because doing work with community partners forced me and taught me a lot to get out of my own voice and my own box. And to figure out what practices enabled people who were different from each other to hear each other. I'm seen as someone who's opening up space because of that work. (Wh, M, H)

The white men faculty members above discuss very different kinds of work in local community settings. The first faculty member enters the urban public school system to advance both the content being taught as well as some unique pedagogical approaches. The second faculty member reports that he develops long-term partnerships with community agency representatives and is seen as "opening up space" for future collaboration by himself and colleagues. The fact that both these last excerpts are from white faculty indicate that race alone guarantees neither resistance to nor acceptance of diversity-related change efforts.

Advocacy external to the local university scene sometimes involve faculty members working for change in their professional or disciplinary associations:

> I am the first Asian female and first Asian executive officer elected there. I believe that by working together we don't have to feel we're pushed out. This is something one individual cannot do by themselves. To make people's opportunities happen, there must be political action ... that's why I'm doing it. (AsAm, W, NS)

There is no mistaking the political nature of this and some of the other advocacy efforts above. As a further illustration, consider the role played by Professor Patricia Gurin as she presented scientific testimony to the US Supreme Court regarding the University of Michigan's student admissions policies (Gurin 1999). Pat Gurin argued on the basis of scientific evidence that there were compelling educational benefits from a diverse student body.

Facing Resistance to Change. Efforts to create change bring with them resistance to change. As Chesler, Lewis, and Crowfoot (2005, 187) argue, "Resistance to multicultural change efforts is normal and should be expected to continue." Such resistance can occur at the individual level or the organizational level, and it can be open and direct or subtle and covert (Thomas and Plaut 2007). As a result, Sturm (2006) calls for "organization catalysts," as she especially highlights the need for internal change advocates to focus on the organizational context of diversity efforts—the reactions of peers and the limits or resistance to change posed by traditional organizational policies and priorities. Such catalysts or change agents tend to be "tempered radicals," advocates who promote change in ways that both challenge current practice and maintain their presence and value in their departments (Meyerson 2001).

Sometimes resistance to diversity advocacy in the classroom comes in the form of departmental or university policies that indicate a general disregard or lack of support for a priority on teaching, especially for innovative teaching:

> I don't think teaching is taken seriously in the institution. When I first got here, I would ask people about teaching, and the standard answer was, "Do whatever you want." Somebody said that if there aren't incentives to be a good teacher, they are not going to spend time on it. There must not be a culture about it. (AfAm, M, SS)

And sometimes resistance surfaces with particular regard to diversity-related work in the classroom, as it did in Boudreau and Eggleston's (2002) report of how their colleagues tried to sabotage their innovative classroom work about race without talking about race as the issue in their objections. As a further example,

> I think a lot of my colleagues just don't think what I teach is important, especially at the undergraduate level where most of the content on diversity happens. I think even the well-meaning people see this as a sort of this fad that hopefully we'll get past in the next couple of years and then we'll get back to the real business of education. (AfAm, W, SS)

Of course, such disregard is not the case for all faculty or all departments. Consider the following:

> I think in this department there is a good ethic about teaching. There is a good departmental culture about it. It has been valued by all the departmental chairs we've had, and we spend a lot of time talking about teaching. That gives those of us who are particularly interested in our teaching a lot of support. (NA, M)

Advocating on departmental issues such as graduate student admissions and faculty hiring also can generate resistance:

> In a search committee there's a particular colleague who at every single meeting says, "So what exactly does affirmative action mean? Does that mean we have to hire a

less qualified person instead of…?" It also comes up when other faculty say things to me with great astonishment, "Such and such a person of color graduate student, faculty member, is really, really, smart." And so I know we are talking about race and we're not talking about race. (Wh, W, SS)

Many who define themselves as diversity advocates, even in this special sample, discuss the ways in which men and women, students and colleagues, whether white or people of color, challenge, resist, or seek to sabotage their efforts.

Diversity advocacy in the community often draws resistance from colleagues who are steeped in a culture of a priority for academically based and directed research.

Unfortunately, the down side was not only did I not get encouragement from my department to do that, I got a letter from my departmental chair saying, "This isn't what you were hired to do." Basically I was told to stop doing this thing. (Wh, M, NS)

This faculty member was sanctioned for work that is not seen as central to his research and teaching role because it does not focus on advancing the frontiers of scientific knowledge but instead on scholarly based efforts to improve minority student performance in local community schools.

Faculty members of all races, genders, and disciplines more often discuss their advocacy work in the classroom (in positive or negative terms) than in other are-nas. This is the most private arena of faculty work and the setting in which the faculty has most control over what does and does not happen. At the same time, numerous colleagues focus on their peers and departments, especially around recruitment and retention of diverse groups of students and faculty. In this more public arena the risks are greater: one's colleagues (or chairs) can withhold support or otherwise sanction advocacy efforts and the individuals promoting them in symbolic or material terms. Far fewer faculty discuss their work in the external community, reflecting in part the low priority on service in R-1 academic research institutions and the traditional gaps between scientific work and locally useful knowledge or social action.

Although explorations of faculty members' views of the meaning of diversity generate some strong emotional reactions, so do conversations about advocacy. Faculty members' considerations of their actions involve both cognitive and affective/emotional reactions, expressed in terms of frustration, anger, fear, malaise, resentfulness, a sense of success, pride, commitment, joy, ambivalence, and concerns about conflict or safety or career implications. Some feel they are not and should not be advocates. Others feel there are issues that they are ready and willing to address and, hence, take them on as challenges. In fact, some see it as their role to be at the forefront for outing the issues, explaining the negative impact of current institutional and classroom arrangements on people of color or white women, and overtly working for change.

Conclusions

Many of the individuals represented here take individual and collective action and are consistent in their thoughts (the meaning of diversity) and their behaviors (diversity advocacy) around diversity concerns in the university. As one might expect on the basis of the sample involved, there is much support for diversity and its advocacy. Despite reports of resistance—or perhaps because of it—many faculty members exhibit tangible commitments to affecting change in racial/ ethnic and gender relations. These activities are not limited to interventions and innovations in the classroom or even elsewhere within the university but extend to the community as well (e.g., running a summer camp program, working in local school systems, helping to organize local political constituencies). Additionally, some faculty talk about how their high levels of advocacy in many years past continue to this day.

White faculty and faculty of color; men and women faculty; and social scientists, natural scientists, and humanities faculty are represented in all categories of the meaning of diversity and in most of the arenas of advocacy. Although there are some relevant trends, especially with regard to discipline, it is clear that race/ethnicity, gender, and discipline do not tightly determine these faculty members' views and actions. Contrary to some reports in the literature and probably due to the nature of this particular sample of faculty selected on the basis of their reputations for diversity work, there is as much if not more diversity in ideology and pedagogy within the ranks of faculty of color as among any other group. And in the face of serious and continuing racial underrepresentation, faculty of color's mere presence may be inspiring to others and represent a quiet form of advocacy—perhaps that is enough. Indeed, some faculty of color have had to work so hard to gain promotion and tenure, especially given the continuing implicit and explicit discrimination as well as the cultural taxation so often visited upon them, that they may not have much time and energy left over. Some faculty of color who consider various forms of advocacy do not want to chance being seen and trivialized as "a race person," "a racist," or be stigmatized as a radical rabble rouser. And finally, some who have advocated before and have seen little progress toward educational justice have withdrawn or become cynical about the prospects of significant change. These hesitancies are by no means limited to faculty of color; they affect many white faculty as well: some white faculty talk about being criticized or alienated by their white colleagues because of their challenges to mainstream cultures and practices. These countervailing pressures often create among justice-minded colleagues a double-bind that involves both hope and concern, pride and guilt, commitment and caution.

Chapter 12

Challenge, Advocacy, and Change

Mark A. Chesler and Alford A. Young Jr.

The problems and dilemmas reported in prior chapters are not etched in stone, nor are they amenable to simplistic analyses or solutions. As Chesler previously stated in the first chapter, although it is important to acknowledge the personal, interpersonal, and organizational forces that so clearly affect the quality of life and pedagogical actions of all faculty members and that fall especially hard on white women faculty and men and women faculty of color, no one should imagine that faculty members of whatever social identity are rendered powerless, disabled, or victims in these daily classroom and peer/departmental struggles. As can be seen in most prior chapters, many faculty members establish and assert agency, find ways to cope with these situations, learn from them, survive and even thrive in their midst, and hopefully improve the quality of life, learning, and social justice in their classrooms and university/collegiate organizations.

Those of us who recognize the existence of injustice in higher education must be prepared to challenge it—in classrooms, corridors and departmental/ organizational meetings, policies, and programs. They—and we—must be prepared to recognize and advocate for change in the content of the disciplines, pedagogies of instruction, and collegial and institutional relationships. The faculty, as key players in the instruction of the young, are a key locus of prevailing cultural traditions and countertraditions, positive and negative, and thus are central agents for making progress in meeting the goals of critical multiculturalism, democratic citizenship, and social justice.

Pedagogical Options

For faculty, the classroom is a key arena in which interaction with a broad range of students and cultural traditions can occur and in which race, gender, and class dominance and injustice can be challenged. For the classroom is not just an arena for knowledge transmission; it also is a social system, with groups of students always interacting with one another and with the faculty member. Their ways of relating, patterns of influence, and expressions of power and privilege, whether real or symbolic, always affect students' classroom participation, performance, and learning. Each classroom has its own culture and norms, its own patterns of participation and interaction, its own means of exercising power and authority. Race/ethnicity, gender, class, and sexuality are all likely to be at play in the teaching-learning process in all classrooms, sometimes overtly and often covertly. In the context of the US higher education system and amidst the larger US society, no classroom is a neutral or culture-free zone: they all reflect core elements of the white-, male-, and affluent-dominated cultural and sociopolitical environment. If left unchallenged, the prevailing forms of culture, interaction, and power that reign in the society at large will also reign in the classroom. When effectively challenged, antiracist (and antisexist) norms, related patterns of more equal and productive student participation, and more effective forms of instructional authority may be realized.

Effective teaching in the context of diversity is not an easy task for faculty members socialized, educated, and working within a system of racial, gender, and class privilege and disadvantage. It requires (adapted from Reed 1996):

- attention to the ways that one's own and others' ethnicity, gender, culture, and conscious or unconscious prejudices shape the ways that students learn and faculty teach;
- acknowledgement of the importance of including curricular content with diverse perspectives wherever possible;
- attention to the ways that multiple differences among students (e.g., race/ethnicity, gender, religion, class, sexual orientation, disability status, age) interact in complex ways within the classroom and elsewhere;
- incorporation of institutional strategies that positively recognize and address differences among students in course activities, assignments, and

interactions and that provide alternative opportunities for learning and demonstrating competence;

- active responses to overt and covert prejudice and discrimination as well as effort to reduce dynamics that perpetuate discrimination, disadvantage, and unmerited privilege in the learning environment, including both those that are intentional and those that are unintentional; and
- challenge to the ways in which disciplinary and institutional policies, traditions, and norms reflect and reproduce societal racism, sexism, classism, and other systematic forms of oppression and exclusion.

This last point is especially important and is often overlooked in discussions and plans to improve teaching. Teaching and learning take place in an organizational context, and unless that context is altered, individual faculty efforts are not likely to have lasting and powerful impact. Chism and Whitney (2005) make this point as they distinguish between typical "faculty development" programs and "organizational development" programs, emphasizing the latter's importance in changing institutional norms as well as individual faculty approaches. We return to this issue later in this chapter.

Faculty efforts to improve the classroom climate around diversity start with *knowledge about one's own social identity and cultural perspectives and their likely impact* on students (Bell et al. 2010). The Athenian challenge to "know thyself" may seem simple enough, but many faculty (especially white and men faculty) often do not consciously think about the meaning and impact of their social identities on their own behavior, on students, on their curricular and pedagogical choices, and even on their use of classroom spaces (note the constitutive elements of classroom conflict described in chapter 3). Faculty members' race, gender, social class, and sexual identities and backgrounds influence the interactions and power dynamics between themselves and students. In turn, they affect the ways in which students think about and respond to faculty members of different social locations and identities. Chapter 4 discusses how white women and men and women of color experience these student dynamics, and chapter 8 reveals some of the impression management and "bodywork" strategies women faculty of color use to protect themselves and advance their credibility and authority with students. Chapter 9 indicates in more detail how differently men of color respond to such situations. Men, especially white men, are not exempt from these challenges but do encounter them less often and do not experience them as seriously.

Faculty members' social identities or perspectives include not only the obvious cultural markers of race and gender but also age and rank in the academic system. More senior faculty or faculty who appear older are likely to receive more immediate and greater respect from students than are younger colleagues. Faculty who understand and can deal with the ways in which their own social identities and outlooks impact their behavior and the reactions of students can improve the reach and depth of their teaching and especially their ability to create a multicultural educational environment. Adequate knowledge of oneself also permits faculty to deal with their own concerns or fears about teaching in general and about teaching in diverse classrooms in particular.

Explicitly with regard to white men faculty, self-knowledge can increase understanding of their privileged status and its potential effects as well as their power to control some common classroom fears and concerns (Weinstein and O'Bear 1992, and see chapter 7) and relationships with colleagues. Faculty of color and white women faculty who also understand these dynamics may be better prepared to deal with the kinds of tests and challenges in relations with students and peers that have been reported in earlier chapters.

In addition to self-knowledge, *knowledge of the students* with whom a faculty member is working is an essential component of good—multicultural or otherwise—teaching. Such acquaintance goes beyond the often lost art of knowing students' names; it also involves understanding the social identities of students in class and the kinds of attitudes and experiences that different groups may bring with them. Tatum (1992) and Hardiman and Jackson (1992) also explicitly suggest that instructors assess—formally or informally—the stage of students' racial identity development, and the same is likely to be true of other dimensions of students' social locations and identities. Tatum (1992) and Osajima (1995) argue that without taking such information into account and without publicly drawing attention to and dealing with racial dynamics, faculty can anticipate students who avoid discussion of race and racism, maintain traditional ideologies of individual merit and achievement, and resist grappling with patterns of group discrimination and privilege in the classroom. Faculty members and students can also benefit from similar assessments of and attention to students' levels of cognitive development and social maturity.

The existence and maintenance of a diverse student body and diverse classroom demographics, or structural/representational diversity, is an important consideration. To be sure, not all classrooms draw diverse student memberships, and not all colleges and universities have adopted admissions' programs that create a large enough diverse pool of students. But creating diverse membership and mixing bodies does not in and of itself guarantee a multicultural environment or positive multicultural lessons. Moreover, although the lack of a diverse student body clearly acts as a barrier to certain kinds of teaching and learning opportunities, it does not eliminate them entirely. Much good work on creating a critically multicultural classroom and academic organization can and must be done with members of the white student majority—with or without the presence of students from minority or disadvantaged backgrounds. In the classroom, inclusive curriculum content, positive student-faculty and student-student interactions, and teaching techniques that focus on issues of social identity and attitudes toward one's own group and others (all components of pedagogy) become vital.

Progress on this agenda is easier in some classes than others. The manifest content of many of the social sciences and some humanities courses make curricular and pedagogical attention to intergroup relationships among students and among groups of students consistent with course objectives—although it is clear that acting on this potential is not common practice in many institutions and classrooms. This is a more difficult integration task in the physical sciences, mathematics, and engineering. Regardless of content, however, these issues are relevant throughout the curriculum (for reports of creative faculty responses to these issues in STEM disciplines see, for example, Jones 2005; Miller 2005; Reddick et al. 2005—all in an excellent and broad pedagogical anthology edited by Ouellett 2005).

Faculty working with diverse groups of students must also be prepared to *adopt diverse and innovative pedagogies,* to teach in ways that respond to different groups of students' preferred learning styles as well as to individual variations in approaches to course material, the instructor, and peer relationships. A social justice or critical multicultural orientation in the classroom must achieve the positive use of differences in the learning process; that is, teaching—including presentations, activities, and evaluations—can be done differently for people from different cultural traditions and can use the diversity represented in the classroom as vehicles for learning.

Faculty members' attention to theory and research on young adult learning styles brings to the fore questions about the ways learning styles may differ, primarily by individuals' cognitive and emotional characteristics but also by their gender, class, and race/ethnicity (Anderson and Adams 1992; Auster and MacRone 1994). These social background factors often combine to provide white and men and middle- to-upper-middle-class students with a greater sense of belongingness and competence in the classroom and, thus, a greater sense of their own power—to learn, to participate, to approach the faculty, to influence others—than is typical for students from less privileged backgrounds. Students of color, cognizant of a history of racism in education and society, may approach faculty, classrooms, and the university itself with greater caution. First-generation college students in particular are also likely to be unfamiliar with the culture and norms of affluent educational systems. Thus, a significant faculty challenge involves designing ways to deal with the unequal material and symbolic resources different groups of students bring to the classroom, generally evident in differential air time, assertiveness in asking for help, and general comfort. A focus on the differences among students as well as on their commonalities requires attention to background factors and to cultural variations in learning and participation styles. But it also needs to avoid stereotyping and essentialism: there typically is as much variation within a group of students from a particular identity or cultural group as there is among students of different groups.

Several scholars also emphasize the ways in which faculty members' own diverse cultural styles or preferences are reflected in the ways they present, work with, and test classroom material. Not just race and gender, but class and sexuality are also involved: the different ontological and epistemological assumptions prevalent in the social sciences, humanities, and natural sciences likewise affect these different cultural styles (see Kolb 1981, and Murray and Renaud 1995, as well as chapters 5 and 6 in this volume for further discussion of how teaching styles and responses may vary by disciplinary focus).

Across these disciplines, engaged, active, and interactive teaching-learning strategies, those that have been labeled "student centered," may be especially useful in diverse classrooms. These approaches often involve students in experiential encounters with course material and their peers, personal reflection on these encounters, and links to relevant scholarly literature on such matters. The result is attention to the individual as well as group-level dynamics in the classroom and to the emotional as well as cognitive aspects of learning. One especially interesting academic innovation is courses using intergroup dialogues—either entire courses focused or distinct modules using this approach (Gurin, Nagda, and Sorensen 2011; Schoem and Hurtado 2001; Zuniga et al. 2007). These designed encounters bring students of different social identities into sustained and depthful contact with one another in ways that build bridges of communication and relationships across group boundaries. Research on these classroom intergroup dialogues indicates that participants also develop more complex forms of thinking. Efforts to bring these innovations in interactive and experiential learning into the pedagogical mainstream should bear significant fruit.

In addition, it is important that faculty clearly *acknowledge and respond— proactively or reactively—to situations, comments, and actions that reflect institutional and personal forms of racism, sexism, homophobism, and other forms of discrimination and bias.* Several chapters in this volume have examined some of the overt and covert ways that students of different identity groups typically relate with one another in the classroom and how faculty members respond to occasional scenes of conflict. Faculty members may be able to head off some negative patterns and incidents by establishing, with students' help, a set of "guidelines" for classroom discussion and interaction. Proactively anticipating and challenging negative and exclusionary patterns (e.g., segregated seating arrangements, monocultural study/work teams, white and male assumptions of entitlement to greater air time and instructor attention, mutual awkwardness) and especially responding actively to overt and covert patterns or incidents (e.g., statements about assumed backgrounds or competencies, name calling, exclusion) is essential. This can be done in ways that are simultaneously challenging and supportive with respect to guidelines of civil exchange and respect in interaction and communication. Nevertheless, "hot moments" will occur, and faculty must be prepared to deal with them and their own concerns about losing control constructively and to use the passion involved in these situations as openings for student growth (Warren 2005; and see chapters 5, 6, 7, and 9).

When adopting multicultural or social justice–oriented teaching pedagogies, faculty often use strategies that surface or consciously raise "cognitive dissonance" between students' incoming attitudes and knowledge of the world as it really is. As a result, faculty engaging in such efforts must be prepared for student resistance (as well as, perhaps, their own). As Wagner (2005, 261–62) argues, pedagogy that undertakes to explore the personal and experiential meaning of racial and gender power and privilege "deviates from the norms of the academy and therefore may be expected to evoke significant resistance, both from students and, more broadly, others situated at varying levels of the academic hierarchy." Strong emotional reactions from students who are unsettled by this approach may raise defenses and work against the very aims of the faculty member. But Wagner (2005) and Gillespie, Ashbaugh, and DeFiore (2002) argue, first, that such unsettlement is essential to the learning process and, second, that faculty should deliberately prepare students for such resistance, indicating that it is a typical response from members of privileged groups.

Portions of chapter 1's discussion of some of the cultural traditions that mark the current higher educational system are illustrated in table 12.1, which summarizes some of the choices involved in more or less multicultural forms of curricular content and pedagogy. In a monocultural approach to pedagogy and the classroom the decisions about classroom content or subject matter of the course is the exclusive concern of the faculty member. Similarly, choices of instructional tactics and interaction patterns are set by the faculty member and are usually rooted in conscious or unconscious enmeshment in or commitment to the dominant white male culture that pervades the larger educational culture and organization. In a transitional approach the instructor is attentive to students' varied cultural identities and styles (and probably his or her own as well) and attempts to be inclusive and adopt a variety of culturally responsive pedagogical tactics. The curriculum may attend to alternative cultural standpoints and some attention is paid to the ways in which students interact in class as well as to the ways students' race and gender may affect such interactions. In a more multi-cultural approach educators pay deliberate, proactive, and sustained attention to how issues of race and gender can or do play out and use alternative teaching and learning styles that are responsive to the needs and desires of varied cultural groups and that help empower all students in the learning process. A colearning environment may be established that seeks to combine academic knowledge with students' personal experiences.

It is clear that these principles must be implemented differently in different institutional, disciplinary, and classroom contexts. What is possible to do varies with the nature of the collegiate institution: large, research-oriented multiversities exist in a different environment and have different goals and resources than do small liberal arts colleges, and urban colleges have different demographics than do rural colleges. And large, lecture-type classes can be organized to deal with these issues differently than can small, discussion-oriented seminars. In some settings these issues can be raised only subtly, perhaps in ways that focus more on norms of classroom participation and engagement than in relation to the content of instruction. Moreover, disciplines such as sociology and psychology deal with subject matters that can approach these issues more directly and as part of the formal curriculum, contrasted with disciplines such as chemistry and physics, for example. In almost any setting, however, the introduction of such content and pedagogical processes can facilitate students' ability to deal with one another and course materials.

Organizational Options

The primary task faced by faculty members committed to challenging discrimination and promoting multiculturalism is to build caring classrooms and faculty communities in the midst of an academic culture of individualism, occasional ignorance, slights (perhaps unintended but institutionally embedded), outright bias or disregard, and considerable competition. This requires attention not only to issues of faculty development (both in terms of knowledge and pedagogical skills) but also to issues of organizational development—to changes in the cultures, structures, and policies of the institution. As Jackson (2005, 5) notes about contemporary institutions' efforts to respond to diversity: "They have come to recognize that individual consciousness-raising, education and behavioral change in support of social justice and diversity must be approached in the context of a set of changes for the whole campus (or system)."

Over and above what they wish for students, faculty must create climates that can support their own pedagogical innovations and social justice efforts. This requires organizational changes at all levels of the institution, ones that alter the monocultural or transitional nature of the collegiate organization; reduce subtle and obvious as well as intentional and unintentional forms of discrimination; and challenge the micro-aggressions so commonly experienced by women faculty and faculty of color, the fears and ignorance expressed by many white and men faculty, and the norms and reward structures that so often relegate teaching and service to second- or third-class status. Chapters 4, 8, and 10 in this volume provide detail on some of these challenges—especially those faced by

Table 12.1 A Model for Multicultural Course Change: Examining Course Components

Component	Stage of Course Development		
	Exclusive (Monocultural)	Inclusive (Transitional)	Transformed (Multicultural)
Content	Gives traditional mainstream experiences and perspectives Adds authors from different backgrounds who confirm traditional perspectives or support stereotypes	Adds alternative perspectives through materials, readings, speakers Analyzes historical exclusion of alternative perspectives	Reconceptualizes the content through a shift in paradigm or approach Presents content through nondominant perspective
Instructional strategies and activities	Mainly lecture and other didactic methods Question-and-answer discussions Instructor as purveyor of knowledge	Instructor as purveyor of knowledge but uses a variety of methods to relate new knowledge to previous experience, engage students in constructing knowledge, build critical thinking skills, and encourage peer learning	Change in power structure so students and instructor learn from each other Methods center on student experience and knowledge, such as analyzing concepts against personal experience
Assessment of student knowledge	Primarily examinations and papers	Multiple methods and alternatives to standard exams and papers, perhaps with student choice	Alternatives that focus on student growth: action-oriented projects, self-assessment, reflection on the course
Classroom dynamics	Focus exclusively on content Avoidance of social issues in classroom Minimal student participation	Acknowledgement and processing of social issues in classroom Promoting equity in student participation	Challenging of biased views and sharing of diverse perspectives Ensuring equity in student participation

*(Adapted from Charbeneau 2009)

195

colleagues of color and women colleagues—and several other chapters describe actions some faculty have taken or may take to deal with them. Vigorous and effective responses to such challenges can improve the quality of education and social life provided for students of all races/ethnicities, genders, class origins, ability statuses, sexual orientations, and religions. They also can ameliorate the pain and struggle many faculty members report regarding the ways in which collegiate life is different for many white women and people of color than it is for most white men. Substantial research and informal commentary points to one of the most important differences, the heavier service load (and sometimes heavier teaching load) reported by white women faculty and men and women faculty of color (see chapter 10). The consistency and persistence of these reports about unequal loads and their effect on faculty research productivity raises questions about the need to alter some of the subtly discriminatory as well as toxic departmental climates that exist as well as some traditional standards for merit reviews and promotions.

Despite the power of contemporary monocultural norms and discriminatory practices, it is clear that innovative approaches to the classroom and organizational cultures and practices described herein are occurring on campuses throughout the nation. One increasingly common approach is the creation of faculty development programs that focus not only on curricular and pedagogical innovations but also on the relationships and social support systems among faculty members and on changes in the academy's organizational structures and policies. Given the power of organizational norms (see chapter 1), faculty development efforts cannot be successful and sustained without complementary efforts at organizational development/change, especially with regard to diversity-related issues.

A number of the earlier comments from faculty support this emphasis on not only the development of alternative pedagogical approaches but also more supportive forms of collegiality and restructuring of the system of rewards for multicultural teaching. After all, if a collegiate culture does not vigorously support and reward teaching as a priority, it certainly will not recognize and reward teaching innovations that support a social justice agenda. In these circumstances faculty development programs will not effectively challenge some of the academy's core norms and traditions, and only relatively few creative outliers will undertake this challenge.

It is difficult to meet the challenges of effective teaching alone, and groups of colleagues working together can not only support one another but also create greater leverage for organizational change. Eliker and colleagues (2009) report on an innovative format for training graduate student instructors for "multiculturally inclusive teaching" but indicate that even some committed participants in this program failed to implement new materials and processes in their classrooms. This is a common critique of many faculty development programs and draws attention to the limits of purely educational approaches to faculty change. Without a supportive and even demanding peer/departmental culture, faculty members are not likely to alter their pedagogical approaches, especially not on issues as sensitive as race and gender inequality/injustice.

In many institutions faculty committed to teaching effectively in diverse classrooms and to a more equitable organizational climate have formed informal (and often invisible) communities dedicated to supporting and (re)educating one another. Such networks are potential antidotes to those toxic environments in which faculty of color and white women faculty encounter "undervaluation of their research interests, approaches and theoretical frameworks, and challenges to their credentials and intellect in the classroom ... isolation, perceived biases in the hiring process, unrealistic expectations of doing their work and being representatives of their group, and accent discrimination" (Turner, Gonzalez, and Wood 2008, 143). Such networking and alliance-building may lead to attempts to alter the peer culture, challenge traditional institutional norms, and create a "teaching counterculture." One example is precisely the network of colleagues on one campus who are recognized for their efforts and represented in the sample of faculty members interviewed in this study, some of whose change-oriented actions are reported in chapter 11. Kaplan and Reed (2005) report on another network venture that was assisted by consultants or counselors, some of whom were faculty development staff members and others were faculty colleagues.

Another typical component of such networks, whether formally formed as an institutional agenda or flowing from developing relationships, is mentoring programs. It appears especially important that support networks and mentoring problems focus not only on general issues but directly on some of the particular issues faced—or faced in more extreme fashion—by white women faculty and men and women faculty of color, such as those issues discussed above.

And if colleges and universities are to go beyond appreciating or accepting the work styles and priorities of white women faculty and men and women faculty of color (which themselves would be positive steps forward from the current status of marginalization) and truly incorporate them, it likely would require new standards for promotion and tenure. As Turner, Gonzalez, and Wood (2008, 149–50) summarize in their review of several decades of research on faculty diversity in higher education, "The literature described new and/or alternative ways of thinking, teaching, writing and just being an academic brought to higher education by current faculty of color. Their new approaches to research, teaching and service are, in many cases, in conflict with traditional approaches leading to poor evaluations and lack of publications. . . . as the faculty diversifies and brings to the academy different ways of knowing, it is important that they be given the opportunity for individual expression." In addition to serving the interests of minority faculty, such embrace might broaden the culture of the academy beyond its historic reliance on Western, white, and male academic standards, thus challenging more of the core norms and traditions of our contemporary higher education system (see also Misra et al. 2011).

Beyond a direct focus on individual faculty members or clusters of colleagues, the forthright actions of senior faculty and administrators can affect the organizational climate. Such collegiate leaders can advocate, sponsor, model, support, and monitor the movement toward a more positive climate for diversity. Students, faculty, and staff need this leadership both in the forms of challenge and of support—push and pull, rewards and sanctions. Presidents and executive officers must make their commitments clear well beyond rhetoric, and deans, chairs, directors, senior and middle managers, and senior faculty must follow suit. Change at every level of the organization—schools or colleges, departments, classrooms, staff units, dormitories and living units—will require the exercise of power in many arenas, with adequate resources and multicultural task teams. Moreover, although such leadership from above is crucial, it is not sufficient; grassroots involvement is required as well, with support, incentives, and empowered action by many people and groups throughout the institution. Because mobilization by students often precedes the faculty and administration on these issues, collaboration with students' energy, experience, and wisdom is essential for this change process—doing not *for* them or *to* them but rather *with* them.

Table 12.2 provides a description of some varied organizational contexts in which teaching takes place and what diversity advocates might consider in developing and supporting a multicultural pedagogical environment. This table can be used both as a diagnostic and prescriptive tool: it can help assess an institution's relative commitment to a multicultural or socially just environment and can help guide a vision for which advocates might strive. The eight organizational dimensions all affect what faculty do, do not do, can imagine doing, and are rewarded or sanctioned for doing in the classroom and in their departments. They represent options related to the core norms of higher educational systems reviewed in chapter 1. Changes that seek environments for more effective teaching and learning involve moving from a monocultural to a multicultural framework along these dimensions. Such change can lead to a more accepting rather than a hostile or indifferent institutional culture for such teaching, research, and service.

Undertaking a critically multicultural or social justice change effort involves attention to a wide range of organizational issues, including membership patterns, local cultures, climates, structures and styles of decision making and power, and resources. It also requires anticipating and planning to deal with conflict and resistance, because such multicultural change efforts challenge the traditional culture in which most members of the academy—faculty, administrative staffs,

Table 12.2 Organizational Stages on the Path to Multiculturalism*

Organizational Dimension	Monocultural	Transitional	Multicultural
		Stage	
Mission	Deliberate exclusion of diverse issues and people Exclusive focus on Western tradition	Diverse student and faculty membership sought Diversity and educational quality are linked	Diverse student and faculty body and service to underrepresented groups valued Diversity and academic excellence are linked Global and social justice perspective advocated Need expressed for change in societal arrangements
Culture	White, male, and Eurocentric norms prevail Prejudice and discrimination unquestioned and prevail Assimilation into dominant traditions encouraged Individual merit and responsibility for performance emphasized	White and male norms questioned but prevail Prejudice and discrimination lessened but continue Comfort/tolerance for minorities sought Group identities reified in separate student groupings/programs	Campus incidents of discrimination constantly confronted publicly and negatively sanctioned Alternative norms embraced White, male, and Eurocentric symbols changed Group identities synthesized with a transcendent community

table continues

Table 12.2 Organizational Stages on the Path to Multiculturalism (continued)

Organizational Dimension	Stage		
	Monocultural	Transitional	Multicultural
Power	White and male throughout	A few minority members reach middle staff and faculty levels	Multicultural teams of faculty and staff leaders
	Others excluded or at the bottom of faculty/staff ranks	White and male leaders sponsor minority and women faculty/staff	Relatively flat and multilevel decision making, with wide access, including students
	Access to "the club" limited	Narrow access to positions of power	Different decisional styles valued
	Strong hierarchy	Conflict occurs between change advocates and power holders	Multiple centers of power engaged
	No designated responsibility for diversity agenda in admissions, hiring, retention, advancement	Special staff/office for diversity programs	Multicultural initiative in all units/levels seen as line function
		Bureaucratic innovations undertaken	Departments/colleges accountable for progress on minority hiring, success
Membership	Exclusionary	Minority recruitment office exists	Plural representation guaranteed
	Token minority presence	Culturally assimilated minorities and women included	Plural sense of community
Social relations/social climate	Segregated social events	Distant but cordial intergroup relations	Proactive inclusiveness in class, dorms, and external relations
	Communication occurs within racial/gender groups	Informal circles open to assimilated minorities	Homogeneous and heterogeneous student and faculty groupings coexist
	No external intergroup contact	Communication on deeply held issues mostly within social identity groups	Much communication across race/gender lines
	Lack of trust across group boundaries	Some external intergroup social contact	Conflict resolution mechanisms widespread
	Emphasis on order and low level of conflict	Cooperation and conflict occur among identity groups	
	Traditional management and meeting style	Attention to intergroup processes	

Technology	Curriculum rooted in Western and classic traditions People required to adapt to the existing technology, which is seen as culture-neutral Segregated work and study teams common Traditional definitions of research excellence prevail	Discussion occurs about ways traditional pedagogy may not fit/serve/reflect diverse groups' needs/styles/histories Desegregated work teams occur Cultural critiques surface of established research and teaching methods Innovative curricular designs supported	New pedagogies adapt to diverse groups' needs/styles and contributions Integrated work teams cherished Curricula responsible to different groups' traditions/histories Active pursuit of plural forms of research responsive to minority communities and their epistemologies
Resources	No special funds for diversity programs Traditional recruitment paths and admissions criteria	Special funds for diversity events Recruitment focused on promising people of color and women Retention efforts focused on minorities Alternative admissions criteria	Diverse membership a priority Multicultural programs built into unit budgets Multicultural retention and mentoring programs common Multiculturalism a priority for resource development/use Funds available for students in need
Boundary management	Traditional separations of work and home No external socializing with diverse peoples Fit in external market and cultures is a priority	Changing demographics of markets/clients/suppliers/members recognized Support for external socializing Contradictions and conflicts in local community life acknowledged	Work and home conflicts resolved creatively Minority suppliers and markets sought New external cultures and municipal policies advocated Global focus Multicultural vision and mission exported to peer institutions

(Chesler, Lewis, and Crowfoot 2005, 70–72, reprinted and adapted with permission from Rowman and Littlefield) and students—have been trained and in which they are accustomed to operating. Institutional transformation does not have to be a consensual change process; indeed, it cannot be, and, in any event, little in the academy is consensual. Reasonable disagreement is to be expected and respected—not obliterated, but respected and countered. As in the classroom, advocates can take advantage of the inevitable conflicts and crises that will occur and use the friction of these teachable moments to create the fire for organizational change.

The literature on organizational change in higher education, especially with regard to issues of diversity and multiculturalism, suggests some core elements of successful systemic change efforts (Adams, Bell, and Griffin 2010; Chesler, Lewis, and Crowfoot 2005; Law, Phillips, and Turney 2004; Smith et al. 2002). Chesler, Lewis, and Crowfoot (2005) summarize these elements as follows:

1. development of a clear vision of desired changes and the linkage of this vision to the organization's mission, core values, and strategic plans—otherwise innovative efforts are likely to be marginalized or rejected;
2. conduct and use of an organizational assessment or audit, one that can identify critical problems, the existence of exclusionary or discriminatory policies and practices, potential "best practices," and potential levers of change (allies);
3. selection of particular change strategies, including both top-down or formal administrative leadership and bottom-up or informal advocacy, potentially combining education and awareness programs, skill development opportunities, persuasion efforts, pressure campaigns, and taking advantage of the opportunities that critical incidents and crises offer;
4. mobilization of resources that permit implementation of change plans and strategies, including resources such as people (administrators, faculty, students, alumni, interest groups—especially aggrieved interest groups and organizational and civic elites), funds, release time and energy, institutional leadership and support, and new ideas or documentations of best practices;
5. actual action steps—not just talking and planning; and
6. ongoing monitoring and assessment that permits corrections and points the way for continued cycles of multicultural change.

These elements constitute an iterative process, neither linear nor finite: as the cycles of change are initiated, progress will occur unevenly along the eight organizational dimensions, and progress and regress will occur constantly.

There is much more to do in transforming the larger organizational culture and operational patterns of our colleges and universities for everyone's benefit. Sánchez-Casal (2002) argues that members of both dominant and marginalized groups must collaborate and ally together as equals in order to create transformative projects. And, we think, such transformative projects, in the form of new and more plural, interactive, and justice-oriented pedagogies and colleagueships, are required to create transformative knowledge and relationships. These outcomes can only arise from the dedicated and legitimated engagement with and integration of multiple and intersecting narratives as well as traditional and oppositional stances, both in and out of classrooms and departments.

References

Adams, M., L. Bell, and P. Griffin, eds. 2010. *Teaching for Diversity and Social Justice,* 2nd ed. New York: Routledge.

ADVANCE. 2002. *Assessing the Academic Work Environment for Women Scientists and Engineers.* Ann Arbor: University of Michigan Institute for Research on Women and Gender.

———. 2008. *Assessing the Academic Work Environment for Science and Engineering and Social Science Faculty at the University of Michigan in 2006: Gender, Race and Discipline in Retention-Relevant Career Experiences.* Women Scientists and Engineers. Ann Arbor: University of Michigan Institute for Research on Women and Gender.

Aguirre, A. Jr. 2000. "Women and Minority Faculty in the Academic Workplace: Recruitment, Retention, and Academic Culture." Washington, DC: ERIC Clearinghouse on Higher Education.

Akbar, N. 2002. "The Psychological Dilemma of African American Academicians." In *Making It on Broken Promises: Leading African American Male Scholars Confront the Culture of Higher Education,* edited by L. Jones, 32–41. Sterling, VA: Stylus Publishing.

Alfred, M. 2001. "Success in the Ivory Tower: Lessons from Black Tenured Female Faculty at a Major Research University." In *Sisters of the Academy: Emergent Black Women Scholars in Higher Education,* edited by O. Mabokela and A. Green, 56–79. Sterling, VA: Stylus Publishing.

Allen, W. 1988. "The Education of Black Students on White Campuses: What Quality the Experience?" In *Toward Black Undergraduate Student Equality in American Higher Education,* edited by M. Nettles, 57–86. Westport, CT: Greenwood Press.

Andersen, M., and P. Collins, eds. 1992. *Race, Class, and Gender: An Anthology.* Belmont, CA: Wadsworth.

Anderson, J., and M. Adams. 1992. "Acknowledging the Learning Styles of Diverse Student Populations: Implications for Instructional Design." *New Directions for Teaching and Learning* 49: 19–33.

Anderson, L., and J. Carta-Falsa. 2002. "Factors That Make Faculty and Student Relationships Effective." *College Teaching* 50, no. 4: 134–38.

Antonio, A. 2001. "Diversity and the Influence of Friendship Groups in College." *Review of Higher Education* 25, no. 1: 63–89.

———. 2002. "Faculty of Color Reconsidered: Reassessing Contributions to Scholarship." *The Journal of Higher Education* 73, no. 5: 582–602.

Antonio, A., H. Astin, and C. Cress. 2000. "Community Service in Higher Education: A Look at the Nation's Faculty." *The Review of Higher Education* 23: 373–89.

Aronson, E., N. Blaney, C. Stephan, J. Sikes, and M. Snapp. 1978. *The Jigsaw Classroom.* Beverly Hills, CA: Sage Publications.

Aronson, J., C. and Steele. 2005. "Stereotypes and the Fragility of Academic Competence, Motivation and Self-Concept." In *Handbook of Competence and Motivation,* edited by A. Elliot and C. Dweck, 436–56. New York: Guilford Press.

Association of American Colleges and Universities. 2002. *Greater Expectations: A New Vision for Learning as a Nation Goes to College.* Washington, DC: Association of American Colleges and Universities.

Astin, H., A. Antonio, C. Cress, and A. Astin. 1997. *Race and Ethnicity in the American Professoriate: 1995–1996.* Los Angeles, CA: University of California Press.

Auster, C., and M. MacRone. 1994. "The Classroom as a Negotiated Setting: An Empirical Study of the Effect of Faculty Members' Behavior on Student Participation." *Teaching Sociology* 22: 289–99.

Balderrama, M., M. Texiera, and E. Valdez. 2006. "Una Luchera de Fronteras [A Struggle of Borders]: Women of Color in the Academy." In *From Oppression to Grace: Women of Color and Their Dilemmas in the Academy,* edited by T. Berry and N. Mizelle, 209–32. Sterling, VA: Stylus Publishing.

Baszile, D. 2006. "In This Place Where I Don't Quite Belong: Claiming the Ontoepistemological In Between." In *From Oppression to Grace: Women of Color and their Dilemmas Within the Academy,* edited by T. Berry and N. Mizelle, 195–208. Sterling, VA: Stylus Publishing.

Bavishi, A., J. Madera, and M. Hebl. 2010. "The Effect of Professors' Ethnicity and Gender on Student Evaluations: Judged Before Met." *Journal of Diversity in Higher Education* 3, no. 4: 245–56.

Beale, R., and D. Schoem. 2001. "The Content/Process Balance in Intergroup Dialogue." In *Intergroup Dialogue: Deliberative Democracy in School, College, Community, and Workplace,* edited by D. Schoem and S. Hurtado, 266–80. Ann Arbor: University of Michigan Press.

Bell, L., S. Washington, G. Weinstein, and B. Love. 2010. "Knowing Ourselves as Social Justice Educators." In *Teaching for Diversity and Social Justice.* 2nd ed., edited by M. Adams, L. Bell and P. Griffin, 381–94. New York: Routledge.

Bellas, M., and R. Toutkoushian. 1999. "Faculty Time Allocations and Research Productivity: Gender, Race and Family Effects." *The Review of Higher Education* 22, no. 4: 367–90.

Berger, P., and T. Luckmann. 1967. *The Social Construction of Identity: A Treatise in the Sociology of Knowledge.* Garden City, NY: Anchor Books.

Berry, T., and N. Mizelle, eds. 2006. *From Oppression to Grace: Women of Color and Their Dilemmas in the Academy.* Sterling, VA: Stylus Publishing.

Bernal, D. 1998. "Using a Chicana Feminist Epistemology in Educational Research." *Harvard Educational Review* 68, no. 4: 555–82.

Bilimoria, D., S. Perry, X. Liang, P. Higgins, and V. Taylor. 2006. "How Do Female and Male Faculty Members Construct Job Satisfaction: The Role of Perceived Institutional Leadership and Mentoring and Their Mediating Processes." *Journal of Technology Transfer* 31: 355–65.

Bird, S. 1996. "Welcome to the Men's Club: Homosociality and the Maintenance of Hegemonic Masculinity." *Gender and Society* 10: 120–32.

Black, L. 1995. "Stupid, Rich Bastards." In *This Fine Place So Far from Home,* edited by B. Dews and C. Law, 263–75. Philadelphia, PA: Temple University Press.

Blumer, H. 1969. *Symbolic Interactionism: Perspectives and Methods.* Englewood Cliffs, NJ: Prentice-Hall.

Bobo, L., J. Kluegel, and R. Smith. 1997. "Laissez-Faire Racism: The Crystallization of a 'Kinder, Gentler' Anti-Black Ideology." In *Racial Attitudes in the 1990s: Continuity and Change,* edited by S. Tuch and J. Martin, 14–42. Westport, CT: Prager.

Bonilla-Silva, E. 2001. *White Supremacy and Racism in the Post-Civil Rights Era.* Boulder, CO: Lynne Rienner Publishers.

———. 2006. *Racism Without Racists: Color-Blind Racism and the Persistence of Racial Inequality in the United States,* 2nd ed. Lanham, MD: Rowman and Littlefield Publishers.

Bonilla-Silva, E., and T. Forman. 2000. "'I'm Not a Racist But…': Mapping College Students' Racial Ideology in the USA." *Discourse and Society* 11: 50–85.

Bordo, S. 1993. *Unbearable Weight: Feminism, Western Culture, and the Body.* Berkeley: University of California Press.

Boudreau, B., and T. Eggleston. 2002. "Traps, Pitfalls, and Obstacles: Challenges to Confronting Racism in Academia." In *Race in the College Classroom: Pedagogy and Politics,* edited by B. TuSmith and M. Reddy, 200–9. Piscataway, NJ: Rutgers University Press.

Bourdieu, P. 1990. *The Logic of Practice.* Cambridge, MA: Polity Press.

Bowman, N. 2010. "Disequilibrium and Resolution: The Nonlinear Effects of Diversity Courses on Well-Being and Orientations Toward Diversity." *The Review of Higher Education* 33, no. 4: 543–68.

Boysen, G., D. Vogel, M. Cope, and A. Hubbard. 2009. "Incidents of Bias in College Classrooms: Instructor and Student Perceptions." *Journal of Diversity in Higher Education* 2, no. 4: 219–31.

Brekhus, W. 1998. "A Sociology of the Unmarked: Redirecting Our Focus." *Sociological Theory* 16, no. 1: 34–51.

Brouwer, N., and F. Korthagen. 2005. "Can Teacher Education Make a Difference?" *American Educational Research Journal* 42, no. 1: 153–224.

Butler, J. 1990. *Gender Trouble: Feminism and the Subversion of Identity.* New York: Routledge.

Callister, R. 2006. "The Impact of Gender and Departmental Climate on Job Satisfactions and Intentions to Quit for Faculty in Science and Engineering Fields." *Journal of Technology Transfer* 31: 367–75.

Carrigan, T., R. Connell, and J. Lee. 1985. "Toward a New Theory of Masculinity." *Theory and Society* 14, 552–604.

Castellanos, J., and L. Jones, eds. 2003. *The Majority in the Minority: Expanding the Representation of Latino/a Faculty, Administrators and Students in Higher Education.* Sterling, VA: Stylus Publishing.

Centra, J., and N. Gaubatz. 2000. "Is There a Gender Bias in Students' Evaluations of Teaching?" *Journal of Higher Education* 71, no. 1: 17–33.

Charbeneau, J. 2009. "The Intersection of White Racial Identity with Pedagogical Practices in Higher Education: White Faculty Teaching in Diverse Classrooms." Unpublished PhD diss., University of Michigan, Ann Arbor.

Charmaz, K. 2005. *Constructing Grounded Theory: A Practical Guide Through Qualitative Analysis.* Thousand Oaks, CA: Sage Publications.

Chesler, M., A. Lewis, and J. Crowfoot. 2005. *Challenging Racism in Higher Education: Promoting Justice.* New York. Rowman and Littlefield.

Chesler, N., and M. Chesler. 2002. "Gender-Informed Mentoring Strategies for Women Engineering Scholars: On Establishing a 'Caring Community'." *Journal of Engineering Education* 91, no. 1: 49–55.

Chin, J. 2002. "(Re)Framing the Issues—Changing Pedagogy, Not Students: A Conversation with Mark Chesler." In *Included in Sociology: Learning Climates That Cultivate Racial and Ethnic Diversity,* edited by J. Chin, C. Berheide and D. Rome, 21–25. Washington, DC: American Association for Higher Education.

Chism, N., and K. Whitney. 2005. "It Takes a Campus: Situating Professional Development Efforts Within a Campus Diversity Program." In *Teaching Inclusively: Resources for Courses, Departments and Institutional Change in Higher Education,* edited by M. Ouellett, 34–45. Stillwater, OK: New Forums Press.

Chronicle of Higher Education, The. 2011. "Race and Ethnicity of Full-Time Faculty Members at More Than 1500 Institutions." September 30.

Clatterbaugh, K. 1996. *Contemporary Perspectives on Masculinity: Men, Women and Politics in Modern Society.* Boulder, CO: Westview Press.

Cleveland, D., ed. 2004. *A Long Way to Go: Conversations about Race by African American Faculty and Graduate Students.* New York: Peter Lang Publishing Group.

Coleman, J. 1990. *Foundations of Social Theory.* Cambridge, MA: Harvard University Press.

Collins, P. 1986. "Learning from the Outsider Within: The Sociological Significance of Black Feminist Thought." *Social Problems* 33: 14–32.

———. 1998. "Race, Class and Gender: Common Bonds, Different Voices." *Ethnic and Racial Studies* 21, no. 1: 175–77.

———. 2004. *Black Sexual Politics: African Americans, Gender, and the New Racism.* New York: Routledge.

Collinson, D., and J. Hearn. 1994. "Naming Men as Men: Implications for Work, Organizations and Management." *Gender, Work and Organizations* 1: 2–22.

Connell, R. 1995. *Masculinities.* Sydney, Australia: Allen and Unwin.

———. 2000. *The Men and the Boys.* St. Leonards, NSW, Australia: Allen and Unwin.

Connell, R., and J. Messerschmidt. 2005. "Hegemonic Masculinity: Rethinking the Concept." *Gender and Society* 19: 829–59.

Conway-Jones, D. 2006. "Being All Things to All People: Expectations of and Demands on Women of Color in the Legal Academy." In *From Oppression to Grace: Women of Color and Their Dilemmas in the Academy,* edited by T. Berry and N. Mizelle, 121–30. Sterling, VA: Stylus Publishing.

Cooley, C. 1902. *Human Nature and the Social Order.* New York: Scribner and Sons. (Revised ed., 1922).

Creamer, E. 2006. "Policies That Part: Early Career Experiences of Coworking Academic Couples." In *The Balancing Act: Gendered Perspectives in Faculty Roles and Work Lives,* edited by S. Bracken, J. Allen, and D. Dean, 73–90. Sterling, VA: Stylus Publishing.

Crenshaw, K. 1995. *Critical Race Theory: The Key Writings that Informed the Movement.* New York: New Press.

Cross, J., and E. Goldenberg. 2009. *Off Track Profs: Nontenured Teachers in Higher Education.* Cambridge, MA: MIT Press.

Darder, A. 1991. *Culture and Power in the Classroom.* Westport, CT: Bergin and Harvey.

Dawe, A. 1978. "Theories of Social Action." In *A History of Sociological Analysis,* edited by T. Bottomore and R. Nisbet, 362–418. New York: Basic Books.

Delgado-Romero, E., L. Flores, A. Gloria, A. Arredondo, and J. Castellanos. 2003. "Developmental Career Challenges for Latina/o Faculty in Higher Education." In *The Majority in the Minority: Expanding the Representation of Latina/o Faculty, Adminstrators and Students in Higher Education,* edited by J. Castellanos and L. Jones, 284–97. Sterling, VA: Stylus Publishing.

DeLoria, P. 1998. *Playing Indian.* New Haven, CT: Yale University Press.

Dews, B., and C. Law, eds. 1995. *This Fine Place so Far from Home.* Philadelphia, PA: Temple University Press.

Doane, A. 2003. "Rethinking Whiteness Studies." In *White Out: The Continuing Significance of Racism,* edited by A. Doane and E. Bonilla-Silva, 1–18. New York: Routledge.

Dovidio, J., and S. Gaertner. 2004. "Aversive Racism." *Advances in Experimental Social Psychology* 36: 1–52.

Duderstadt, J. 2007. *The Michigan Mandate: Looking Back and Looking Forward.* Ann Arbor: University of Michigan Press.

Duster, T. 1991. *The Diversity Project.* Berkeley, CA: University of California at Berkeley Institute for the Study of Social Change.

Eliker, J., M. Thompson, A. Snell, and A. O'Malley. 2009. "A Framework and Follow-Up Observation for Multiculturally Inclusive Teaching." *Journal of Diversity in Higher Education* 2, no. 2: 63–77.

Emerson, R., R. Fretz, and L. Shaw. 1995. *Writing Ethnographic Fieldnotes.* Chicago: University of Chicago Press.

Emirbayer, M., and J. Goodwin. 1994. "Network Analysis, Culture, and the Problem of Agency." *American Journal of Sociology* 99, no. 6: 1411–54.

Emirbayer, M., and A. Mische. 1998. "What Is Agency?" *American Journal of Sociology* 104: 962–1023.

Essien, V. 2003. "Visible and Invisible Barriers to the Incorporation of Faculty of Color in Predominantly White Law Schools." *Journal of Black Studies* 34, no. 1: 63–71.

Feagin, J. 2000. *Racist America: Roots, Current Realities and Future Reparations*. New York: Routledge.

Feagin, J., and C. Feagin. 1986. *Discrimination American Style*. Englewood Cliffs, NJ: Prentice-Hall.

Feagin, J., and H. Vera. 1995. *White Racism*. New York: Routledge.

Feagin, J., H. Vera, and N. Imani, 1996. *The Agony of Education: Black Students at White Colleges and Universities*. New York: Routledge.

Fenstermaker, S., and C. West. 2002. *Doing Gender, Doing Difference: Inequality, Power, and Institutional Change*. New York: Routledge.

Fiske, S., A. Cuddy, P. Glick, and J. Xu. 2002. "A Model of (Often Mixed) Stereotype Content: Competence and Warmth Respectively Follow from Perceived Status and Competition." *Journal of Personality and Social Psychology* 82, no. 6: 878–902.

Flagg, B. 1993. "Was Blind but Now I See: White Race Consciousness and the Requirement of Discriminatory Intent." *Michigan Law Review* 91: 953–56.

Forman, T., and A. Lewis. 2006. "Racial Apathy and Hurricane Katrina: The Social Anatomy of Prejudice in the Post–Civil-Rights Era." *DuBois Review* 3, no. 1: 175–202.

Fox, H. 2009. *"When Race Breaks Out": Conversations about Race and Racism in College Classrooms*. New York: Peter Lang Publishing Group.

Frankenberg, R. 1993. *White Women, Race Matters*. Minneapolis: University of Minnesota Press.

Freire, P. 1970. *Pedagogy of the Oppressed*. New York: Seabury.

Fuchs, S. 2001. "Beyond Agency " *Sociological Theory* 19, no. 1:24-40..

Gallagher, C. 2003. "White Reconstruction in the University." In *Privilege,* edited by M. Kimmel and Abby Ferber, 299–318. Boulder, CO: Westview Press.

Giddens, A. 1984. *The Constitution of Society*. Cambridge, MA: Polity Press.

Gillespie, D., L. Ashbaugh, and J. DeFiore. 2002. "White Women Teaching White Women about White Privilege, Race Cognizance and Social Action: Toward a Pedagogical Pragmatics." *Race Ethnicity and Education* 5, no. 3: 237–53.

Giroux, H. (1997. "Racial Politics and the Pedagogy of Whiteness." In *Whiteness: A Critical Reader,* edited by M. Hill, 294–315. New York: New York University Press.

Gitli, G. 2002. "Menaced by Resistance: The Black Teaching in the Mainly White School/ Classroom." In *Race in the College Classroom: Pedagogy and Politics,* edited by TuSmith, B., and M. Reddy, 176–188. New Brunswick, NJ: Rutgers University Press.

Glaser, B., and A. Strauss. 1976. *The Discovery of Grounded Theory: Strategies for Qualitative Research*. Chicago: Aldine Publishing Company.

Goffman, E. 1963. *Stigma: Notes on the Management of Spoiled Identity*. Englewood Cliffs, NJ: Prentice-Hall.

Goodman, D. 1995. "Difficult Dialogues: Enhancing Discussions about Diversity." *College Teaching* 43, no. 2: 47–52.

Graff, G. 1992. *Beyond the Culture Wars: How Teaching the Conflicts Can Revitalize American Education*. New York: Norton.

Grahame, K. 2004. "Contesting Diversity in the Academy: Resistance to Women of Color Teaching Race, Class and Gender." *Race, Gender and Class* 11, no. 3: 54–73.

Gramsci, A. 1971. *Selections from the Prison Notebooks.* New York: International Publishers.

Grazian, D. 2005. *Blue Chicago: The Search for Authenticity in Urban Blues Clubs.* Chicago: University of Chicago Press.

Guiffrida, D. 2005. "Other Mothering as a Framework for Understanding African American Students' Definitions of Student-Centered Faculty." *Journal of Higher Education* 76, no. 6: 701–23.

Gunning, S. 2000. "Now That They Have Us, What's the Point?" In *Power, Race, and Gender in Academe: Strangers in the Tower,* edited by S. Lim, M. Herrera-Sobek and G. Padilla, 171–82. New York: Modern Language Association.

Gunter, R., and A. Stambach. 2003. "As Balancing Act and as Game: How Women and Men Science Faculty Experience the Promotion Process." *Gender Issues* 21, no. 1: 24–42.

Gurin, P. 1999. "Selections from 'The Compelling Need for Diversity in Higher Education, Expert Reports in Defense of the University of Michigan: Expert Report of Patricia Gurin.'" *Equity and Excellence in Education* 32, no. 2: 37–62.

Gurin, P., E. Dey, S. Hurtado, and G. Gurin. 2002. "Diversity and Higher Education: Theory and Impact on Educational Outcomes." *Harvard Educational Review* 72, no. 8 (Fall): 330–66.

———. 2004. "The Educational Value of Diversity." In *Defending Diversity,* edited by P. Gurin, J. Lehman, and E. Lewis, 97–188. Ann Arbor: University of Michigan Press.

Gurin, P., B. Nagda, and G. Lopez. 2004. "The Benefits of Diversity in Education for Democratic Citizenship." *Journal of Social Issues* 60, no. 1: 17–34.

Gurin, P., B. Nagda, and N. Sorensen. 2011. "Intergroup Dialogue: Education for a Broad Conception of Civic Engagement." *Liberal Education* 97, no. 2 (Spring): 46–51.

Hardiman, R., and B. Jackson. 1992. "Racial Identity Development: Understanding Racial Dynamics in College Classrooms and on Campus." *New Directions for Teaching and Learning* 52: 21–28.

Harding, S. 1991. *Whose Science? Whose Knowledge? Thinking from Women's Lives.* Ithaca, NY: Cornell University Press.

Harlow, R. 2003. "'Race Doesn't Matter but … ': The Effect of Race on Professors' Experiences and Emotion Management in the Undergraduate College Classroom." *Social Psychology Quarterly* 66, no. 4: 348–63.

Harris, T. 2007. "Black Feminist Thought and Cultural Contracts: Understanding the Intersections and Negotiations of Racial, Gendered and Professional Status in the Academy." *New Directions for Teaching and Learning* 110 (Summer): 55–64.

Harris-Lacewell, M. 2001. "No Place to Rest: African American Political Attitudes and the Myth of Black Women's Strength." *Women and Politics* 23, no. 3: 1.

Harvard University. 2007. *A Compact to Enhance Teaching and Learning at Harvard, Proposed by the Task Force on Teaching and Career Development to the Faculty of Arts and Sciences.* Cambridge, MA.

Headley, C. 2004. "Delegitimizing the Normativity of Whiteness: A Critical Africana Philosophical Study of the Metaphoricity of Whiteness." In *What White Looks Like:*

African American Philosophers on the Whiteness Question, edited by G. Yancey, 87–106. New York: Routledge.

Hendrix, K. 2007. "'She Must Be Trippin': The Secret of Disrespect from Students of Color Toward Faculty of Color." *New Directions for Teaching and Learning* 110 (Summer): 85–96.

Hickcox, L. 2002. "Personalizing Teaching Through Experiential Learning." *College Teaching* 50, no. 4: 123–28.

Hobson-Horton, L. 2004. "Avoiding the Clock-Stoppers: How to Prepare for, Endure, and Survive the First Years of the Professoriate." In *A Long Way to Go: Conversations about Race by African American Faculty and Graduate Students,* edited by D. Cleveland, 94–109. New York: Peter Lang Publishing Group.

hooks, b. 1990. *Yearning: Race, Gender, and Cultural Politics.* Boston: South End Press.

hooks, b. 1994. *Teaching to Transgress: Education as the Practice of Freedom.* New York: Routledge.

Howard, G. 1999. *We Can't Teach What We Don't Know: White Teachers, Multiracial Schools.* New York: Teachers College Press.

Hubbard, S., and F. Stage. 2009. "Attitudes, Perceptions and Preferences of Faculty at Hispanic Serving and Predominantly Black Institutions." *The Journal of Higher Education* 80, no. 3: 270–89.

Hurtado, S. 2001. "Research and Evaluation on Intergroup Dialogue." In *Intergroup Dialogue: Deliberative Democracy in School, College, Community, and Workplace,* edited by D. Schoem and S. Hurtado, 22–36. Ann Arbor: University of Michigan Press.

Ibarra, R. 2003. "Latina/o Faculty and the Tenure Process in Context." In *The Majority in the Minority: Expanding the Representation of Latina/o Faculty, Administrators and Students in Higher Education,* edited by J. Castellanos and L. Jones, 207–20. Sterling, VA: Stylus Publishing.

Jackson, B. 2005. "The Theory and Practice of Multicultural Organizational Development in Education." In *Teaching Inclusively: Resources for Courses, Departments and Institutional Change in Higher Education,* edited by M. Ouellett, 3–20. Stillwater, OK: New Forums Press.

Jacobs, L. J. Cintron, and C. Canton, eds. 2002. *The Politics of Survival in Academia: Narratives of Inequality, Resilience and Success.* Lanham, MD: Rowman and Littlefield.

Jayakumar, U., T. Howard, W. Allen, and J. Han. 2009. "Racial Privilege in the Professoriate: An Exploration of Campus Climate, Retention and Satisfaction." *The Journal of Higher Education* 80, no. 5: 538–63.

Johnson, A. 2006. *Privilege, Power, and Difference.* New York: McGraw-Hill.

Johnson-Bailey, J., and R. Cervero. 2008. "Different Worlds and Different Paths: Academic Careers Defined by Race and Gender." *Harvard Educational Review* 78, no. 2: 311–34.

Johnsrud, L. 1993. "Women and Minority Faculty Experiences: Defining and Responding to Diverse Realities." *New Directions for Teaching and Learning* 53 (Spring): 3–16.

Jones, Lee, ed. 2002. *Making It on Broken Promises: Leading African American Male Scholars Confront the Culture of Higher Education.* Sterling, VA: Stylus Publishing.

Jones, Leslie. 2005. "Science in the Interest of Social Justice: Untangling the Biological Realities of Race and Gender." In *Teaching Inclusively: Resources for Courses, Departments and Institutional Change in Higher Education,* edited by M. Ouellett, 460–72. Stillwater, OK: New Forums Press.

Jones, S., V. Torres, and J. Arminio. 2006. *Negotiating the Complexities of Qualitative Research in Higher Education: Fundamental Elements Issues.* New York: Routledge.

Jordan, G., and D. Bilimoria. 2007. "Creating a Productive and Inclusive Academic Work Environment." In *Transforming Science and Engineering: Advancing Academic Women,* edited by A. Stewart, J. Malley, and D. LaVaque-Manty. Ann Arbor: University of Michigan Press.

Kane, R., S. Sandretto, and C. Heath. 2002. "Telling Half the Story: A Critical Review of Research on the Teaching Beliefs and Practices of University Academics." *Review of Educational Research* 72, no. 2: 177–228.

Kaplan. M., and B. Reed. 2005. "But How Can I Talk with Faculty about That? Approaches to Consulting around Multicultural Issues." In *Teaching Inclusively: Resources for Courses, Departments and Institutional Change in Higher Education,* edited by M. Ouellett, 366–81. Stillwater, OK: New Forums Press.

Kardia, D., and T. Sevig. 2001. "Embracing the Paradox: Dialogue that Incorporates Both Individual and Group Identities." In *Intergroup Dialogue: Deliberative Democracy in School, College, Community, and Workplace,* edited by D. Schoem and S. Hurtado, 247–65. Ann Arbor: University of Michigan Press.

Kardia, D., and M. Wright. 2003. "Gender, Identity and Teaching: What Are Students Rating?" *SWS Network News* 20, no. 1, 7–10.

Kendall, F. 2006. *Understanding White Privilege: Creating Pathways to Authentic Relationships Across Race.* New York: Routledge.

Kimmel, M. 1996. *Manhood in America: A Cultural History.* New York: The Free Press.

Kimmel, M., J. Hearn, and R. Connell, eds. 2005. *Handbook of Studies on Men and Masculinities.* Thousand Oaks, CA: Sage Publications.

Kimmel, M., and M. Messner. 2007. *Men's Lives,* 7th ed. Boston: Pearson Allyn and Bacon.

Kitano, M. 1997. "What a Course Would Look Like after Multicultural Change." In *Multicultural Course Transformation in Higher Education: A Broader Truth,* edited by A. Morrey and M. Kitano, 18–34. Needham Heights, MA: Allyn and Bacon.

Kochman, T. 1981. *Black and White: Styles in Conflict.* Chicago: University of Chicago Press.

Kolb, D. 1981. "Learning Styles and Disciplinary Differences." In *The Modern American College: Responding to the Realities of Diverse Students and a Changing Society,* edited by A. Chickering and Associates, 232–55. San Francisco, CA: Jossey-Bass.

Kolodny, A. 2000. "Raising Standards while Lowering Anxieties: Rethinking the Promotion and Tenure Process." In *Power, Race and Gender in Academe: Strangers in the Tower,* edited by S. Lim and M. Herrera-Sobek, 83–111. New York: The Modern Language Association.

Krysan, M., and R. Farley. 2002. "The Residential Preferences of Blacks: Do They Explain Persistent Segregation?" *Social Forces* 80, no. 3: 937–80.

Kumashiro, K. 2003. "Against Repetition: Addressing Resistance to Anti-Oppressive Change in the Practices of Learning, Teaching, Supervising, and Researching." In *Race and Higher Education: Rethinking Pedagogy in Diverse College Classrooms,* edited by A. Howell and F. Tuitt, 45–60. Cambridge, MA: Harvard Educational Review.

Laden, B., and L. Hagedorn. 2000. "Job Satisfaction among Faculty of Color in Academe: Individual Survivors or Institutional Transformers?" *New Directions for Institutional Research* 105: 57–66.

Lather, P. 1991. *Getting Smart: Feminist Research and Pedagogy With/in the Postmodern.* New York: Routledge.

Law, I., D. Phillips, and L. Turney. 2004. "Tackling Institutional Racism in Higher Education: An Antiracist Toolkit." In *Institutional Racism in Higher Education,* edited by I. Law, D. Phillips, and L. Turney, 93–104. Sterling, VA: Trentham Books.

Lea, V., and J. Helfand, eds. 2006. *Identifying Race and Transforming Whiteness in the Classroom.* Washington, DC: Peter Lang Publishing Group.

Lewis, A. 2002. "What Groups? Studying Whiteness in the Era of Color-Blindness." *Sociological Theory* 22, no. 4: 623–46.

Li, L., and G. Beckett, eds. 2006. *"Strangers" of the Academy: Asian Women Scholars in Higher Education.* Sterling, VA: Stylus Publishing.

Lindholm, J., A. Astin, L. Sax, and W. Korn. 2002. *The American College Teacher: National Norms for the 2001–2002 HERI Faculty Survey.* Los Angeles, CA: Higher Education Research Institute, University of California.

Lindholm, J., and H. Astin. 2008. "Spirituality and Pedagogy: Faculty's Spirituality and Use of Student-Centered Approaches to Undergraduate Teaching." *The Review of Higher Education* 31, no. 2, 185–207.

Lindholm, J., and K. Szelenyi. 2006. "Disciplinary Differences in Faculty Use of Student-Centered Pedagogy." Unpublished manuscript. Los Angeles, CA: Higher Education Research Institute, University of California.

Lindholm, J., K. Szelenyi, S. Hurtado, and W. Korn. 2005. *The American College Teacher: National Norms for the 2004–2005 HERI Faculty Survey.* Los Angeles, CA: Higher Education Research Institute, University of California.

Lippin, L. 2006. "Making Whiteness Visible in the Classroom." In *Identifying Race and Transforming Whiteness in the Classroom,* edited by V. Lea and J. Helfand, 109–31. Washington, DC: Peter Lang Publishing Group.

Mabokela, R., and A. Green, eds. 2001. *Sisters of the Academy: Emergent Black Women Scholars in Higher Education.* Sterling, VA: Stylus Publishing.

MacDonald, A., and S. Sánchez-Casal, eds. 2002. *Twenty-First-Century Feminist Classrooms: Pedagogies of Identity and Difference.* New York. Palgrave MacMillan.

Maher, F., and M. Tetrault. 1997. "Learning in the Dark: How Assumptions of Whiteness Shape Classroom Knowledge." *Harvard Educational Review* 67, no. 2: 321–49.

Margolis, E., and M. Romero. 1998. "The Department is Very Male, Very White, Very Old and Very Conservative: The Functioning of the 'Hidden Curriculum' in Graduate Sociology Departments." *Harvard Educational Review* 68, no. 1: 1–23.

Marin, P. 2000. "The Educational Possibility of Multi-Racial/Multi-Ethnic College Classrooms." In *Does Diversity Make a Difference? Three Research Studies on Diversity in College Classrooms,* edited by G. Maruyama, J. Moreno, R. Gudeman, and P. Marini, 61–83. Washington, DC: American Council on Education and American Association of University Professors.

Maruyama, G., and J. Moreno. 2000. "University Faculty Views about the Value of Diversity on Campus and in the Classroom." In *Does Diversity Make a Difference? Three Research Studies on Diversity in College Classrooms,* edited by G. Maruyama, J. Moreno, R. Gudeman, and P. Marini 9–36. Washington, DC: American Council on Education and American Association of University Professors.

Mason, M., M. Goulden, and K. Frasch. 2009. "Why Graduate Students Reject the Fast Track." *ACADEME* 95, no. 1 (January/February): 11–16.

Massey, D., and N. Denton. 1993. *American Apartheid: Segregation and the Making of the Underclass.* Cambridge, MA: Harvard University Press.

Massey, W., A. Wilger, and C. Colbeck. 1994. "Overcoming 'Hollowed' Collegiality: Departmental Cultures and Teaching Quality." *CHANGE* 26, no. 4 (July–August): 11–20.

Mathieson, G. 2004. "Reconceptualizing our Classroom Practice: Notes from an Antiracist Educator." In *Identifying Race and Transforming Whiteness in the Classroom,* edited by V. Lee and Judy Helfand, 235–56. New York: Peter Lang Publishing Group.

Maxwell, K. 2004. "Deconstructing Whiteness: Discovering the Water." In *Identifying Race and Transforming Whiteness in the Classroom,* edited by V. Lea and J. Helfand, 153–68. New York: Peter Lang Publishing Group.

Mayhew, M. and H. Grunwald. 2006. "Factors Contributing to Faculty Incorporation of Diversity—Related Course Content." *Journal of Higher Education* 77, no. 1: 48–168.

McAllister, G., and J. Irvine. 2000. "Cross-Cultural Competency and Multicultural Teacher Education." *Review of Educational Research* 71, no. 1: 3–24.

McCune, P. 2001. "What Do Disabilities Have to Do with Diversity?" *About Campus* 6, no. 2 (May–June): 5–12.

McFalls, E., and D. Cobb-Roberts. 2001. "Reducing Resistance to Diversity through Cognitive Dissonance Instruction." *Journal of Teacher Education* 52, no. 2, 164–72.

McKinney, M. 2002. "Whiteness on a White Canvass: Teaching Race in a Primarily White University." In *Race in the College Classroom: Pedagogy and Politics,* edited by M. Reddy and B. TuSmith, 126–39. Piscataway, NJ: Rutgers University Press.

McPherson, M., and R. Jewell. 2007. "Leveling the Playing Field: Should Student Evaluation Scores Be Adjusted?" *Social Science Quarterly* 88, no. 3: 868–81.

Mead, G. 1934. *Mind, Self and Society from the Standpoint of a Social Behaviorist,* edited by C. Morris. Chicago: University of Chicago Press.

Messner, M. 2000. "White Guy Habitus in the Classroom." *Men and Masculinities* 2, no. 4: 457–69.

Meyers, S. 2003. "Strategies to Reduce and Prevent Conflict in College Classrooms." *College Teaching* 51, no. 3: 94–98.

Meyerson, D. 2001. *Tempered Radicals: How People Use Difference to Inspire Change at Work.* Cambridge, MA: Harvard Business School Press.

Miller, A. 2005. "The Multicultural Lab: Diversity Issues in STEM Classes." In *Teaching Inclusively: Resources for Courses, Departments and Institutional Change in Higher Education,* edited by M. Ouellett, 451–59. Stillwater, OK: New Forums Press.

Miller, F. 1994. "Preface: Why We Chose to Address Oppression." In *The Promise of Diversity,* edited by E. Cross, J. Katz., F. Miller, and E. Seashore, xxv–xxix. New York: Irwin Professional Publishers.

Mills, C. 1997. *The Racial Contract*. Ithaca, NY: Cornell University Press.

Milner, H. 2007. "Race, Culture and Researcher Positionality: Working Through Dangers Seen, Unseen, and Unforeseen." *Educational Researcher* 36, no. 7: 388–400.

Mintz, B. and E. Rothblum, eds. 1997. *Lesbians in Academia: Degrees of Freedom*. New York: Routledge.

Misra, J., J. Lundquist, E. Holmes, and S. Agiomavritis. 2011. "The Ivory Ceiling of Service Work." *Academic Online.* http:www.aaup.org/AAUP/pubres/academe/2011/JF/feat/misr.htm.

Monroe, K., S. Ozyurt, T. Wrigly, and A. Alexander. 2008. "Gender Equality in Academia: Bad News from the Trenches, and Some Possible Solutions." *Perspectives on Politics* 6, no. 2: 215–33.

Murray, H., and R. Renaud. 1995. "Disciplinary Differences in Classroom Teaching Behaviors." *New Directions for Teaching and Learning* 64 (Winter): 31–39.

Myers, L. 2002. *A Broken Silence: Voices of African American Women in the Academy*. Westport, CT: Bergin and Harvey.

Nagda, B., P. Gurin, and G. Lopez. 2003. 'Transformative Pedagogy for Democracy and Social Justice." *Race Ethnicity and Education* 6, no. 2: 165–91.

Nagda, B., X. Zuniga, and T. Sevig. 1995. "Bridging Differences Through Peer-Facilitated Intergroup Dialogues." In *Peer Programs on College Campuses: Theory, Training and "Voice of the Peers,"* edited by S. Hatcher, 378–414. San Jose, CA: Resource Publications.

Nakanishi, D. 1993. "Asian Pacific Americans in Higher Education: Faculty and Administrative Representation and Tenure." *New Directions for Teaching and Learning* 53: 51–59.

Niemann, Y. 1999. "The Making of a Token: A Case Study of Stereotype Threat, Stigma, Racism and Tokenism in Academe." *Frontiers: A Journal of Women Studies* 20, no. 1: 111–34.

Niemann, Y., and J. Dovidio. 1998. "Tenure, Race/Ethnicity and Attitudes toward Affirmative Action: A matter of Self-Interest?" *Sociological Perspectives* 41, no. 4: 783–96.

O'Brien, E. 2006. "'I Could Hear You If You Would Just Calm Down': Challenging Eurocentric Classroom Norms Through Passionate Discussions of Racial Oppression." In *Identifying Race and Transforming Whiteness in the Classroom,* edited by V. Lea and J. Helfand, 63–68. New York: Peter Lang Publishing Group.

Omi, M. and H. Winant. 1994. *Racial Formation in the United States from the 1960s to the 1990s*. New York: Routledge.

Ong, M. 2005. "Body Projects of Young Women of Color in Physics: Intersections of Gender, Race, and Science." *Social Problems* 52, no. 4: 593–617.

Orfield, G., and N. Gordon. 2001. *Schools More Separate*. Cambridge, MA: Harvard University Press, The Civil Rights Project.

Osajima, K. 1995. "Racial Politics and the Invisibility of Asian Americans in Higher Education." *Educational Foundations* 91, no. 1: 35–53.

Ouellett, M., ed. 2005. *Teaching Inclusively: Resources for Courses, Departments and Institutional Change in Higher Education*. Stillwater, OK: New Forums Press.

Owen-Smith, P. 2004. "What Is Cognitive-Affective Learning (CAL)?" *Journal of Cognitive Affective Learning* 1 (Fall): 11.

Padilla, A. 1994. "Ethnic Minority Scholars, Research and Mentoring: Current and Future Issues." *Educational Research* 23, no. 4: 24–27.

Padilla, R. 2003. "Barriers to Accessing the Professoriate." In *The Majority in the Minority: Expanding the Representation of Latina/o Faculty, Administrators and Students in Higher Education,* edited by J. Castellanos and L. Jones, 179–206. Sterling, VA: Stylus Publishing.

Paige, R. 1986. "Training Competencies: The Missing Conceptual Link in Orientation." *International Journal of Intercultural Relations* 10, no. 2: 135–58.

Park, J., and N. Denson. 2009. "Attitudes and Advocacy: Understanding Faculty Views on Racial/Ethnic Diversity." *The Journal of Higher Education* 80, no. 4: 415–38.

Parker, W. 2003. *Teaching Democracy: Unity and Diversity in Public Life.* New York: Teacher's College Press.

Patton, T. 2004. "Reflections of a Black Woman Professor: Racism and Sexism in Academia." *The Howard Journal of Communication* 15: 185–200.

Peckham, I. 1995. "Complicity in Class Codes: The Exclusionary Function of Higher Education." In *This Fine Place so Far From Home,* edited by B. Dews and C. Law, 263–75. Philadelphia, PA: Temple University Press.

Pedraza, S. 2000. "Beyond Black and White: Latinos and Social Science Research on Immigration, Race, and Ethnicity in America." *Social Science History* 24, no. 4, 697–726.

Perry, G., H. Moore, C. Edwards, K. Acosta, and C. Frey. 2009. "Maintaining Credibility and Authority as an Instructor of Color in Diversity-Education Classrooms: A Qualitative Inquiry." *The Journal of Higher Education* 80, no. 1: 80–105.

Pike, K. and D. Johnson. 2003. "Asian American Women and Racialized Femininities: 'Doing' Gender across Cultural Worlds." *Gender and Society* 17, no. 1: 33–53.

Pleck, J., and J. Sawyer, eds. 1974. *Men and Masculinity.* Englewood Cliffs, NJ: Prentice-Hall.

Porter, S. 2007. "A Closer Look at Faculty Service: What Affects Participation on Committees?" *Journal of Higher Education* 78, no. 5: 523–40.

Prince, M. 2004. "Does Active Learning Work? A Review of the Research." *Journal of Engineering Education* 93, no. 3: 223–32.

Purwar, N. 2004. "Fish in or out of the Water: A Theoretical Framework for Race and the Space of Academia." In *Institutional Racism in Higher Education,* edited by I. Law, D. Phillips, and L. Turney, 49–58. Sterling, VA: Trentham Books.

Rankin, P., J. Nielsen, and D. Stanley. 2007. "Weak Links, Hot Networks, and Tacit Knowledge." In *Transforming Science and Engineering: Advancing Academic Women,* edited by A. Stewart, J. Malley and D. Lavaque-Many, 31–47. Ann Arbor: University of Michigan Press.

Reddick, L.,W. Jacobson, A. Linse, and D. Young. 2005. "A Framework for Inclusive Teaching in STEM Disciplines." In *Teaching Inclusively: Resources for Courses, Departments and Institutional Change in Higher Education,* edited by M. Ouellett, 435–50. Stillwater, OK: New Forums Press.

Reed, B. 1996. "Faculty Initiatives and Institutional Change." *The Diversity Factor* 5, no. 1: 15–20.

Reid, L. 2010. "The Role of Perceived Race and Gender in the Evaluation of College Teaching on RateMyProfessors.com." *Journal of Diversity in Higher Education* 3, no. 3: 137–52.

Rhoads, R. 1997. "Toward a More Inclusive Vision of Affirmative Action: Improving Campus Environments for Lesbian, Gay and Bisexual People." In *Affirmative Action's Testament of Hope: Strategies for a New Era in Higher Education,* edited by M. Garcia, 181–204. Albany: State University of New York Press.

Rich, M., and A. Cargile. 2004. "Beyond the Breach: Transforming White Identities in the Classroom." *Race, Ethnicity and Education* 7, no. 4: 351–65.

Richardson, L., and E. A. St. Pierre. 2005. "Writing: A Method of Inquiry." In *The Sage Handbook of Qualitative Inquiry,* 3rd ed., edited by N. Denzin and Y. Lincoln, 959–78. Thousand Oaks, CA: Sage Publications.

Riley, D. 2003. "Employing Liberative Pedagogies in Engineering Education." *Journal of Women and Minorities in Science and Engineering* 9, no. 2: 137–58.

Roberts, A., and K. Smith. 2002. "Managing Emotions in the College Classroom: The Cultural Diversity Course as an Example." *Teaching Sociology* 30, no. 3: 291–301.

Rubin, J., D. Pruitt, and S. Kim. 1986. *Social Conflict: Escalation, Stalemate and Settlement.* New York: McGaw-Hill.

Russ, T., C. Simonds, and S. Hunt. 2002. "Coming Out in the Classroom: An Occupational Hazard? The Influence of Sexual Orientation on Teacher Credibility and Perceived Student Learning." *Communcation Education* 51, no. 3: 311–24.

Sadao, V. 2003. "Living in Two Worlds: Success and the Bicultural Faculty of Color." *Review of Higher Education* 26, no. 4: 397–418.

Sánchez-Casal, S. 2002. "Unleashing the Demons of History: White Resistance in U.S. Latino Studies Classrooms." In *Twenty-First Century Feminist Classrooms: Pedagogies of Identity and Difference,* edited by A. MacDonald and S. Sánchez-Casal, 59–85. New York: Palgrave MacMillan.

Scheurich, J., and M. Young. 2002. "White Racism among White Faculty." In *The Racial Crisis in American Higher Education* (revised), edited by W. Smith, P. Altbach, and K. Lomotey, 221–242. Albany: State University of New York Press.

Schoem, D., L. Frankel, X. Zuniga, and E. Lewis, eds. 1993. *Multicultural Teaching in the University.* Westport, CT: Praeger.

Schoem, D., and S. Hurtado, eds. 2001. *Intergroup Dialogue: Deliberative Democracy in School, College, Community, and Workplace.* Ann Arbor: University of Michigan Press.

Schrock, D., and M. Schwalbe. 2009. "Men, Masculinity and Manhood Acts." *Annual Review of Sociology* 35: 277–95.

Schwalbe, M. 2005. "Identity Stakes, Manhood Acts, and the Dynamics of Accountability." In *Studies in Symbolic Interaction,* edited by N. Denzin, 65–81. New York: Elsevier.

Schwalbe, M., and M. Wolkomir. 2001. "The Masculine Self as Problem and Resource in Interview Studies of Men." *Men and Masculinities* 4: 90–103.

———. 2002. "Interviewing Men." In *Handbook of Interview Research: Content and Method,* edited by J. Gubrium and J. Holstein, 203–20. Thousand Oaks, CA: Sage Publications.

Segura, D. 2003. "Navigating Between Two Worlds: The Labyrinth of Chicana Intellectual Production in the Academy." *Journal of Black Studies* 34, no. 1: 28–51.

Seifert, T., and P. Umbach. 2008. "The Effects of Faculty Demographic Characteristics and Disciplinary Content on Dimensions of Job Satisfaction." *Research in Higher Education* 49, no. 4: 357–81.

Settles, I., L. Cortina, A. Stewart, and J. Malley. 2007. "Voice Matters: Buffering the Impact of a Negative Climate for Women in Science." *Psychology of Women Quarterly* 31: 270–81.

Sleeter, C. and C. Grant. 2009. *Making Choices for Multicultural Education: Five Approaches to Race, Class, and Gender.* Hoboken, NJ: John Wiley and Sons.

Smith, D., S. Parker, A. Clayton-Pederson, N. Osei-Kofi, G. Richards, D. Teraguchi, and M. Figueroa. 2002. *Campus Diversity Initiative Evaluation Project Resources Kit.* Claremont, CA: Claremont Graduate University School of Educational Studies.

Smith, E., and S. Witt. 1993. "A Comparative Study of Occupational Stress among African-Americans and White Faculty: A Research Note." *Research in Higher Education* 34, no. 2: 229–41.

Smith, W. 2004. "Black Faculty Coping with Racial Battle Fatigue: The Campus Racial Climate in a Post–Civil Rights Era." In *A Long Way to Go: Conversations About Race by African American Faculty and Graduate Students,* edited by D. Cleveland, 171–92. New York: Peter Lang Publishing Group.

Solorzano, D., M. Ceja, and T. Yosso. 2000. "Critical Race Theory, Racial Microaggressions and Campus Racial Climate." *Journal of Negro Education* 69, no. 1/2: 60–73.

Stanley, C. 2006a. "An Overview of the Literature." In *Faculty of Color: Teaching in Predominantly Colleges and Universities,* edited by C. Stanley, 1–29. Boston: Anker.

———, ed. 2006b. *Faculty of Color Teaching in Predominantly White Colleges and Universities.* Boston, MA: Anker Books.

Stanley, C., M. Porter, N. Simpson, and M. Ouelett. 2003. "A Case Study of the Teaching Experiences of African American Faculty at Two Predominantly White Research Universities." *Journal of Excellence in College Teaching* 14, no. 1: 151–78.

Stassen, M. 1995. "White Faculty Members and Racial Diversity: A Theory and Its Implications." *The Review of Higher Education* 18, no. 4: 361–91.

Steele, C. 1997. "A Threat in the Air: How Stereotypes Shape Intellectual Identity and Performance. *American Psychologist* 52, no. 6: 613–29.

———. 2007. "Stereotype Threat and African American Achievement." In *The Inequality Reader: Contemporary and Foundational Readings in Race, Class, and Gender,* edited by D. Grusky and S. Szelenyi, 252–57. Boulder, CO: Westview Press.

———. 2010. *Whistling Vivaldi: And Other Clues to How Stereotypes Affect Us.* New York: W. W. Norton and Company.

Strauss, A. 1959. *Mirrors and Masks: The Search for Identity.* Glencoe, IL: Free Press.

Strauss, A., and J. Corbin, J. 1998. *Basic of Qualitative Research: Techniques and Procedures for Developing Grounded Theory.* Thousand Oaks, CA: Sage Publications.

Sturm, S. 2006. "The Architecture of Inclusion: Advancing Workplace Equity in Higher Education." *Harvard Journal of Law and Gender* 29: 247–334.

Sue, D., G. Torino, C. Capodilupo, D. Rivera, and A. Lin. 2009. "How White Faculty Perceive and React to Difficult Dialogues on Race: Implications for Education and Training." *The Counseling Psychologist* 38, no. 8: 1090–1115.

Takiff, H., D. Sanchez, and T. Stewart. 2001. "What's in a Name? The Status Implications of Students' Terms of Address for Male and Female Professors." *Psychology of Women Quarterly* 25: 134–44.

Tate, W. 1994. "From Inner City to Ivory Tower: Does My Voice Matter in the Academy?" *Urban Education* 29, no. 3: 245–69.

Tatum, B. 1992. "Teaching about Race, Learning about Racism: The Application of Racial Identity Development Theory in the Classroom." *Harvard Educational Review* 62: 1–24.

Thomas, D., and R. Ely. 2002. "Making Differences Matter: A New Paradigm for Managing Diversity." In *Harvard Business Review on Managing Diversity,* 33–66. Cambridge, MA: Harvard Business Publishing.

Thomas, G., and C. Hollinshead. 2001. "Resisting from the Margins: The Coping Strategies of Black Women and Other Women of Color Faculty Members at a Research University." *Journal of Negro Education* 70, no. 3: 166–75.

Thomas, K., and V. Plaut. 2007. "The Many Faces of Diversity Resistance in the Workplace." In *Diversity Resistance in Organizations,* edited by K. Thomas, 1–23. New York: Psychology Press.

Thomas, R. 2002. "From Affirmative Action to Affirming Diversity." In *Harvard Business Review on Managing Diversity,* 1–31. Cambridge, MA: Harvard Business Publishing.

Thompson, B. 2001. *A Promise and a Way of Life: White Anti-Racism.* Minneapolis: University of Minnesota Press.

Thompson, C., and E. Dey. 1998. "Pushed to the Margins: Sources of Stress for African American College and University Faculty." *Journal of Higher Education* 69, no. 3: 324–45.

Thompson, C., E. Schaefer, and H. Brod. 2003. *White Men Challenging Racism: 35 Personal Stories.* Durham, NC: Duke University Press.

Tierney, W., and E. Bensimon. 1996. *Promotion and Tenure: Community and Socialization in Academe.* Albany: State University of New York Press.

Tillman, L. 2001. "Mentoring African American Faculty in Higher Education." *Race in Higher Education* 42, no. 3: 295–325.

Trower, C., and R. Chait. 2002. "Faculty Diversity—Too Little for Too Long." *Harvard Magazine* (March–April): 33–37.

Trujillo, C. 1986. "A Comparative Examination of Classroom Interactions Between Professors and Minority and Non-Minority College Students." *American Educational Research Journal* 23: 629–42.

Turk, T. 1981. "Women Faculty in Higher Education: Academic Administration and Governance in a State University System, 1966–1977." *Pacific Sociological Review* 24, no. 2: 212–36.

Turner, C. 2002. "Women of Color in Academe: Living with Multiple Marginality." *The Journal of Higher Education* 73, no. 1: 74–94.

———. 2003. "Incorporation and Marginalization in the Academy: From Border Toward Center for Faculty of Color?" *Journal of Black Studies* 34: 112–25.

Turner, C., J. Gonzalez, and L. Wood. 2008. "Faculty of Color in Academe: What 20 Years of Literature Tells Us." *Journal of Diversity in Higher Education* 1, no. 3: 139–68.

Turner, C., and S. Myers. 2000. *Faculty of Color in Academe: Bittersweet Success.* Boston, MA: Allyn and Bacon.

TuSmith, B., and M. Reddy, eds. 2002. *Race in the College Classroom: Pedagogy and Politics.* New Brunswick, NJ: Rutgers University Press.

Valian, V. 1998. *Why So Slow? The Advancement of Women.* Cambridge, MA: MIT Press.

Valle, M. 2002. "Antiracist Pedagogy and Concientizacion: A Latina Professor's Struggle." In *Twenty-First-Century Feminist Classrooms: Pedagogies of Identity and Difference,* edited by A. McDonald and S. Sánchez-Casal, 155–73. New York: Palgrave Macmillan.

Vargas, L., ed. 2002. *Women Faculty of Color in the White Classroom: Narratives on the Pedagogical Implications of Classroom Diversity.* New York: Lang.

Verdugo, R. 2003. "Discrimination and Merit in Higher Education: The Hispanic Professoriate." In *The Majority in the Minority: Expanding the Representation of Latina/o Faculty, Administrators and Students in Higher Education,* edited by J. Castellanos and L. Jones, 241–56. Sterling, VA: Stylus Publishing.

Wagner, A. 2005. "Unsettling the Academy: Working Through the Challenges of an Anti-Racist Pedagogy." *Race, Ethnicity and Education* 8, no. 3: 261–75.

Warren, L. 2005. "Strategic Action in *Hot Moments.*" In *Teaching Inclusively: Resources for Course, Department, and Institutional Change in Higher Education,* edited by M. Ouellet, 620–30. Stillwater, OK: New Forums Press.

Waters, M. 1990. *Ethnic Options: Choosing Identities in America.* Berkeley: University of California Press.

Weinstein, G., and K. O'Bear. 1992. "Bias Issues in the Classroom: Encounters with the Teaching Self." *New Directions in Teaching and Learning* 52: 39–50.

Whitehead, S., ed. 2006. *Men and Masculinities: Critical Concepts in Sociology.* New York: Routledge.

Winkler, J. 2005. "Faculty Reappointment, Tenure, and Promotion: Barriers for Women." *Professional Geographer* 52, no. 4: 737–50.

Zamudio, M., and F. Rios. 2006. "From Traditional to Liberal Racism: Living Racism in the Everyday." *Sociological Perspectives* 49, no. 4: 483–501.

Zinn, H. 1980. *A People's History of the United States.* New York: Harper and Row.

Zuniga, X., B. Nagda, M. Chesler, and A. Cytron-Walker. 2007. *Intergroup Dialogue in Higher Education.* ASHE Higher Education Series 32, no. 2. New York: Wiley.

Index

About the Editors and Contributors

Ruby Beale (PhD) is Chair of the Department of Business Administration at Hampton University, which incorporates undergraduate and graduate students. She received her MA and PhD from the University of Michigan. She has consulted with numerous corporations, national, state and local agencies, not-for-profit and grassroots organizations, universities, and school districts. Her research interests include work with diverse populations as it relates to teaching effectiveness, academic and work performance, and financial literacy. Her work has appeared in *Review of Business Research* and *Proceedings of the Academy for Economics and Economic Education.* She has co-authored *Developing Competencies to Manage Diversity: Readings, Cases and Activities* (1997, Berrett-Koehler).

Corissa Carlson (BA) received her BA from the University of Michigan and currently is enrolled in a graduate clinical psychology doctoral program at Wayne State University. Her research interests include forensic psychology and the successful reintegration of offenders into society.

Jessica Charbeneau (PhD) received her BA from the University of Texas at Austin, her MAT from Texas State University, and her PhD in Sociology from the University of Michigan. Her research focuses on pedagogical issues related to how students and faculty in higher education learn and teach within and about structures of race, ethnicity, class, and gender. A recent publication appeared in *Teaching Sociology.*

Mark A. Chesler (PhD) is Arthur F. Thurneau Professor of Sociology and Project Director in the Program on Intergroup Relations at the University of Michigan and Executive Director of Community Resources Ltd. He received his his PhD in Social Psychology from the University of Michigan. His research interests include organizational change around issues of race and gender equity, whiteness and multicultural teams and coalitions, and the psychosocial dynamics of childhood cancer. He is active as a consultant, workshop leader, and lecturer on issues of multicultural teaching and organizational change. His publications include *Intergroup Dialogue in Higher Education: Meaningful Learning about Social Justice* (2007, ASHE/Wiley), *Challenging Racism in Higher Education: Promoting Justice* (2005, Rowman and Littlefield), and *Cancer and Self-Help: Bridging the Troubled Waters of Childhood Illness* (1995, University of Wisconsin Press).

Kristie A. Ford (PhD) is Associate Professor of Sociology and Director of the Intergroup Relations Program at Skidmore College. She received her BA from Amherst College and her MA and PhD from the University of Michigan. Her research explores the connection between race, gender, and intersecting social identities in relationship to (1) body management practices and (2) pedagogical approaches to teaching and learning. Recent publications have appeared in *Symbolic Interaction,* the *Journal of Equity and Excellence in Education,* and the *Journal of Higher Education.*

Megan Furhman received her BA from the University of Michigan, with honors, in Sociology. She joined Teach for America in the New York City public school system. She currently is a Founding Teacher at an Expeditionary Learning School in New York City.

Laura Hirshfield (PhD) is Visiting Assistant Professor of Sociology at the New College of Florida. She received her BA from Swarthmore College and the PhD in Sociology and Social Psychology from the University of Michigan. Her research focuses on women's experiences in the workplace, specifically in the academy and in STEM disciplines, issues of gender, emotion, science and organizations, and how authority and expertise are established and portrayed in scientific settings. Recent publications have appeared in *Journal of the American College of Surgeons, International Journal of Gender, Science and Technology,* and *Ethnic and Racial Studies.*

Tiffany Joseph (PhD) is currently a Robert Wood Johnson Foundation Health Policy Scholar at Harvard University and Assistant Professor of Sociology at SUNY Stony Brook. She received her BA from Brown University and the MA and PhD in Sociology from the University of Michigan. Her research interests include comparative frameworks of race in the Americas, how Latin American and Caribbean immigrants adapt to the US racial system, immigrants' health, and the experiences of faculty of color and women in academia. Recent publications have appeared in *Ethnic and Racial Studies, Race and Social Problems,* and *Gender and Education.*

Kelly Maxwell (PhD) is faculty member in the Psychology Department and Academic Codirector of the Program on Intergroup Relations at the University of Michigan. She received her MS in Higher Education in Student Affairs from Florida State University and the PhD in Educational Leadership and Policy Studies from Arizona State University. She teaches courses in intergroup issues, including social identity, privilege, and power, and she trains students to facilitate campus intergroup dialogues. Her research interests include dialogue and intergroup issues in higher education and change processes in religious and white racial identity dialogues. Her publications include *Facilitating Intergroup Dialogues Bridging Differences, Catalyzing Change* (2011, Stylus).

Penny A. Pasque (PhD) is Associate Professor of Adult and Higher Education in the Departments of Educational Leadership and Policy Studies and Gender Studies at the University of Oklahoma. Her research addresses in/equities in higher education, dis/connections between higher education and society, and complexities in critical qualitative inquiry. She received her PhD in Higher and Continuing Education at the University of Michigan. Her work has appeared in the *Review of Higher Education, Qualitative Inquiry,* the *Journal of College Student Development,* and *Multicultural Perspectives.* Her recent books include *American Higher Education, Leadership and Policy: Critical Issues and the Public Good* (2011, Palgrave Macmillan) and *Empowering Women in Higher Education and Student Affairs* (2011, Stylus).

Elizabeth Ramus (MSW) received her BA in Sociology and MSW in Management of Human Services and Mental Health at the University of Michigan. She currently works as a grant writer for a local human services agency, and her interests include affordable housing, Not In My Back Yard attitudes, and connectedness between serious mental illness and homelessness. She has published in *Diversity and Democracy.*

Alford A. Young Jr. (PhD) is Arthur F. Thurnau Professor and Chair of the Department of Sociology at the University of Michigan, with a joint appointment in the Department of AfroAmerican and African Studies. He received his BA from Wesleyan University and his MA and PhD in Sociology from the University of Chicago. His research focuses on low-income, urban-based African Americans,

African American scholars and intellectuals, and the classroom-based experiences of faculty as they pertain to diversity and multiculturalism. His work appears in *Sociological Theory,* the *Annual Review of Sociology, Symbolic Interaction,* and *Ethnic and Racial Studies.* His publications also include *The Minds of Marginalized Men: Making Sense of Mobility, Opportunity, and Future Life Chances* (2004, Princeton University Press), and he is completing a book manuscript, *From the Edge of the Ghetto: African Americans and the World of Work.*